The Impact of Accounting Research on Practice and Disclosure

Financial support of the Symposium by Haskins & Sells Foundation is gratefully acknowledged.

The Impact of Accounting Research on Practice and Disclosure

A. Rashad Abdel-khalik and
Thomas F. Keller, editors

Duke University Press   Durham, N.C.   1978

© 1978, Duke University Press

L.C.C. card no. 77–85520
I.S.B.N. 0–8223–0396–5

Printed in the United States of America
by Kingsport Press

Contents

vi   Contents

Part IV. Where to Go from Here

Part V. Conference Synthesis

Preface

"The Impact of Accounting Research in Financial Accounting and Disclosure on Accounting Practice," a symposium held at Duke University on December 3 and 4, 1975, financially supported by the Haskins & Sells Foundation, brought together for two days thirty accounting professors and practitioners to evaluate systematically the interaction between research in accounting and the practice of accounting. The research examined was that resulting from three classes of investigation, (1) a priori research, (2) experimental research, and (3) the analysis of past observations.

The areas chosen encompass the major research approaches and methods of the past ten years. The authors were asked to address the assigned topic in terms of a review of past research and their perception of its impact on practice. As is to be expected, the impact of certain topics in accounting research on practice is reasonably obvious, and at other times the relationship is quite subtle. The discussion following each paper was spirited and thought-provoking. The gist and spirit of the discussion are contained in the individual papers following each article, though no transcript was made of the complete discussion.

After discussing the state of the art, we examined future directions for accounting research. The final paper presents a synthesis of the conference.

We want to take this opportunity to thank the participants for providing a wealth of stimulating ideas both in the formal papers and in the informal discussion which ensued. The confidence and support of Hector Anton, Kenneth Stringer and Robert Pivik were invaluable in financing the conference. Without the support of the Haskins & Sells Foundation, the conference would not have been possible. To the many individuals, especially Carl L. Nelson and our colleagues at Duke, who discussed with us the ideas for the conference, we must say thank you. These ideas contributed immeasurably to the success of the conference.

At Duke we have a commitment to increase the effectiveness of communication between academics and professionals. This conference has been a first step, and we believe an important one in that direction. We hope that the publication of these papers will increase the level of under-standing among a broader audience that we could not reach during the course of the conference.

A. Rashad Abdel-khalik
Thomas F. Keller
Codirectors of the Duke Symposium

Participants

Hector R. Anton, *Haskins & Sells*
Norton M. Bedford, *University of Illinois, Urbana*
R. Lee Brummett, *University of North Carolina, Chapel Hill*
William J. Bruns, Jr., *Harvard University*
John C. Burton, *Securities and Exchange Commission*
Sidney Davidson, *University of Chicago*
Nicholas Dopuch, *University of Chicago*
Thomas R. Dyckman, *Cornell University*
Charles T. Horngren, *Stanford University*
Robert S. Kaplan, *Carnegie-Mellon University*
Robert S. Kay, *Touche Ross & Co.*
Albert A. Koch, *Ernst & Ernst*
Kermit D. Larson, *University of Texas, Austin*
Raymond C. Lauver, *Price Waterhouse & Co.*
Richard C. Lyle, *The Institute of Certified Public Accountants*
Robert K. Mautz, *Ernst & Ernst*
Maurice Moonitz, *University of California, Berkeley*
Felix Pomeranz, *Coopers & Lybrand*
Lawrence Revsine, *Northwestern University*
David Solomons, *University of Pennsylvania*
Robert R. Sterling, *Rice University*
William Stewart, *Haskins & Sells*
Robert T. Sprouse, *Financial Accounting Standards Board*
Kenneth W. Stringer, *Haskins & Sells*
Robert J. Swieringa, *Cornell University*
Roman L. Weil, *Georgia Institute of Technology*
Charles A. Werner, *Alexander Grant & Co.*
Frank T. Weston, *Arthur Young & Co.*
Arthur R. Wyatt, *Arthur Andersen & Co.*

From Duke University

A. Rashad Abdel-khalik
Robert L. Dickens
Thomas F. Keller
Wayne J. Morse
James H. Scheiner
Robert E. Taylor

PART I
The Impact of A Priori Research

The Impact of A Priori Theory and Research on Accounting Practice

Norton M. Bedford

The notion that accounting research has an impact on accounting practice is a fascinating thought. While it is quite obvious that a priori theory is used to support both authoritative and nonauthoritative accounting rules and procedures, it is not at all obvious that a priori research causes rules and procedures to be promulgated. To the contrary, a survey of the accounting literature over the past ten years (Appendix A) provides little reason to believe a priori research causes changes in accounting practice.

There are two possible roles which a priori accounting research can take to affect accounting practice. First, a priori research results could be deposited in the accounting literature, as a data base, from which practical men of affairs could select publications to support or refute a proposed accounting rule or procedure. Second, a priori research could play a more direct role, one similar to that of research in the natural sciences, where research determines what practice should be and practice adjusts to the a priori research results.

Given the great differences in the quality of accounting literature, it would appear that the first role might not be particularly meaningful and that progress in accounting practice would depend more on the ability of practical men to select the "right" a priori theory and research than on the quality of the theory and research itself. Only in the sense that the practical men in some way are restricted, in their search for justification of a proposed accounting rule, to the accumulated accounting literature can it be maintained that a priori research has any impact on accounting practice. The inference is that an examination of the impact of accounting theory and research on accounting practice should place more emphasis on the second possible role of accounting research.

It is not necessary that a study of the relationship between research and practice be confined to an examination of the extent to which a priori research causes practice to change. There may well be other highly sophisticated relationships between accounting research and practice. For example, it could be maintained that "a priori" research does not have to precede practice to have impact on it. It could be that the impact is merely the support the research provides in sustaining an existing or newly authorized practice, but this type of impact is difficult to evaluate. Also, to the extent that "a priori" research includes a value-judgment indoctrination process, which is a questionable research process at best, it could be maintained that a priori research influences practice because a priori research results taught in the classroom or on the job may ultimately be adopted in practice. But one then wonders why only students believe "a priori" research results. It seems that the second, more direct causal view of the relationship between research and practice is the appropriate way to relate accounting research and practice, particularly when that relationship is referred to as an "impacting" relationship. It seems reasonable to conclude that both "justification of practice" and "value-judgment indoctrination" processes hardly qualify as research-influencing methods. To have any direct impact on practice, research would have to precede practice and this study is based on that premise.

Before starting this analysis, it seems desirable to clarify the meaning of the terms "theory" and "research." Essentially, *theory* is an *explanation*. It explains why something *is* as it is or why something *should* be such and such. This notion of theory as explanation is in accord with everyday use of the term. We have all heard and possibly made the statement, "I've got a theory for that," meaning we have an explanation for something. These explanations or theories vary in quality. Some are at the *speculative* level, such as statements that "bad weather is caused by the explosion of atomic bombs" or that "the economic system would operate better if human-asset accounting were adopted." The distinguishing characteristic of "speculative" theory is that it asserts an explanation that *might* be valid. In contrast to the "might be" or speculative theory is *conclusive* theory for which there is objective evidence indicating with a high level of confidence that the explanation is valid.

In accounting literature, the level of accounting theories varies indiscriminately from the speculative to the conclusive with no accompanying indication of the level or quality of any enunciated theory. While some may contend there is no means of providing evidence of the quality of a theory, success in other fields suggests that accountants need to try.

Consistent with the view of theory as explanation, research represents means of developing theories or explanations of things. The various available research methods of developing theories can be gathered together under three categories: (1) empirical, (2) behavioral, and (3) "a priori."

While it has been suggested that "a priori" refers to a method of reasoning and is not a method of research at all, the point is that new accounting knowledge may be developed by the "a priori" process, and if research is viewed as a process of knowledge development, "a priori" research is not an unacceptable notion. In this context the task undertaken by the investigation supporting this paper was to examine the "a priori" research-based theory and determine its impact on accounting practice. For purposes of the investigation, all accounting explanations not based on empirical and behavioral research were treated as "a priori" research.

As an aside, to deal with the confusing notion that a priori research is all research not based on mathematical analysis, any theory developed by any of the three research methods can be expressed verbally or quantitatively. Also any theory, however developed, can be expressed in terms of everyday language or even in terms of symbolic logic as a set of relations. Further, the conclusion that accounting theory has little impact on practice may apply to theory based on all three types of research methods. But this study is confined to a priori research and the limited conclusion is that only by the development and use of a theory of accounting theories can a priori research be expected to have a direct impact on accounting *practice*.

With the foregoing as guidance, the analysis will be developed according to the following sequence of topics:

1. The *need* to use a theory-of-theories approach because a priori research may have no impact.
2. The *meaning* of a theory-of-theories in the selection and development of a theory.
3. The *criteria* for a theory-of-theories that will determine the acceptability of a theory.
4. The *scope* or *types* of economic-based or information-based accounting theories to which the criteria apply.
5. The *evolution* or *historical* perspective leading up to the theory-of-theories approach.
6. The characteristics of a theory of accounting theories.
7. Conclusions regarding means whereby a priori theory and research might achieve impact on accounting practice.

To begin the analysis, it must be recognized that a study of the impact of a priori accounting research on accounting practice is a difficult and frustrating undertaking. Not only is it difficult to develop a research design to test the proposition, but the implications of the findings are frustrating because they relate to the quality and even survival of this research method.

If the quality of a research method is defined in terms of the acceptance of the research results, a finding that a priori research has had no impact on accounting practice would suggest a low quality research method. Contrariwise, a finding that accounting practice rapidly accepts the results of a priori studies might imply a high quality research method. Unfortunately, no convincing method or research design can be developed to test the proposition. It is rather easy, of course, to search out the a priori research proposals or conclusions that have appeared in the accounting literature in the past ten years and compare them with new development in accounting practice at later dates (Appendix A). When a new practice is discovered that is in accord with a previously developed a priori research proposition, one might conclude that a priori research had an impact on practice. The problem is that there is no proof that any "impacting" at all took place. In fact, when one attempts to establish in a systematic manner a causal relationship between a priori research and practice, that causal relationship cannot be determined in a statistical sense. An interesting aspect of such a study is that one can almost conclude the reverse relationship, that practice has impact on a priori research because much of the a priori research follows and attempts to justify practice. That is, there may be reason to suspect that theories developed a priori are based more on expediency than on reason and that one should be more impressed with their quantity than with their quality. In any event, there appears to be precious little a priori research in the past ten years that can be pointed to as the cause of the multitude of accounting rules and regulations issued to guide practice.

Need for a Theory-of-Theories Approach

Faced with the practical impossibility of developing a causal relationship between the mass of a priori research and accounting practice because some a priori research precedes practice, some follows it, and some is never used, another approach to the problem of relating a priori research and accounting practice seems to be needed. The problem takes the form of determining the type of a priori research that has or should be immediately accepted in practice. To select this type, some criteria are needed to distinguish the relevant theories. In this sense a theory of accounting theories, one that will identify the "good" theories, is needed before any worthwhile discussion of the impact of "a priori" research on practice is feasible. While there is now no systematic way of saying that "a priori" accounting research influences accounting practice, it is possible to support the notion, because it is appealing, by suggesting a few instances where intuitively it appears that practice follows a priori research, and this has been done. But if one has limited faith in intuition, one must conclude that the practical problem is really that of determining which a priori theory is "right," and this calls for a well-developed theory of accounting theories.

The notion of a theory of accounting theories is a relatively new approach to the development of a structure of accounting thought. It implies a comprehensive theory which relates to all theories but which is not a general theory since it does not contain within itself all the substance of all theories. Rather it is just a theory of accounting theories. A background perspective of its development may justify its use. To begin, it should be noted that throughout the history of the subject, the speculations of scholars on the nature of accounting have varied from naive assumptions to sophisticated analysis: from Pacioli's explanation that for every debit there is a credit because such is the nature of things to Paton and Littleton's systematic enunciation of corporate accounting standards and on to ASOBAT's ill-structured general relativity framework of accounting thought. Currently, the accounting literature is replete with deductively derived theories of varying levels of quality, and a great deal of it is based on little more than speculation. Some of it is blatantly self-serving and some is poorly reasoned. Some of it is subtle and some is appealingly written. As a consequence, discernment of the questionable theories to be ignored is time consuming and difficult. To deal with the problem, a substantial body of accounting thought has been developed in the last ten years, suggesting three approaches to the a priori development of accounting theory. First, several accountants inclined toward a priori research have become convinced that a general relativity structure, which deductively explains accounting as a broad information development and communication process, is the appropriate approach to the development of accounting theory. All theories developed otherwise would be irrelevant. They praise the scope, adaptability to user needs, and compatibility with multiple authoritative pronouncements of such a view of accounting. But the house of a priori research is divided because in the same ten-year period other a priori researchers, particularly those who fully absorbed the Paton and Littleton deductive structure, have become dubious of such an ASOBAT type of relativity framework and contend that other deductively derived basic overall explanations can be developed and fitted into a deterministic framework to provide a better description of accounting. Only these theories would be accepted. The third approach lies somewhere between the extremes of those who prefer a closely reasoned deductive theory, such as the rather well structured Paton and Littleton framework, and those who prefer a broader, less tightly knit formulation, such as that of ASOBAT. This growing number of a priori researchers and scholars have adopted a neutral position. Declining to support one view over another because of their insistence that any good accounting theory must be accepted and used as a guide for accounting practice, they examine all concepts and theories as a totalility They hope to discover some of the common elements of the various acceptable accounting proposals and use the common elements as a base for a priori research that will deductively derive an accounting theory of relevant accounting theories. The final objective of their efforts, still unattained, and the partial success of their efforts, largely unpublished, is a theory that will improve the quality of accounting theories. The a priori research on this theory-of-accounting-theories approach has brought forth some new conceptions of the nature of accountancy and, more important, it seems to be a powerful process for determining in a systematic manner which of the various accounting theories are acceptable candidates for being a desirable theory. The most interesting effect of a priori research on the theory of accounting theories is the development of criteria for determining the acceptability of a concept or a theory and the explanations of why certain criteria are appropriate. Indeed, a theory of criteria selection might well represent the entire theory of accounting theories in the sense that it would provide a basis for suggesting the appropriateness of various sets of accounting propositions.

Meaning of Theory of Accounting Theories

The effect of the theory-of-theories approach to a priori accounting research has been to expand the scope of accounting concepts, expand the scope of the area within which accounting methods may be applied, and refine the precision of various accounting notions. And it has had an impact on the thinking of both practicing accountants and researchers, though it is not yet possible to determine if the impact is of slight or of substantial benefit. But certainly the implicit use of the theory-of-theories approach by the Trueblood Committee in developing the objectives of financial statements did much to emphasize the notion that accounting reports are related to user needs. Conceptually, that committee report served as authoritative, objective evidence that accounting theory must span both objectives of accounting information and means of developing the information. Operationally, it questioned such well-accepted knowledge as the matching concept, not on the grounds that it contains logical errors but on the grounds that the results do not relate to the accounting objective. In doing so, the committee report is in accord with the theory-of-theories view that because people have different *objectives, make different observations,* and *use different fact-finding methods,* different explanations (theories) of things are inevitable. The theory of accounting theories would require that a theory specify its *objectives, observational techniques,* and *experimental method used* so that the selection of the most appropriate accounting theory may be facilitated.

Other impacts of the foregoing feature of the theory-of-theories approach may and have been implied. For example, the emergence of expanded footnotes and treatment of leases in the balance sheet have been justified by the a priori research proposition that, because different accounting theories exist, greater disclosure is appropriate. Also, the criterion of different objectives, observations, and methods has been used to suggest that change in business practices can change accounting concepts of assets and liabilities. Uses of the criteria inherent in the theory-of-accounting-theories approach are extensive, although seldom referred to as such. The criteria are evident in the FASB discussion memorandum on materiality and in various research studies published by the AICPA and the AAA. A few simplified a priori research illustrations of the use of the criteria feature of the theory-of-theories approach may be appropriate. One such illustration, in that it influenced existing theory to the extent that theoretical views of price-level accounting approached more closely the criteria for a desirable theory, is Sterling's (1975) explanation of the distinction between general purchasing-power accounting and current-value accounting. It had been generally recognized that the theory of general purchasing-power accounting was a different thing from current-value accounting. But Sterling's explanation, complying with the theory-of-theories criterion of being self-consistent, that the two represented different theories was effective. He pointed out that general purchasing-power accounting, which aims merely to standardize the accounting measuring unit, could be applied to either historical cost or to current value. This meant that it was inconsistent to contend that general purchasing-power accounting was a substitute for current-value accounting or vice versa. This clarified the conflicting theories to some degree. That is, Sterling suggested little new knowledge but, whether he intended to do so or not, by using the theory-of-theories *criterion of self-consistency,* he was able a priori to clarify prevailing accounting thought on the issue. Similarly Bradford's (1974) discussion of accounting for inflation questioned the previous a priori accounting theory for measuring monetary gains and losses by using the theory of interest. He suggested that the interest rate anticipates inflation and so the monetary gain or loss on holding net monetary items should be offset by the inflation element in the higher inflation-induced interest receipts or payments. The implied a priori-developed theory is somewhat compatible with the *prime criterion of a theory, that of being in correspondence with relevant real-world phenomena,* and thus more acceptable to accounting practice. A third routine use of a desirable theory criterion to evaluate a priori research is implied in Davidson and Weil's explanation of the net monetary gain accruing to utility companies with large debt financing. The study called attention to the real-world phenomenon of growing reliance on debt financing in the United States, where the average debt-equity ratio has increased from 25% to 41% in the past 10 years. Their analysis questioned the relevance of the conventional theory of general purchasing-power accounting by revealing that utilities have been motivated to expand debt financing as a means of coping with inflation. The implication is that theories of general purchasing-power accounting lack scope and that a broader theory needs to be developed that would prevent the business motivational aspects of inflation on corporation planning and on accounting from going undisclosed to society at large. In this respect the a priori aspects of their study tend to move existing theory and practice more toward compliance with the theory-of-accounting-theories *criterion of being comprehensive.*

While these authors did not specify why they wrote as they did, the limited practical success of unbounded a priori research based on speculation and intuitive judgments must have influenced them to use the broad concept of systematic criteria as a means of substantiating their reasoning.

The theory-of-theories approach to the development of accounting thought comprises much more than demonstrations of the inadequacy of a given theory or of the relevance of conflicting theories to different situations. It also makes a priori research and theory construction more readily acceptable to accounting practice. For example, once the a priori research on present value measures was expressed in compliance with the *criterion of being in accord with well-developed theories in insurance, bond invest-ments, and other fields,* the theory became more acceptable to practice.

This may explain why practitioners rejected Sprouse and Moonitz's support of present value in 1963 and yet adopted it ten years later. While the criterion of relevance was not included in the list of criteria useful for a theory of accounting theories because it seemed vague and imprecise, it was used by ASOBAT and adopted four years later by APB Statement No. 4, apparently because relevance was then seen to be in accord with the criterion of being in correspondence with the real world.

Theory-of-Accounting-Theories Criteria

The notion of a theory of accounting theories to which a priori accounting research seems to be moving is not unambiguous. It is not a meta-theory in abstract form. Rather it is more in the nature of a comprehensive framework for developing reliable accounting theories. It seems to offer hope for the development of accounting theories more directly related to accounting practice and more acceptable to practicing accounting authorities. A considerable amount of research on the notion is needed, and the emerging a priori research on the theory of accounting theories in the last ten years is, taken as a whole, rather complex. It has been suggested that it is a theory of theory selection in that it may indicate when each theory is appropriate or why some theory is inadequate. Broadly stated, the theory of accounting theories holds among other features that the better a theory of accounting meets the following criteria, the better it is: (1) the criterion of being in correspondence with the real world; (2) the criterion of having the capability to build models; (3) the criterion of being comprehensive; (4) the criterion of being self-consistent; (5) the criterion of being consistent with well-developed theories in other disciplines; (6) the criterion of not rejecting the basic framework of the field, sometimes referred to as the limiting criterion.

1. The Real-World Criterion. The criteria that make an accounting theory desirable are not held to be a closed set, and the foregoing list may well have to be expanded. Criteria also change from time to time but, as with all kinds of theories, the first and primary criterion is that of being in accord with observations in the real world. For this notion to be operational, it is important to recognize that the criterion of a real-world base has changed over the years and will continue to change as *observational techniques* and *experimental methods* improve our capacity to know what the real world is. In the 40s and 50s Paton and Littleton could observe, as the real world, the information needs of undefined public users as they were reflected in the prevailing accounting practice and use those observations, plus a bit of creativity and a priori reasoning, to establish that their statement of corporate accounting standards was "the" theory of accounting. By the middle of the 60s, observational techniques had become much more precise, and the area seems almost to have emerged as a field of study in itself, with the result that data-collection methods became sufficiently developed to show that managerial information needs for planning purposes were not being met by Paton and Littleton's statement of corporate accounting standards. ASOBAT's broad framework, which introduced a considerable amount of flexibility into accounting, recognized these newly observed information needs but provided neither definitive accounting practices nor principles to deal with the newly perceived real world. Moreover, the ASOBAT structure asserted the observational existence of a multifaceted real world where various attributes of it required different measures and disclosures for different purposes, an assertion having wide intuitive support and rapidly verified to the highest level of accuracy possible with the research methods then available—situation analysis and intuitive reasoning. In the decade since, the accelerating advance of accounting knowledge has given rise to improved observation and data-collection techniques in the form of research instruments and knowledge-development methods for accounting, such as survey research, controlled experiments, normative analyses, and field studies that can suggest the behavioral impact of a bit of information on specified decision-makers, determine the reaction of the financial markets to specific accounting disclosures, and reveal to some extent the social consequences of various accounting disclosures. As these *observation techniques* and *experimental research methods* have developed, a priori research views of the real world have been expanded beyond the traditional areas in which the deductive process of reasoning from basic premises and definitions has been applied. Creative effort has been directed toward the definition of the real world underlying accounting thought. The need to expand the scope of a priori research may have been motivated by the realization that the "real world" as conceived by accountants was overly constricted, as was evidenced by their unwillingness to accept the propositions of Moonitz (*The Basic Postulates of Accounting*) and Sprouse and Moonitz (*A Tentative Set of Broad Accounting Principles for Business Enterprise*). In any event, shortly after the publication of their wholistic real-world views, Chambers, Ijiri and Sterling expanded the search for a base for accounting research that could relate the results of research to accounting practice. In the process, they broadened the base of a priori research with borrowing from such basic disciplines as philosophy, the behavioral sciences, mathematics, and formal logic. In the process, there slowly emerged the widespread realization that underlying the notion of a priori research was evidence of a real world with unlimited characteristics, the discernment of which requires the inclusion of a great deal of creativity in accounting research. As a result, at the leading edge of current a priori research is some substantial creative inquiry into the nature of the real world which transcends any speculative collection of "good ideas" or hypotheses which can be subjected to empirical testing. In fact, much current a priori research deals with metaphysical propositions about the real world which are tinged with value judgments and with goals and objectives (Trueblood Committee Report, 1973) that cannot be tested. Possibly current a priori research might best be thought of as creatively initiated and deductively derived accounting propositions having intuitive appeal to qualified accountants as being in accord with exigent real-world requirements.

A priori research is distinctive in that its tools of research are frequently not those of statistical analysis, though some researchers do use them. Rather the accepted tools are carefully developed and deductively derived judgments, finely tuned phrases, and intuitively appealing generalizations that aim to persuade through an appeal to reason rather than through empirically developed brute facts. Desirable as it would be to trace the impact of this type of research on accounting practice, there are limited means of establishing the extent to which specific new accounting practices can be traced back to specific a priori research conclusions. In the broad sense it is possible to assert that current accounting practice has been strongly influenced by the real world as portrayed in Paton and Littleton's *Introduction to Corporate Accounting Standards*. Yet note that the FASB Standard No. 2 on "Accounting for Research and Development Costs" rejected Paton and Littleton's matching concept, and this action may have opened the floodgates for attempts to develop a theory of accounting theories which would identify those theories that are in accord with real-world observations.

But what is the nature of the real world? To deal with the question, recall the flurry of a priori research and court cases that preceded and followed the FASB Standard No. 4 on gains and losses from extinguishment of debt. On the other hand, years before FASB Standard No. 5 was issued, a priori researchers had been calling for improved accounting for contingencies. A review of the references in the discussion memorandums of the FASB suggests that some a priori research on the subject had taken place as much as 25 to 30 years prior to the memorandums but that the preponderance of the a priori research referenced was less than ten years old. The implication is that the "real world" is not stationary and may change so much in ten years that the real world observed and painted by the a priori research of the past becomes irrelevant (Appendix B). While the FASB emphasis on more current a priori research could be due to the inadequacy of the FASB library research, a systematic examination of the background support for the references, the literature referenced in the discussion memorandums on leases and research and development, suggests that in this one case, at least, effective a priori research is applied within ten to fifteen years. When one examines specific a priori research propositions, one finds no clear discernible pattern which would indicate which a priori research is most acceptable. But it does appear appropriate to conclude from such an examination that unless the conclusions of a priori research are quickly adopted in practice, they tend to lose their distinctiveness because they are soon modified or adjusted to new environmental situations. This lack of stability in a priori propositions may be unfortunate because, of the four time spans with which accounting research should be concerned (distant future, near future, present, and past), a priori research is virtually the only research method which attempts to deal with the distant future and, to a large extent, the near future. To the extent that the future is being constantly modified, it is difficult to determine the validity of the initial conclusions proposed.

Essential as a priori research is to any growing and evolving field, the unsuccessful attempts to use it to "make a case" for almost any proposition and the frequent discovery that propositions developed a priori are not in accord with the subsequently discovered real-world facts led to a scholarly effort to replace it with more rigorous methods of knowledge development. As these methods develop, it is easy to understand why the area of concern for a priori research tends to shift to other unresolved issues at the leading edge of accounting thought. Such is the current state of affairs: new research instruments and tools have fostered a new generation of accounting standards which are slowly tightening the observational processes of accountants so that their perceptions of the real world have become more accurate and are advancing data-collection criteria to the point where the relevance of their observations is vastly improved.

In general, the theory of accounting theories suggests that to be relevant to the practical world of affairs any comprehensive accounting theory, by whatever research method it is developed, must be able to encompass newly discovered economic and social phenomena in which accounting must play a role: social indicators, new concepts of assets and liabilities (leases), public right-to-know doctrine (disclosure), inflation, energy shortages, pollution, professional liabilities, other environmental aspects, and even the total socioeconomic system.

2. The Model-Building Criterion. The second criterion of accounting theory is the capability to build models. The inference is that a priori-developed accounting theory must foster rather detailed models to accommodate the information phenomena appropriate for specific situations. Otherwise, it tends not to be accepted. To the extent possible, these models should be relevant to practical problems, but conceptually, some a priori researchers contend they need not be precise: at this stage it is more important that accounting theory have the capability to yield, foster, or build models that relate to specific situations. The theory must be such that the concepts and relationships it displays can be used to develop detailed descriptions of solutions for practical problems. The above is established as a criterion because to gain general acceptance an accounting theory must be capable of being related to many specific situations; therefore it must be both *comprehensive* and *self-consistent.* Trueblood (1960) stated the problem well, ". . . there is [sic] today no generally accepted criteria for the design of an integrated information system for a firm—for deciding what information is needed, how frequently the information is required, how accurate it needs to be. . . ." This is the practical demand which a priori-developed theory must meet if it is to survive. Unfortunately, to do so, much of the a priori research has had to be expressed at some level of abstraction in order to provide a grasp of the overall phenomena and to assure self-consistency. And therein lie many of the problems of accounting. Excessive abstraction reduces the ability of various users to apply the theory, with the result that it may exist in isolation unused and untrusted. Also, depending upon the process by which it is developed, the abstractions may not be a good reflection of the real-world situation and thus may not be applicable. Whether because of excessive abstraction or because it is unrealistic, a theory may be rejected. Less abstract theoretical propositions on the other hand frequently do not meet the criterion of being able to build models because of their limited scope.

The criterion of ability to build models, if applied systematically, would do much to improve the quality of a priori-developed accounting theory. Work by an AAA Committee on Accounting Theory Construction and Verification (1971) dealt with this topic in recent years. It specified that a decision model must include the following general requirements: (1) the optimization rule, decision criterion, or goal of the decision-maker; (2) all feasible acts available to the decision-maker; (3) all possible events or states that may occur over the decision horizon; (4) probability distributions relating to the set of possible events; (5) set of payoffs, conditional upon the state and act. These requirements can be used to evaluate an accounting theory in terms of whether or not the theory will be able to provide a substrate upon which a valid model can be built.

3. The Comprehensive Criterion. The third criterion of accounting theory is that it be comprehensive. Unless a theory can be related to the whole field of accounting, it cannot be applied to the neglected areas. Since the scope of the field changes, perfect compliance with the third criterion can never be achieved; but in theory selection or in the creation of new theories, the more comprehensive theory would be preferred to a less comprehensive one.

The requirement of comprehensiveness is rather rigorous, and normally most accounting theories can only approach it. For a theory to be comprehensive, it must both *span the field* and subsume *measurement rules* which can be operationalized. To span the field, it must be of such a nature that an analyst can deduce an outcome relevant to every possible situation from the basic assumptions of the theory about the nature of the universe within which accounting operates. If the needs of the specific situation are not in accord with the deduced outcome, the theory is wrong and must be corrected. This self-correcting process must be a part of any a priori theory of accounting theories. As an illustration of the shortcomings of a less-than-comprehensive theory, one of the main criticisms of an APB-proposed pronouncement on leases (APB No. 7), aside from the use of words that permitted alternative interpretation, was that it did not span the entire field of executory contracts. As a consequence, the supporting theory could not be used to deal with the contractual arrangements that produced the same effect as a lease though technically not a lease. An example of an inadequate conceptual accounting theory is the income-smoothing hypothesis, which lacks measurement rules capable of indicating which of the alternative accounting procedures should be used in a particular situation.

4. The Self-Consistent Criterion. The fourth criterion, self-consistency is the most frequently used criterion in evaluating a priori theory and research. It was almost the only criterion used in past a priori theory development. That is, much of the past a priori research consisted of arguing that because one procedure was used in one situation it should be used in another in order to be consistent. The literature abounds with demonstrations of inconsistencies in accounting reasoning. But the interesting aspects of these analyses is the variety of definitions of consistency that exist. Distilling them and confining the term to self-consistency, as contrasted with the broader notion of consistency, the self-consistency criterion in the theory of theories would hold that to be self-consistent a theory must be internally consistent in a logical sense. To be self-consistent, the theory must consistently predict or provide the same outcome for every similar situation or experiment. In other words, a theory must call for similar procedures or measures of the same thing or similar things under similar situations to arrive at the same result, which is different and broader than consistent procedures over successive periods of time. Another confusing feature in the a priori research literature dealing with self-consistency is a tendency to confuse verbal self-consistency with content or substance self-consistency. The theory-of-theories criterion would require content self-consistency. To illustrate the distinction, consider the theoretical proposition that expense should be measured in terms of historical cost. Verbal self-consistency would require merely that expense be measured in terms of historical cost. In substance or content, there may be several historical costs. For example, it is inconsistent for an accounting theory of historical costing of expense to be used to measure depreciation and also be used to measure repairs expense because two concepts of historical cost are involved: original acquisition cost of the item depreciated versus the replacement (restoration) acquisition cost of the restored part. The theory of historical costing of expenses, to the extent that it measures different things, does not comply with the criterion of content or substance self-consistency.

5. The Multi-Disciplines Criterion. The fifth criterion of accounting research and theory requires agreement with fundamental theoretical knowledge. When the accounting aspects of the theory are "dropped"—that is, when it is assumed that accounting does not exist—the nonaccounting aspects of the theory and its principles should be consistent with the principles of the information development process proposed by basic discipline findings, such as those in economic and psychological studies which deal with organizational motivation and behavior. Specifically, it seems reasonable to propose that, as the ultimate objective, for an a priori accounting theory to be useful in the total information systems of future society, it will have to be expressed in terms or methods that will permit a meshing with economics and pyschology, particularly, with the principles of utility theory, uncertainty, perception, and organization behavior. That is, a priori research must be consistent with other disciplines.

6. The Limiting Criterion. The sixth criterion of accounting theory holds that to gain general acceptance, an accounting theory should not violate the standards of an existing theory which it cannot supplant. For example, it could be held that a theory's propositions should not come in conflict with the matching concept Paton and Littleton proposed for use in measuring income. A theory having this property of compatibility with the Paton and Littleton *Introduction of Corporate Accounting Standards* would be said to fall within the Paton and Littleton limit. Not all accounting theories have this property. One not meeting the Paton and Littleton limit would be a theory contending that the operating concept of income is identical with all-inclusive concept of income, which is an obvious disagreement with the existing theory that has yet to be supplanted.

To summarize, the a priori research of the past decade suggests that a currently acceptable accounting theory would have to be in correspondence with the real world, have the capability to build models, be complete, be self-consistent, agree with findings in other disciplines and not exceed without justification the prevailing limits of the field. These six criteria may be used to categorize accounting theories as either desirable or undesirable. A great many accounting theories are essentially undesirable because they do not meet one or more of the criteria. Such theories should henceforth be ignored.

The Scope of Various Accounting Theories

The a priori research literature (e.g., Committee on Foundations of Accounting Measurement Report, *Accounting Review Supplement,* 1971) suggests that the scope of desirable a priori theories of accounting can be separated into two types: *economic-based theories* and *information-based theories*. The former attempt to measure economic activity while the latter aim to provide information. In general terms, an information-based accounting theory is one in which the accounting process is treated as synonymous with the process of developing and communicating quantitative information that directly motivates a decision-maker to act. The information may or may not be purely economic in nature. Conceptually, income measures, variance-analysis calculations, unit costs and indeed any accounting information one cares to imagine all aim to provide information to meet various types of human needs and wants, and do not serve merely as disclosures of economic events and activities independent of concern for the behavioral impact of the disclosure on individuals and groups. ASOBAT's relativity structure has some characteristics of an information-based theory, and there are other such behavioral views of accounting theory. Each information-based theory differs from the others in the same way different psychological views of the nature of human wants exist but may be construed as giving rise to an overall view of human behavior.

Economic-based theories are by definition those based on the assumption that human information needs are known and that reports on income, resources and obligations, and similar economic phenomena will meet the needs of society. Traditionally, accounting theories have been economic-based, but there are emerging a priori studies which indicate a need to shift from economic-based theories to behavioral or information-based theories. It may be helpful to dwell a bit more on the notion of information-based theories.

In the total world society system, accounting has been a relatively weak system compared to such fields as law and medicine. But it has a robustness that has caused it to survive and grow. Nevertheless, the predictions of any accounting information-based theory applicable to the whole world system probably should be analyzed using the assumption that the theory has a comparatively constricted scope. Various attempts have been made in a priori research to broaden the scope of the accounting information system. The AICPA Study Group on the Objectives of Financial Statements, dealing with the public disclosure function, stated that "the basic objective of financial statements is to provide information useful for making economic decisions." The significance of the statement is that it does not state that the prime objective is to prepare financial statements which reveal economic activity or status. Rather, by the a priori reasoning of the Study Group, the objective is to provide useable information. The scope is limited to information which may serve as a basis for economic decisions, and there is an implication that a substantial portion of the information should be in quantitative form.

The Historical Perspective

Now for those still "hanging in there," it may be well to trace the trend of a priori research over the past few years, first conceptually, then with documentary support. Conceptually the following rather distinct steps, types, or levels are evident in the literature:

1. The attempt to develop the basic postulates and principles of accounting (Moonitz, and Sprouse and Moonitz).
2. The attempt to broaden the base of the accounting discipline and relate it to the basic disciplines (Chambers, Ijiri, and Sterling).
3. The attempt to formalize accounting theory into a more abstract form with characteristics of relativity (Mattessich, Williams, and Demski).
4. The attempt to politicalize accounting theory for practical use in bargaining by preparers and users of accounting information (FASB, Horngren).
5. The attempt to develop a theory of accounting theories (FASB, Churchman).

Documentary support for the first three types of a priori research may be found in Carl Nelson's analysis of the subject at the University of Illinois conference in 1971 and the critiques by Yuji Ijiri and Kermit Larson. These three types of a priori research are quite distinct and each used a deductive process in developing theoretical proposals. Moonitz openly asserted an intent to develop the basic postulates from which principles could be deductively derived, and Sprouse attempted to establish a deductive relationship between the postulates and the principles of accounting. Intuitively appealing as both efforts seemed in the search for a broad framework of accounting theory, they could not be applied to specific situations, and a priori research of another type attracted the attention of the fundamental researcher, though various authors had taken this approach well before Moonitz and Sprouse had drawn together the literature on the postulates–principles–practices type of theory. In any event, the belief arose that accounting should have its base in the basic disciplines. Essentially, this type of a priori research differed from the Moonitz-Sprouse type only in that it assumed that its basic postulates could be found in the basic disciplines and that its principles could deductively be derived from the finding of the basic disciplines. But this type of a priori research went further. It attempted to integrate accounting into something of a world-wide and interdisciplinary general theory. While this general-theory type of accounting theory proved interesting and undoubtedly improved the academic status of accounting professors on the campus, the findings of the relevant social-science disciplines are not unequivocal, and the deduced accounting theory represented an unstable mass. Out of this condition arose the notion of empirical research—more accurately it arose prior to the proclamation of the limitations of the general-theory approach by skeptics who refused to accept the general-theory approach at all—whence the idea emerged that accounting research should "get the basic facts," and articulate these first into minor theories with the ultimate objective that some day the empirically verified facts would be drawn together into a well-structured statement which would represent the theory of accounting.

Whether merely an intellectual exercise, or an attempt to clarify the general theory, or an effort to provide a means for integrating the findings of empirical research into a grand theory, the axiomatic type of a priori research sought to develop a formal symbolic structure initially devoid of meaning in itself but capable of being translated into real-world substance as needed. Its advantage lay in its ability to articulate the symbols according to the rules of logic or mathematics and subsequently reveal new insights, when transposed, into accounting.

Largely out of frustration with prior efforts, but also because of the pressure of the practicing arm of the profession to provide generally accepted accounting principles, and in compliance with the Financial Accounting Standards Board's determination of what was acceptable to preparers and users of accounting data, a priori researchers turned to a political type of a priori research. As Horngren states categorically (1973), "My hypothesis is that the setting of accounting standards is as much a product of political action as of flawless logic or empirical findings. Why? Because the setting of standards is a social decision. Standards place restrictions on behavior; therefore, they must be accepted by the affected parties." His a priori theory is that Congress, the SEC, the Department of Treasury, other federal agencies, and the lobby groups of industry can and do change accounting principles and standards. Then he points to the essence of the political type of accounting theory when he calls for consideration of the "marketing" or "selling" of accounting principles. That is to say, a political type of accounting research should include within itself the means for gaining acceptance of what it has produced. Given the dual function of "production" and "marketing" as inherent elements of a priori research, it becomes apparent that they impinge on each other. What can be produced depends ultimately upon what can be sold and what can be sold requires adequate production. In Horngren's view, the base for political a priori research and theory rests on the following premise: "In the 1960's and early 1970's researchers in accounting borrowed heavily from quantitative methods and the behavioral sciences. I hope that the 1970's see some concentration on the optimal methods for wielding accounting power in a democratic society." Subsequently, Gerboth suggested (1973) that accountants expect too much from formalized accounting research and pointed to the shortcomings of accounting research which led to the downfall of the Accounting Principles Board. His view that accounting inquiry can no longer be confined to the determination of the verity of the accounting rules, but must be expanded to include acceptability of the rule-making process itself, gained considerable support. He pointed out quite clearly that the effectiveness of accounting standards or principles, however developed, depends not on technical competence but on political competence. His proposition was that "rationality as well as prudence lies not in seeking final answers, but rather in compromise—essentially a political process."

The political type of a priori research has devastating effects, for it implies that no fact can be proved in physical or social-sciences research unless it is accepted. General acceptance and that alone is the criterion of good a priori research. Mautz asserted the same view when he held that while a new idea may be "golden" to an academic, it is of no interest to a practitioner unless it is "generally accepted." As Gerboth recognized, the political type of a priori research seems "terribly unscientific." It was his belief that "current orthodoxy in accounting inquiry stresses, at least as an ideal, rigorous analysis and determinate solutions of the type popularly supposed to comprise inquiry in the much-envied natural sciences" and that "next to that ideal, political analysis and intuitive solutions seem to compare unfavorably." It is generally recognized that politics and intuition as tools of inquiry are in themselves in need of an underlying discipline. That is, the fundamental concepts of politics and intuition need to be organized into a systematic, validated structure. Because this structure is not available and because it is believed that the scientific method does have the needed rigorousness, an unease prevails about political solutions. To the scientifically inclined researcher any intuitively based movement of a priori research into politics seems an unscientific and unworthy endeavor. But the a priori research of the political type continues to search for the discipline that underlies politics, and its supporters emphasize the usefulness of the results. They rest their case on the view that much accounting scientific research yields irrelevant conclusions and point out that no criterion of science requires that the most advanced analytical techniques must be used in accounting inquiry regardless of their suitability. Usefulness of results rather than rigorous analysis is considered more meaningful.

There are many supporters of the political type of a priori research. Representative of others who joined in this effort to develop a political type of a priori research are certain members of the staff of the Financial Accounting Standards Board who diligently seek out the views of financial analysts and corporate executives on proposed accounting standards. The resulting discussion memoranda by the Financial Accounting Standards Board frequently reflect this political data, which is then used by the Board to issue standards for public accounting. A review of the basis of the conclusion by the FASB that "all research and development costs encompassed by this Statement (Standard No. 2) shall be charged to expense when incurred" reveals constant reference to "respondents to the Discussion Memorandum" (on which the Standard was based) and to the fact that the "Board agreed" or the "Board agrees with this view and the change is reflected in paragraph ———." Now there is nothing "wrong" with the political type of a priori research if the attempt is to formulate a theory, a principle, or a standard that will be generally accepted. If general acceptance is to be the sole criterion by which theory is to be evaluated as desirable or undesirable, the political type of a priori research does give the appearance of yielding acceptable theory almost by definition. It qualifies as a priori research in that it is presented as a judgmental deductive process involving reasoning from a variety of derived facts. But as Bierman and Dukes (1975) subsequently pointed out, this particular deductive process did not meet the requirements of research and development because it did not adequately define the basis for the deductive process. The possibility of this type of error may explain the general lack of confidence in the political type of a priori research, although the error persists in a great number of articles and research conclusions.

Characteristics of the Theory of Accounting Theories

Returning to the theory-of-accounting-theories type of a priori research, which may be with us for some time, it seems appropriate to consider some of its characteristics and the questions with which it is concerned. The most obvious characteristic previously noted is that it seeks to establish criteria for evaluating theory. Attention was directed to this development by the 1969–70 AAA Committee on Accounting Theory Construction and Verification when it stated that the "process of theory construction and verification has for many years been the subject of analysis—recently [it] has become a topic for research and discussion in accounting." While the committee was attempting to establish the beginnings of an empirical base for accounting theory development and verification, the committee report itself represented an a priori argument for its concept of a theory.

Once this approach of criteria development was introduced to a priori research, it spread rapidly. It is significant that the FASB discussion memorandum did not deal with the principle of materiality itself but with the "criteria" for determining materiality. A review of the literature in the *Accounting Review, Journal of Accountancy, Journal of Accounting Research,* and *The International Journal of Accounting* reveals the growing tendency for a priori research to consist of comparative analysis which uses variously derived criteria in making comparisons. In addition to the AICPA study on the objectives of financial statements, which sought criteria that could be used in selecting appropriate accounting standards and procedures, the FASB efforts to develop a conceptual framework for subsequent standards seem likewise to be searching for criteria to justify their pronouncements.

Specific examples of efforts to develop a base for a theory of accounting theories include Ijiri's (*Logic and Sanctions in Accounting*) distinction between previous accounting theory and accounting policy; only the latter involves the definition and means of implementing goals. The inference is that only a theory-of-theories type of a priori research can treat both as one theoretical subject matter. Another example is the effort by the Accountants International Study Group to establish uniform guidelines and to point out the need for different and distinctive criteria for international theories of accounting. Although it includes a great deal of the political type of a priori research, the Fourth Directive of the European Economic Community (Commission of the European Economic Community, 1970), dealing with the preparation of annual reports, also includes an effort to establish criteria for selecting appropriate accounting principles and procedures. Another example is Samuelson's (1973) proof that properly discounted present values of assets fluctuate randomly established a criterion which can be used to prefer one accounting valuation theory over another. Baumol and Klevorick's overview (1970) of the literature, dealing with the Averch-Johnson Model of the firm under rate-of-return regulation, indicated that the criterion used by Averch-Johnson was not the most significant one and carried with it an implication that some means for distinguishing the appropriateness of a theory was needed. Cowan's (1968) call for a pragmatic approach to accounting theory amounts to little more than a call for attention to the existence of alternative criteria for evaluating a priori research studies but, when one attempts to establish these criteria, what emerges is the need for a systematic, interrelated structure of criteria which would then represent the theory for theory selection. Wheeler (1970) supports the use of broad economic and social goals as criteria for selecting among alternative accounting theories those appropriate for the development of information for optimum decision models, though he does not present these broad goals as a supertheoretical structure nor does he advocate a theory of accounting theories. He merely leaves his thought with us.

Hakansson (1969), having proposed a family of normative models of the individual's economic decision problem under risk, thereby providing a means for improving the observational capacity of accountants, suggests that these models contain an induced theory of accounting. He contends that criteria for investment, for financing, and for consumption need to be established to develop, evaluate, select, and coordinate accounting theories. Because he uses a deductive process, his paper, although normatively based, provides an overall model of how a theory of accounting theories could be adduced from current accounting practice. Charnes, Colantoni, Cooper, and Kortanek (1972) have illustrated a variety of possibilities for modeling (theorizing) and have related these models to one another, leaving the implication that a theory of accounting theories could be the structure that ties all the theories together. One must infer that this must be done a priori. Lounderback (1971) calls attention to the prevalence of projectability as a criterion for selecting income measurement methods, and questions it. In so doing, it is apparent he is contributing to a theory of theories by improving the criteria for measuring income. Colantoni, Manes, and Whinston (1971) propose a framework "within which one can work on both the theoretical issues concerned with extending accounting to provide more types of information and the practical issues surrounding the efficient implementation of an accounting system" which is something of a framework for accounting theories. Feltham and Demski (1970) use models as a basis of information evaluation and in so doing contribute a criterion useful to a priori research on a theory of theories.

From the foregoing, the following characteristics of the theory of accounting theories seem to emerge: (1) the theory establishes criteria for evaluating theories; (2) the theory subsumes properties of both goals and means theories; (3) the theory identifies and clarifies all alternative theories for the evaluation process or for further development; (4) the theory is an open-ended structure in respect to *observational tools, concepts for determining needed theories, means of developing theories,* and the *type of philosophy to accept.*

Overall, the expansion of a priori research or a reorientation of its objective is still in process of development. But the strong impression is that a theory of accounting theories is a necessity for the development of meaningful a priori theory and research. Not only at the theory-of-theories level, but at the level of authoritative principles, which are issued for the guidance of accounting practice, there have been a priori developments which have supported a broader concept of assets (leases) and more precise definitions, and which have extended the applicability of accounting measures to new areas (cost-benefit analysis).

In conclusion, it does appear that a priori research is performing well its function of expanding the scope of accounting thought and is pointing to a number of acreas in need of empirical study and analytical treatment. If a theory of accounting theories can be developed, it will narrow the time gap between valid research and accounting practice until it becomes apparent that research has caused practice to change. Only then can it be maintained that a priori research has impact on accounting practice in a direct sense. Overall, the attempted contribution of a priori thought may be so great that it may have been too much for the empiricists and the practitioners to absorb, and this may account for the limited direct impact of a priori research on accounting practice.

Appendix A. Empirical Support for the Proposition That A Priori Research Does Not Have Impact on Accounting Practice

One hundred and eighty-three articles, pamphlets and other material appearing in the last ten years (1965–75) were selected as a priori research or theory contributions. The search algorithm used to identify a priori theory or research consisted of these questions: "Does the article include empirical or behavioral findings," and "Has the substance of the article been published previously?" A double "no" answer was required for selection. A limitation to this process of literature selection is that a significant element of subjective judgment had to be applied.

The 183 articles were reviewed and 33 which seemed to use comparatively less of the deductive reasoning process of a priori research were excluded from consideration. Of the 150 remaining, 57 were judged to be "a priori" research which confirmed or justified an existing or proposed accounting practice. Eighty-one seem to coexist with new or proposed changes in accounting practices. Some supported and some opposed the changes. This left only 12 items that could be said to precede a new accounting practice. But this was only the beginning of the "good news." Efforts to select the significant idea(s) in each a priori item and to trace the flow and development of a priori findings were not successful because a great deal of disagreement exists over the origin of an idea. Similarly, it was not possible to establish criteria which an idea would have to meet to say it derived from another idea.

It was then decided to make a list of all the noted problems of accounting practice, whether or not they were ultimately dealt with in an authoritatively backed rule or regulation, and then seek out the a priori accounting literature that dealt with the problem before it was recognized as a problem. Of 100 problems noted in the 1963–73 period, only 16 had been dealt with in the a priori literature either before or after a solution to the problem was necessary. (The 100 problems were not selected on a random basis but were drawn from a file of problems selected from time to time over the ten-year period.)

The inference of these surveys is that a priori research does not: (1) cover the scope of practical problems observed; (2) deal with practical problems in advance of an authoritative proposal in an effective way. As the following illustrative data show, the agonizing fact is that "a priori" research needs a guiding theory for the *evaluation* of a priori theories and to stimulate the development of relevant a priori theory and research. The proposal is awesome in its implications: the change in direction necessary for a priori research to achieve impact on practice directly is fully as great as the change that occurred when alchemy was changed to chemistry.

Appendix B. The Matching Concept: A Test Case

The matching concept developed through a priori research by Paton and Littleton is frequently cited as evidence that in the long run a priori research has impact on practice in many ways. Theirs was a broad conception and indeed many authoritative practices cite Paton and Littleton as theoretical support for their existence. But the uncited fact is that Paton and Littleton from time to time insisted that their *Introduction to Corporate Accounting Standards* was derived from existing practice. Several scholars have suggested that Paton and Littleton provided a rationale that justified existing practice. Because practices varied extensively in the early 1930s, one could contend that several variant practices were changed to comply with the Paton and Littleton framework. In this rather special sense, one could contend that Paton and Littleton's enunciation of the matching concept did influence practice. One must however, maintain a bit of skepticism, in that the Paton and Littleton a priori proposal of the matching concept would not have influenced practice had the concept not been in accord with existing practice.

If doubt can exist that the Paton and Littleton study influenced practice, the question arises as to whether any a priori research influences practice. To test this question in a quick and easy way, a survey of the a priori research publications in 1950 was made to see what was being proposed at that time. The collected list was then compared with a similar list of the a priori publications in 1965. As the data below indicate, the carry-through over the 15 year period was very small. (If an a priori research proposal of 1950 had been adopted in practice, it was included as being in existence in 1965 even though not in the 1965 literature.) While the search technique used to scan the accounting literature was a simple one and more sophisticated techniques may provide more reliable data, the very small carry-through of a priori research suggests that much of it is soon forgotten. If one then moves to 1975 to examine practice, one finds that few of the a priori proposals developed in 1950 have been adopted in practice. At the same time one finds a host of current accounting problems for which no a priori research existed in the 1950 literature. The situation may be presented diagrammatically as follows:

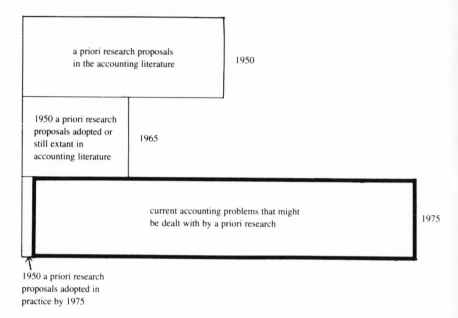

a priori research proposals
in the accounting literature   1950

1950 a priori research
proposals adopted or
still extant in   1965
accounting literature

current accounting problems that might
be dealt with by a priori research   1975

1950 a priori research
proposals adopted in
practice by 1975

References

AAA Committee. *A Statement of Basic Accounting Theory.* American Accounting Association, 1966.

AAA Committee. "Report of the Committee on Accounting Theory Construction and Verification." *Accounting Review Supplement,* 1971.

AAA Committee. "Report of the 1966–68 Committee on External Reporting." *Accounting Review Supplement,* American Accounting Association, 1969.

AAA Committee. "Report of the Committee on Foundations of Accounting Measurement." *Accounting Review Supplement,* 1971.

AAA Committee. "Report of the Committee on Managerial Decision Models." *Accounting Review Supplement,* American Accounting Association, 1969.

AICPA Committee. *Report of the Committee on Scope and Structure.* American Institute of Certified Public Accountants, 1974.

AICPA Study Group. *Objectives of Financial Statement.* American Institute of Certified Public Accountants, October 1973.

Abdel-khalik, A. R. "The Entropy Law, Accounting Data, and Relevance to Decision Making." *Accounting Review* (April 1974).

Averch, H., and L. L. Johnson. "Behavior of the Firm under Regulatory Constraint." *American Economic Review* (December 1962).

Barefield, R. M., and E. E. Comiskey. "The Smoothing Hypothesis: An Alternative Test." *Accounting Review* (April 1972).

Baumol, W. J., and A. K. Klevorick. "Input Choices and Rate-of-Return Regulation: An Overview of the Discussion." *Bell Journal of Economics and Management Science* (Autumn 1970).

Bierman, H. B., and R. E. Dukes. "Accounting Research and Development Costs." *Journal of Accountancy* (April 1975).

Bradford, W. D. "Price-Level Restated Accounting and the Measurement of Inflation Gains and Losses." *Accounting Review* (April 1974).

Braithwaite, R. B. *Scientific Explanation: A Study of the Function of Theory, Probability and Law in Science.* New York: Harper and Brothers, 1960.

Buckley, J. W., P. Kirchner, and R. L. Mathews. "Methodology in Accounting Theory." *Accounting Review* (April 1968).

Butterworth, J. E. "The Accounting System as an Information Function." *Journal of Accounting Research* (Spring 1972).

Chambers, R. J. *Accounting, Evaluation and Economic Behavior.* Englewood Cliffs, N.J.: Prentice-Hall, 1966.

Chapter 6 of the 1970 Fourth Draft of Chapter 6 of the *Societé Européen* published by the Commission of the European Economic Community.

Charnes, A., C. Colantoni, W. W. Cooper, and K. O. Kortanek. "Economic Social and Enterprise Accounting and Mathematical Models." *Accounting Review* (January 1972).

Colantoni, C. S., R. P. Manes, and A. Whinston, "A Unified Approach to the Theory of Accounting and Information Systems." *Accounting Review* (January 1971).

Copeland, R. M. "Income Smoothing" in *Empirical Research in Accounting: Selected Studies.* Chicago: University of Chicago Press, 1968.

Cowan, T. K. "A Pragmatic Approach to Accounting Theory." *Accounting Review* (January 1968).

Demski, Joel. "The General Impossibility of Normative Standards." *Accounting Review* (October 1973).

Demski, J. S. "Choice among Financial Reporting Alternatives." *Accounting Review* (April 1974).

Devine, C. T. "Research Methodology and Accounting Theory Formulation." *Accounting Review* (July 1960).

Feltham, G. A., and J. S. Demski. "The Use of Models in Information Evaluation." *Accounting Review* (October 1970).

Financial Accounting Standards Board. *Criteria for Determining Materiality, Discussion Memorandum.* 1975.

―――. *Statement of Financial Accounting Standards No. 4 and No. 5.* March 1975.

Gerboth, Dale L. "Research Intuition and Politics in Accounting Inquiry." *Accounting Review* (July 1973).

Greenball, M. N. "The Predictive-Ability Criterion: Its Relevance in Evaluating Accounting Data." *Abacus* (June 1971).

Hakansson, Nils H. "An Induced Theory of Accounting under Risk." *Accounting Review* (July 1969).

Ijiri, Yuji. "Physical Measures and Multi-Dimensional Accounting," in *Readings in Accounting Measurement*. American Accounting Association, 1966.

————. *The Foundations of Accounting Measurement*. Englewood Cliffs, N.J.: Prentice-Hall, 1967.

————. *Theory of Accounting Measurement*. American Accounting Association, 1975.

Lambert, S. J. "Basic Assumptions in Accounting Theory Construction." *Journal of Accountancy* (February 1974).

Lewis, Edwin A. "The Evolution (and Revolution) of the Accounting Profession." *Selected Papers 1974*. Haskins and Sells, 1975.

Littleton, A. C. *Structure of Accounting Theory*. American Accounting Association, 1953.

Lounderback, J. G. "Projectability as a Criterion for Income Determination Methods." *Accounting Review* (April 1971).

Mattessich, R. *Accounting and Analytical Methods*. Richard D. Irwin, 1964.

————. "Methodological Preconditions and Problems of a General Theory of Accounting." *Accounting Review* (July 1972).

May, R. G., G. G. Mueller, and T. H. Williams. *A New Introduction to Financial Accounting*. Englewood Cliffs, N.J.: Prentice-Hall, 1975.

McDonald, D. L. "Feasibility Criteria for Accounting Measures." *Accounting Review* (October 1967).

Moonitz, M. *The Basic Postulates of Accounting*. American Institute of Certified Public Accountants, 1961.

Nelson, Carl L. "A Priori Research in Accounting," *Accounting Research 1960–1970: A Critical Evaluation,* ed. N. Dopuch and L. Revsine. Urbana, Ill.: Center for International Education and Research in Accounting, Department of Accountancy, University of Illinois, 1973.

Paton, W. A., and A. C. Littleton. *An Introduction to Corporate Accounting Standards*. American Accounting Association, 1940.

Revsine, Lawrence. "On the Correspondence Between Replacement Cost Income and Economic Income." *Accounting Review* (July 1970).

Ronen, J., and G. H. Sorter. "Relevant Accounting." *Journal of Business* (April 1972).

Samuelson, Paul A. "Proof that Properly Discounted Present Values of Assets Vibrate Randomly." *Bell Journal of Economics and Management Science* (Autumn 1973).

Snavely, Howard J. "Accounting Information Criteria." *Accounting Review* (April 1967).

Sprouse, R. T., and M. Moonitz. *A Tentative Set of Broad Accounting Principles for Business Enterprises*. American Institute of Certified Public Accountants, 1962.

Staunton, J. J. "Realization: A Misapplied Concept in Accounting." *Abacus* (December 1973).

Stent, G. S. *The Coming of the Golden Age.* American Museum of Natural History, 1969.

Sterling, Robert. "On Theory Construction and Verification." *Accounting Review* (July 1970).

———. "Relevant Financial Reporting in an Age of Price Changes." *Journal of Accountancy* (February 1975).

Trueblood, R. M. "Operations Research—A Challenge to Accounting." *Journal of Accountancy* (May 1960).

Wheeler, J. T. "Accounting Theory and Research in Perspective." *Accounting Review* (January 1970).

Williams, T. H., and C. H. Griffin. "On the Nature of Empirical Verification in Accounting." *Abacus* (December 1969).

Discussion

Hector R. Anton

Norton Bedford's paper advances the proposal that a priori research be evaluated in terms of some concept of a theory or theories. That is a pregnant thought. Unfortunately, he has apparently not had the time to do more than hint at its possibilities, and frankly here he only makes some rather speculative assertions, largely unsupported, based upon the works of certain researchers. For example, Bedford's assertion that "substantial literature suggests that within the last ten years many accountants inclined toward a priori research have become convinced that a general relativity structure is the appropriate view of accounting" is a subjective judgment that he can certainly make. But, to extend this to state that a "number of a priori researchers and scholars have adopted a neutral position (between Paton & Littleton's 'closely reasoned deductive theory' and ASOBAT's 'loose formulation')[1] . . . . declining to support one view over the other because of their intent that accounting theory be accepted and used as a guide for accounting practice" is sheer frivolity. I doubt that anyone would "decline to support" because of any such intent—rather I would venture to say that both Paton and Littleton and ASOBAT were inclined to guide accounting practice (see for example Bedford's agreement with this on pp. 5–6). Obviously, Bedford has no evidence, though it might be a testable hypothesis. Where, for example, is the evidence of the "impact on both practicing accountants and researchers" of the theory of theories? And from where does he get "the notion that accounting reports [were deemed] unrelated to user needs" by earlier a priori researchers such that these notions had to be "dispelled" by a priori research on the objectives of accounting? Paton and Littleton, and earlier, Sanders, Hatfield, and Moore put heavy emphasis on users and usefulness. Of course, both monographs *assumed* certain users—*but so do the Study Group and ASOBAT!* The sentence, "Similarly, the emergence of expanded footnotes and treatment of leases in the balance sheet can be traced back to a priori research propositions that greater disclosure is appropriate and that change in business practices can change accounting concepts of assets and liabilities," is equally gratuitous. Greater disclosure

1. All quotes are from the Bedford paper unless otherwise noted. All emphasis is mine unless otherwise noted.

has been urged for more than thirty years, and the growth of footnotes is directly attributable to SEC policy. The treatment of leases in the balance sheet is an exercise in substance over form, and owes its theoretical support to present value theories of the twenties and thirties, which in turn were based on the Swedish school's economic theory of income.

Also, why is Sterling's explanation that the "theory of general purchasing power was a different thing than current-value accounting" any more "self-consistent" than Edwards and Bell's more rigorous treatment of the same concepts almost 20 years earlier? Possibly Sterling was able to "clarify prevailing accounting thought on the issue" because he published in the *Journal of Accountancy* and in more lucid prose—but that is due to *communication* and not to a "theory of theories." Similarly Bedford's assertions that Bradford's (1974) "implied a priori-developed theory" ("that the interest rate anticipates inflation so that the monetary gain or loss on holding net monetary items should be offset by the higher inflation induced interest receipts or payments") is "more acceptable to accounting practice" because it is "more in correspondence with real-world phenomena" (and presumably supports the "theory of theories") is dream stuff. Bedford assumes so, subjectively. Certainly many would accept that interest rates attempt to reflect inflation factors and *may* (or may not) be more in accord with real-world phenomena, but does this make it "more acceptable to accounting practice"? I doubt it. Similarly the reference to Davidson and Weil's study is flawed. Is any study with empirical data a "criteria view of a priori research?" Will their study *"prevent* the business motivated influences on corporate planning and on accounting in times of inflation from going undisclosed to society at large"? And *must* "the limited practical success of unbounded a priori research based on speculation and intuitive judgments. . . . have influenced them to use the broad concept of systematic criteria as a means of substantiating their reasoning"? Again, this is "pure intuitive judgment" and "unbounded a priori" speculation by Bedford. One last picky comment with respect to present value measures: There were "well-developed theories (and applications) in insurance, bond investments, and other fields" thirty or more years ago, and, therefore, their being "expressed in terms of the criterion of being in accord with" these theories could not have been the reason for their more recent adoption, and could not have influenced (one way or the other) the rejection of Moonitz and Sprouse and Moonitz in 1963 by the APB.

Notwithstanding that Bedford's case was not made, his criteria (on page 4) are useful for testing theories, and I will venture that they may be found useful by theory-constructors in the future. But that is not the subject of this conference.

Here, we must try to see how a priori research may be useful in providing *more efficient* (economic) direction for other research, both a priori and empirical. Years ago I mentioned at a Chicago conference that much of the ERA work constituted "data in search of a theory." As Dyckman implies in his paper, that statement, unfortunately, is still too true. A "relativistic accounting theory," to adapt Bedford's terms, may indeed be used as a blueprint for abstract notions of what needs to be studied, where certain aspects fit into the mosaic that may eventually lead to a comprehensive theory, and to point out where practical and theoretical limits exist, and how practical practice problems may be incorporated.

Bedford is quite right that a priori accounting research has been venturing further and further away from our traditional (seventh-grade bookkeeping) model. The need for venturing, moreover, can be explained on an a priori basis.

Take the simplest purposive model possible: A state of the world, a data bank (system), a user (of the data bank's information), an action affecting the state of the world.[2]

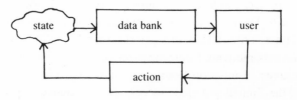

Certain minimum requisites are: (1) a selection method to determine what information from the state of the world shall constitute input into the data bank; (2) a device (code) to use for the input data, for the data bank, and for output from the data bank; (3) data bank capacity (storage memory and perhaps learning); (4) knowledge by the user of the code, so that he *knows* (cognition) what the output means (in terms of its reflection of the state of the world); (5) a means of using the output to affect

2. A fuller discussion is given in H. R. Anton, "Activity Analysis of the Firm: A Theoretical Approach to Accounting Development," (1961) reprinted in H. R. Anton and P. F. Firmen, eds., *Contemporary Issues in Cost Accounting,* Houghton-Mifflin, 1966; and H. R. Anton, "Information Theory and Business Organizations," in H. Kloidt, ed., *Essays in Honor of Erich Kosiol,* Berlin, 1969.

action (utility functions and decision functions); (6) a resulting action (transformation function); and (7) time dimension.

If the system is closed, it becomes tautological; therefore some externality is needed. Many researchers, though not using this model, speak of aiding "the decision process"—which can then be compared to a decision function (say $y = f(x)$). Thus, in early computing days we often heard the general expression, "Tell us what information you want (all or a part of x) and we'll provide the system" (everything up to the user's getting x), or in accounting, "finding out what the user" needs—again getting (x). But as one can readily see, that is not enough—one really needs to know the entire action, and how the decision will affect it, and prior to that, that the user knows and recognizes the code and what it means in terms of the data system *and* the state of the world. Moreover, the user (simplistic one) has a utility function (how he perceives and uses data and how he wants to affect (y). Each of these elements and their interrelations are important in the system—and they keep constantly changing. The study of these elements and interrelationships can form the blueprint for accounting (and, more generally, information) research.

What about accounting practice? Well, complicating the simple model will *not* solve the basic problems; the search for "Everyman" is fruitless. The "objectives of accounting," once determined, will *not* be a panacea—they will be conventionally useful—but only for a limited time until conditions, functions, and users change. Accounting will continue to be subject to "future shock," and research will go on gloriously forever.

Now let me show one other attribute of this elemental model. Let's use it to "test" the results of research. If "research" is the input into the system, it is input by "researchers"—with their own unique codes (jargon, beta's, statistical significance tests, external validity, and all the rest of their meta-language); it must be available in the data bank (laboratories, computers, etc.). Its output (learned journals, research volumes, newspapers, etc.) must be "read" by the user (presumably a practitioner, if we want adoption in practice) who must understand the code and be able to fit it into *his* utility function, and then be able to use it to achieve a "desired" (by whom?) action (adoption of the research results), and thus the output is used to affect the state of the world.

Thus, *any* adoption of research results by practice is dependent not only on the state of the art (the system) but also on perception and cognition by the users (in this case the "adopters" of accounting principles) as they perceive their needs (and indirectly, it is to be hoped, the needs of the rest of the world) and are *able* to influence that world (for example, the politics of the FASB or the SEC vis-à-vis implementation).

One obviously cannot take a short-run view of research, or a naive view of its adoption or lack thereof. Implementation lags are frequently long; for example, the adoption of present values has taken over thirty years, of the entity theory of consolidations about twenty, of funds statements over twenty-five, and market and other current values have actually cycled. In times of inflation current values are always appealing—at other times historical cost finds great support. The academic researcher should keep that long-run perspective, and not be disheartened by apparent lack of appreciation.

Discussion

Maurice Moonitz

Bedford's paper contains much food for thought, too much, in fact, to be digested at one sitting. Much about the paper I like, for example, his six criteria (p. 10) for a correct theory of accounting; his classification of a priori research (pp. 11–12); and his dissection of the "political type of a priori research" (p. 14).

Essentially his paper is a discussion of theory for theorists. It deals with a search for "a total theory," a general all-embracing theory. On page 0, for example, Bedford talks about a growing number of scholars who "examine all concepts and theories as a totality, hoping thereby to discover some of the common elements of the various proposals which can be used as a base for a priori research to derive accounting theory deductively." The "objective of their efforts, still unattained, and the partial success of their efforts, largely unpublished, [might be called] a theory that would improve the quality of accounting theories." An effort of this type is clearly in order at some point in the development of the field of accounting.

Partial theories of accounting abound, many of them not at all the product of research by accountants. I have in mind an area such as economic accounting, the product of work done primarily by economists interested in measuring the national income in its different aspects. Accountants had practically nothing to do with the development of economic accounting, yet it uses the double-entry framework which is the unique contribution of accounting to the classification and analysis of economic phenomena. Another area is cost accounting, developed primarily (or at least originally) by the industrial engineers who needed a vehicle to carry their formulas for scientific management. Up to World War II, cost accounting textbooks included testimony to the origin of the subject in a chapter on wage-incentive plans, in which Taylor's differential piece-rate plan, and later refinements by Gantt, Halsey, Bedaux, and others, were described and illustrated. In a related development, the more recent field of managerial accounting is essentially an offshoot of the work done by microeconomists in their detailed analysis of cost-revenue-volume relationships. Fifty years ago J. M. Clark in his *Economics of Overhead Costs* developed the importance of fixed and variable costs and the concept of different costs for different purposes. It would indeed be worthwhile to have a theory that would unite these disparate partial theories.

But the discussion of a general theory of accounting is not the central theme of this conference. We are here to talk about the impact of accounting research on accounting practice. To deal with this theme we need to consider the *process* by which research and practice interact, i.e., the link between them. We need to pay some attention to the forces at work in the real world, not confine ourselves to the methodological problems of accounting theory.

Education

One of the more obvious routes by which theory influences practice is through formal education. As Vatter points out in the opening paragraph of his *Fund Theory of Accounting:*

Every science, methodology, or other body of knowledge is oriented to some conceptual structure—a pattern of ideas brought together to form a consistent whole or a frame of reference to which is related the operational content of that field. Without some such integrating structure, procedures are but senseless rituals without reason or substance; progress is but a fortunate combination of circumstances; research is but fumbling in the dark; and the dissemination of knowledge is a cumbersome process, if indeed there is any "knowledge" to convey.

In the typical classroom setting in a postsecondary school, the fruits of research find their way into the textbooks, lectures, and class discussion. Some of the graduates of this type of instruction wind up as practitioners, and, no doubt, some of what they learned in class influences them in their professional activities. Certainly the writers on accounting, such as Sprague, Cole, Hatfield, Montgomery, Paton, Finney, and the like, had an impact through the classroom. They also had a direct impact on practice. Hatfield, for example, commented on the attitude of one reviewer who praised his *Modern Accounting* for its "high moral tone." Hatfield was not aware, so he told us, of any moral stance in his book on a subject as neutral as accounting, but the reviewer found one. No doubt he had and other readers were influenced by this aspect of Hatfield's work. Furthermore, those of us who have been teaching for many years have heard from former students who tell us of instances in which their treatment of an issue in practice was influenced by a discussion in class.

Another way in which the educational process works is through instruction on the job by one's colleagues or superiors. This type of instruction may be highly structured, rivaling or surpassing the kind of instruction given in most colleges and universities. It may also be less formal, consisting essentially of guidance in the solution of specific problems, indoctrination in the kind of "conceptual structure" and the "pattern of ideas" that Vatter refers to. In the nature of the case, however, it is virtually impossible to measure the impact of education, formal or informal, on anyone's actions in later life.

Research by Practitioners and Their Organizations

A great deal of research is done by CPA firms and by accounting associations, such as the American Institute of CPAs, and related bodies such as the Cost Accounting Standards Board and the Financial Accounting Standards Board. Certainly this has been true in recent decades. We should expect to find a close relationship between this type of research and accounting practice because much of the research is tailor-made to help solve a pressing practical problem. Even small firms and sole practitioners now do a fair amount of research in the sense of a preliminary determination of the facts. Virtually everyone in the field today needs to "research" a tax problem or to determine the position of the Financial Accounting Standards Board or of the Securities and Exchange Commission on a problem of financial reporting or disclosure. This type of research is a necessary step toward determining what options are available before the exercise of judgment on what decision is appropriate in the circumstances.

Except for the largest firms, however, research beyond this fact-finding mission is difficult to justify on economic grounds. Accordingly, we find a strong tendency to shift further research to organizations such as a committee of a state society, a division of the American Institute of CPAs, or of the FASB. These organizations, along with the larger firms, are in a position to finance ongoing studies of problems and issues not directly related to the practitioner's daily practice.

Even so, a difficult problem faces these organizations in carrying on research projects of wide applicability, and that is the problem of remaining disinterested, of letting the chips fall where they may, of letting reason alone dictate the conclusions. In the past, certainly, much of the research done by professional groups has been in the nature of a lawyer's brief, a search for ways to support a predetermined position. As one result, a good deal of the research carried on by professional groups has not been productive. As another result, the burden of carrying on basic or disinterested or broadly conceived research rests mainly on faculty members in our colleges and universities. As Bedford points out in his paper, there is a great deal of activity on that front at the present time, but so far, the basic problems of constructing a general theory have not been solved.

The Past

Let us examine a few cases in which we can trace some of the interaction between research and practice. The cases I have chosen, solely because I am somewhat familiar with them, are (1) consolidated financial statements, (2) the investment tax credit, and (3) price-level accounting.

1. Consolidated Financial Statements. The documentation for much of this section of my remarks is taken from the first chapter of my monograph, *The Entity Theory of Consolidated Statements,* published in 1944 by the American Accounting Association. The history of the development of the use of consolidated statements is largely the history of the holding company in the United States. Widespread use does not appear until the first decade of the twentieth century. U.S. Steel, formed in 1901, presented consolidated statements from its inception. Since then, consolidated statements have been a familiar feature of corporate reports. A little later, from 1917 on, the Federal income-tax laws and regulations affected the popularity of consolidated statements by their attitude toward consolidated tax returns. There is little question that in those early days, the original ideas, experiments, and practices were developed by the companies themselves and their outside auditors. Formal theory played little or no part in the process until practice was fairly well established.

In the 1930s I became interested in the subject from an academic point of view, first as the subject of a master's thesis at Berkeley, then as a coauthor with Perry Mason of the section of the *Accountants Handbook* devoted to consolidations. In the early 1940s I was asked to do a monograph for the American Accounting Association.

The result was a piece of work that was normative in spirit, although relying heavily on data from practice for its framework. What I did was to devise a theory of consolidation based upon what accountants evidently were trying to do, namely, treat a group of closely allied corporations as a distinct economic or accounting entity, despite the existence of legal lines of separation among the constituent parts. Some of the principal findings of this type of analysis were: (1) One hundred per cent elimination of intercompany markups from assets, with the elimination charged back against the company which booked the profit in the first place; (2) Treatment of control and minority interests in a subsidiary on a co-ordinate basis, share for share; (3) Inclusion of all of the intangible values implied by the price paid by the parent for its interest in a subsidiary; (4) Shares of a parent held by a subsidiary to be treated as treasury shares in consolidation; (5) Parent's investment in a subsidiary to be carried on the equity basis. None of these findings were prevailing practice at the time. In the years that followed, however, virtually all of them were gradually introduced into practice, so that by 1959, ARB No. 51 could recommend or sanction them.

Was there a direct connection between the 1944 monograph and ARB No. 51? From all available evidence, probably not. My own inquiries in the early 1960s in New York convinced me that few, if any, of the members of the Committee on Accounting Procedure that issued ARB No. 51 were aware of the existence of the 1944 monograph. But the ideas had been floating around for at least fifteen years, so that when practical developments called some of the traditional procedures into question, a theoretical framework was at hand to show the way to an alternative that was in many respects more logical and sensible. The earlier rules and procedures, developed piecemeal as specific issues arose, gave rise to a confusing array of alternative and sometimes contradictory standards. The absence of a generally accepted explanation of the nature, purpose, and limitations of consolidated statements hampered the easy and proper resolution of new issues. The entity theory supplied the framework; ARB No. 51 supplied the "principles" for the guidance of practitioners.

2. The Investment Tax Credit. The Accounting Principles Board almost died aborning in late 1962 because of the split over the proper accounting treatment of the investment tax credit. Academic researchers of whatever stripe or persuasion were of absolutely no use whatsoever in the resolution of the dispute. I cannot recall a single article in any journal that discussed the investment tax credit until after APB issued Opinion No. 2. At the same time, the practitioners were not much better. They had no background in experience with a provision like the investment tax credit. In one sense, each member of the APB had to construct his own framework to justify the position he took. The academics had no theory broad enough to encompass the investment credit; the practitioners had no basis in practice for a sound decision. Both arms of the profession suffered a resounding defeat as a result, a defeat from which we have not yet recovered.

3. Price-Level Accounting. By "price-level accounting" I mean the type of accounting recommended by the APB in its Statement No. 3 (June 1969) and by the FASB in its Exposure Draft (December 31, 1974). In many respects the interaction between research and practice in this field is classic.

A good place to start the story is with the great inflation of the early 1920s in Germany. A young graduate student at Columbia University, Henry W. Sweeney, became interested in the accounting problems created by the hyperinflation in Germany. He examined the various devices used on the accounting level to adapt to inflation (e.g., use of a more stable currency, such as the Swiss gold franc, as the unit of account; use of replacement costs instead of historical costs as a basis; etc.). In a series of articles culminating in a book, Sweeney set forth most of the conditions for a satisfactory way to report what was happening in an inflation. The book was published in 1936 by Harper under the title, *Stabilized Accounting,* and reprinted in 1964 by Holt, Rinehart and Winston. In his publications, Sweeney set forth most of the ideas we use today: (1) distinction between changes in relative prices and in the exchange-value of money; (2) sharp focus on the shift in the size of the measuring unit; (3) use of a general index rather than a specific or specialized index to measure the changes in the size of the dollar; (4) recognition of the phenomenon of gains or losses on monetary items.

The mid-1930s, however, was no time to kindle interest in inflation accounting. Sweeney's work lived only in a few specialized advanced accounting seminars. After World War II, however, interest revived. The Committee on Concepts and Standards of the American Accounting Association recommended something akin to Sweeney's formula; and the Study Group on Business Income made a strong bid for price-level depreciation. The AAA received a foundation grant to make some field studies. These were undertaken initially by Ralph Jones of Yale and completed later with the collaboration of Perry Mason, then at Berkeley. The financial statements of New York Telephone, of Armstrong Cork, of

Sargent & Co., and of Reece Corporation were restated, using the AAA Committee's formulas, and the results published. Perry Mason then published a "Primer" to show others how to restate financial statements. The APB authorized a research study in the early 1960s, published as ARS No. 6 in 1963. Later, AICPA made field studies of its own as an extensive test of the practicality of the methods proposed in ARS No. 6. Furthermore, some of the large CPA firms made use of these studies in connection with audits of clients in certain Latin-American countries.

About the time the FASB issued its Exposure Draft recommending that supplemental price-level financial statements be required for fair reporting, similar developments were occurring in the United Kingdom. Further experimentation and testing occurred on both sides of the Atlantic.

The process is still going on under our very eyes. Everyone, it seems, is getting into the act. An enormous amount of effort at all levels, from abstract theory to narrowly based practice, is being expended. Whether or not we will get "price-level accounting" is an open question at this moment, but if we do, there is not the slightest doubt that the practitioners will be able to prepare the required financial statements without too much difficulty. In this area, the field of accounting has been well served. The issues have been explored, debated, analyzed, tested, reduced to practice, introduced into the standard textbooks, and the proposed solutions subjected to intense scrutiny, praise, and condemnation. And the process is still going on. I am continually amazed to see the new nooks and crannies of this subject that are being explored, to good purpose, as the "practicality" of the topic becomes manifest to all interested parties.

The interaction between research and practice has been continuous; it has been fruitful. I doubt if anyone can disentangle the lines of force, but I have no doubt that the pioneering work of Sweeney, of Ralph Jones, and of Perry Mason laid out the framework, developed the model, if you will, gave direction to the work, both theoretical and applied, that has been done in the past 30 years in this field.

The Present

In connection with "the present" (more accurately, the recent past), I call attention to just two cases in which the results of research were brought to bear on pressing practical issues. The first in point of time is William Beaver's pair of articles on accounting for marketable equity securities in the *Journal of Accountancy,* October 1971 and December 1973. In May 1971 the AICPA's committee on insurance accounting and auditing recommended the use of a moving average of past prices (and yields) as the basis of valuation of marketable equity securities, on the grounds that past actual experience was the best available indicator of realizable value. Beaver demonstrated that there is no basis, either in theory or in experience, for such a position. Instead, he demonstrated that current market value is a better indicator of realizable value than any kind of average of past prices or yields. In his analysis, he used both a priori and empirical research. He did not say that current market value is the best of all possible values; merely that current market value is superior to any kind of past price for the purposes set forth by the AICPA committee. I have no way of knowing whether the policy-makers will pay any attention to Beaver's analysis, or whether they have made their own analysis to support or refute his findings. If they do not pay attention or make their own analyses, they proceed at their own peril. In this case, theory and research have done their job.

The second case is the analysis by Harold Bierman and Roland Dukes of the way to account for research and development costs, published in the *Journal of Accountancy,* April 1975. Bierman and Dukes start from the kind of evidence used by FASB to support its ill-conceived Financial Accounting Standard No. 2, "Accounting for research and development costs." By an appeal both to a priori reasoning and to experience, Bierman and Dukes demonstrate that the FASB was guilty of assuming that what was true of one research and development project was true of the aggregate of all such projects undertaken by a company, that what was true for one item in a portfolio was true of the aggregate portfolio. Bierman and Dukes were able to demonstrate that the evidence relied upon by FASB, as set forth in Statement No. 2, leads to precisely the opposite conclusion from the one reached, that instead of expensing all R and D, FASB should have prescribed capitalization (and subsequent amortization). Here the theoretical analysis by Bierman and Dukes came after the policy decision by FASB. The questions that intrude at this point are: Why didn't Bierman and Dukes, or someone else, including the staff of the FASB, make the same kind of analysis *before* FASB acted? If the staff did in fact make such an analysis, why did not FASB follow reason instead of merely adopting the practice of the majority of companies in industry today?

If we could in fact answer questions such as these at this conference, we would have a better grasp of the way in which research influences or does not influence practice. We would have a clearer idea of the steps to take to improve the interaction between the two, and Bedford and the other toilers in the field of theory would have a better view of the probable fate of their efforts, if, in fact, they do succeed.

PART II

The Impact of Experimental and Survey Research

Experimental and Survey Research in Financial Accounting: A Review and Evaluation

Thomas R. Dyckman, Michael Gibbins and
Robert J. Swieringa

1. Introduction

There is a passage in Somerset Maugham's *A Writer's Notebook* that unfortunately may apply to many researchers. It reads: "She plunged into a sea of platitudes, and with the powerful breast stroke of a channel swimmer, made her confident way towards the white cliffs of the obvious" (Maugham, 1967: p. 174).[1] The intent of this paper is to review and evaluate the recently published experimental and survey research literature in financial accounting with a view to trying, in part, to determine whether we too have been paddling powerfully towards the white cliffs of the obvious.

We will review a substantial amount of literature to see what the recent experimental and survey research has to tell us about present reporting problems and about the alleged impact of financial data on individual decision-making. We will examine alternative reporting models and disclosure practice to see what choices are indicated and what improvements are suggested. We will attempt to identify important issues addressed by this research and to note any advances in our understanding of these issues.

The next three sections of the paper will review the experimental and survey research that has been done. First, we will look at the research that has focused on financial statement disclosure and use. We will then turn our attention to research that has focused on accounting principles and alternative accounting models. The final portion of our state-of-the-art review will examine research that has focused on several special topic areas that are not easily subsumed in the previous sections.

Following this review, we will examine briefly certain aspects of the research methods used because they are important factors in explaining

1. We are indebted to Karl Weick for bringing this description and its chilling implications to our attention.

why we have not progressed further, what must be done in the future, and why progress will not be easy. Finally, we will evaluate the relevance and impact of this line of research on financial accounting practice. Frankly, we believe that the data support the contention that experimental and survey research has made only a modest contribution to the resolution of reporting and disclosure issues. Moreover, the results may even have been counterproductive in several instances. Our evaluation will focus on the nature of the research task, on the characteristics of the researchers themselves, and on the nature of the environment in which the research task and the researchers interact.

Both our charge and our choices have constrained the scope of this review. We were asked to limit our review to developments over the past decade. Fortunately, this period includes almost all of the research activity in the area. We admit to cheating only in rare instances where we believe additional studies must be included to understand the historical perspective of more recent efforts. A review of the three bibliographies at the end of this paper will indicate the literature covered in this review. The studies which serve as the basis for our review are listed in the first bibliography. The reader will note that we have not included all the research that has been done. We have, for example, elected to omit unpublished doctoral dissertations from our review. In part, we have done this because of the unavailability of much of this research. Selective inclusion would inevitably have produced an unknown bias in our review. In addition, we have decided to restrict our review to papers that have passed the normal review process so that we would not place ourselves in the role of referees. A list of the doctoral dissertations in the area for which we have references is contained in the second bibliography.[2]

The approach we have taken generally is to evaluate the state of our knowledge and the overall contribution of the research to date. This same overview approach has been followed in the brief methods section. It could be argued that each study included should be evaluated in terms of its explicit and implicit assumptions, its research methods, its statistical tests, and so on.[3] But we believe that this would have been an inappropri-

2. The third bibliography contains those papers to which we refer but which do not represent experimental or survey research. We have also included here a few papers that are relevant to our review but which were not yet available to us. Our review has not been extended to the sizable number of survey articles published by regional or special interest journals.

3. To our knowledge such reviews have been successful only when restricted to a very few studies. Reviews of numerous studies often fail to capture adequately what

ate, if not impossible, approach given the time, the space, and the task allotted us. Our charge was to "examine the benefits of recent accounting research . . . and to provide guidelines for future research." It is only as the conclusions of several studies begin to suggest directions and patterns that they assist us in this task. Indeed, the same comment also applies to review papers such as ours. This paper is only a recent attempt to review and evaluate the growing literature in the area. Review papers by Birnberg and Nath (1967), Hofstedt (1972a, 1975), Rhode (1972), Green (1973) and by Gonedes and Dopuch (1974) provide further insights into the contributions and the limitations of experimental and survey research in financial accounting.

2. Financial Statement Disclosure and Use

We begin by examining research that has focused primarily on financial statement disclosure and use. Included in this research are studies that have dealt with four overall issues: (1) the adequacy of financial statement disclosure, (2) the usefulness of financial statement data, (3) attitudes about corporate reporting practices, and (4) materiality judgments. In focusing on these issues, several different conceptual and methodological approaches have been used. Of particular relevance to this paper is the usefulness of these approaches in improving the quality of information provided to users of financial statements.

2.1. Adequacy of Disclosure. There is almost unanimous agreement that there is more financial disclosure in corporate annual reports today than in the past. A recent survey by Opinion Research Corporation for Arthur Andersen & Company reveals that 96% of the "key publics" and 98% of the corporate executives interviewed stated that their overall impression is that there is more disclosure today than there was five to ten years ago (Opinion Research Corporation, 1974). Yet, during the last decade, there has been considerable controversy about the extent to which financial data available to investors and the public have been adequate to meet their requirements.

---

specific studies have found, let alone adequately evaluate their research methods. A substantive review of one or two research papers is itself a substantial task, as a brief examination of any issue of the *Empirical Supplement to the Journal of Accounting Research* will show.

Studies that have focused on the adequacy of disclosure include Horngren (1955, 1956, 1957), Cerf (1961), Bradish (1965), Ecton (1969), Singhvi and Desai (1971), Buzby (1974), and Opinion Research Corporation (1974). Three overall approaches have been used in these studies. One approach has been to develop a description of how users analyze financial statements to evaluate the assumptions underlying their analysis, and to assess the implications of their analysis for various disclosure issues. This approach was used by Horngren (1955, 1956, 1957) who surveyed written reports of financial analysts and who interviewed analysts to obtain information about their use of financial statement data. He then developed a description of their use of these data, evaluated the underlying reasoning, and assessed its implications for the inclusion of funds-flow statements, price-level accounting, and disclosure of capital expenditures, depreciation, and so forth.

Another approach has been to focus on certain interest groups and to survey their perceptions and attitudes about disclosure. Studies by Bradish (1965), Ecton (1969), and Opinion Research Corporation (1974) provide examples of the use of this approach. Both Bradish and Ecton conducted open-ended interviews with limited numbers of expert users of financial statement data. Bradish interviewed several financial analysts to determine what types of information they considered inadequately disclosed. Ecton interviewed the chief lending officers of seven commercial banks to determine their views of the adequacy of disclosure in financial statements submitted to them. Both Bradish and Ecton discuss specific areas of criticism and solutions proposed by the analysts and lending officers.

The survey by Opinion Research Corporation was more general in nature and broader in scope. Telephone interviews were conducted with individual shareholders and personal interviews were conducted with "key public" individuals, including corporate executives, professors, institutional investors and portfolio managers, stockbrokers and investment analysts, securities lawyers, CPAs, government officials, editors and writers, and social activists. The survey focused on overall opinions which individuals held on the adequacy of disclosure as well as on specific changes in disclosure, such as the inclusion of SEC Form 10-K, information in annual reports and forecasts of future earnings.

A third approach has been to determine the extent to which specific items of important information are disclosed in corporate annual reports. An index of disclosure is developed and then used to measure the extent of disclosure in the annual reports of a sample of companies. This approach was initially used by Cerf (1961), who developed a 31-item index of disclosure on the basis of interviews with financial analysts, an examination of analysts' reports, and a survey of a random sample of analysts. Cerf then rated the disclosures of 527 individual companies in terms of a percentage score based on the number of items in the index that were included in their annual reports. Those scores were used to calculate differences in disclosure among companies and to analyze the relationships among these differences and several other variables.

More recently, this approach has been used by Singhvi and Desai (1971) and Buzby (1974). Relying heavily on the index developed by Cerf and on interviews with four expert analysts, Singhvi and Desai developed a 34-item index which they used as a composite measure of the extent of disclosure in the annual reports of 100 listed and 55 unlisted corporations. Singhvi and Desai analyzed the relationships between disclosure and several other variables, including fluctuations in security prices.

Buzby asked a sample of financial analysts to indicate (on a five-point scale) the relative importance of 39 selected items of information in evaluating an investment in a company's common stock. He then used the responses of 131 analysts to develop a set of weighted disclosure criteria and applied these criteria to a sample of annual reports of 88 small and medium-sized companies. Buzby analyzed the extent to which each item was disclosed, the average disclosure for the items taken as a whole, and the relationship between the relative importance of an item and the extent to which it was disclosed.

Research on the adequacy of disclosure has produced at least three overall conclusions. The first is that there does not appear to be a burning desire for drastic revisions or changes in the form and content of financial statements.[4] Most users of financial statements believe that adequate financial data are available today. In addition, it appears that most of the criticism about financial disclosure is not that there is necessarily something wrong with what is presently reported, but that relevant data are left out. However, there is relatively little agreement about what these relevant data are. Where some users would like to have more detail about what is

---

4. It is interesting to note that even though there have been many improvements and increases in disclosure in recent years, this conclusion is essentially the same as that offered by Roper (1948) and Sanders (1948) almost three decades ago. Perhaps, this indicates the difficulties people have in forecasting the future "state of the art."

presently reported (e.g., more statistical breakdowns), others would like to have data that are presently unreported (e.g., replacement cost data) because they think these data would better help them evaluate a company's future prospects.

A second conclusion is that the trend toward increased financial disclosure apparently has not resulted in overcomplicated financial statements. Many observers have expressed concern about financial statements becoming too complex and too difficult to understand because of increased financial disclosure. Yet, responses to substantive questions on content suggested to some researchers that readers of financial statements may have little difficulty understanding these statements, although we ourselves do not entirely agree with this finding. Further, research indicates that the investing public generally is not very critical of the complexity of these statements.

A third conclusion is that there appear to be significant differences in financial disclosure between companies and that many of these differences tend to be a function of such variables as company size (as measured by total assets or number of shareholders), profitability (as measured by rate of return or earnings margin), size of the CPA firm auditing the company, and the listing status of the company. In general, companies that are larger, more profitable, audited by large CPA firms, and whose shares are traded on the New York Stock Exchange tend to be significantly better disclosers than companies that are smaller, less profitable, audited by small CPA firms, and whose shares are traded either over the counter or closely held. However, it is important to realize that these variables are probably highly intercorrelated. For example, companies traded on the New York Stock Exchange are generally those that have the largest asset size and the widest ownership distribution, and tend to be audited by large CPA firms. Thus, observed differences in disclosure between companies may merely reflect differences in listing status and the involuntary disclosure requirements associated with that status.

2.2 Usefulness of Financial Statement Data. During the last decade, there has been considerable controversy about the extent to which financial data available to investors and the public are useful in decision-making. Studies that have focused on the usefulness of financial statement data include Soper and Dolphin (1964), Pankoff and Virgil (1970), Smith and Smith (1971), Falk (1972), Haried (1972, 1973), Falk and Ophir (1973a, 1973b), Baker and Haslem (1973), Abdel-khalik (1973, 1974a,

1974b), Ronen and Falk (1973), Chandra (1974), Oliver (1974), and Libby (1975a, 1975b). Several approaches have been used in these studies.

One approach has been to ask users of financial statements to indicate the relative importance of various factors or information items in investment analysis. A list of information items or factors is developed and a sample of users of financial statements is asked to indicate (usually on a five-point scale) the relative importance of these items in making investment decisions. The mean responses for each item are used to determine the degree of importance attributed to it. In some cases, the mean responses of different samples of users or preparers of financial statements are compared. This approach, which is similar to that used by Cerf (1961) and Buzby (1974) in developing their indices of disclosure, has been used by Baker and Haslem to determine the relative importance of 33 factors to a sample of common stock investors and by Chandra to determine the relative importance of 58 information items to a sample of CPAs and to a sample of Chartered Financial Analysts (CFAs).

A second approach in the attempt to determine whether financial statement data are used in decision-making and whether their use is affected by other variables is to create a representation of a "decision" under quasi-laboratory conditions and then to study the behavior of the subjects who make the "decisions." Pankoff and Virgil (1970), to investigate the demand for information and the effects of information on expectations and on the quality of forecasts and decisions, constructed a laboratory stock market in which subjects purchased information, predicted closing market prices, and chose portfolios. Falk and Ophir (1973a, 1973b) used a representative investment setting to investigate the relationship between the degree of risk involved in an investment and the demands of the investor for information and the frequency of his requests for this information. Libby (1975a, 1975b) used a field experiment to investigate the use of five accounting ratios by 43 professional lending officers in evaluating the likelihood of failure of 60 firms (and ten repeat firms). Abdel-khalik (1973, 1974a, 1974b) and Ronen and Falk (1973) have used the concept of entropy as a basis for experiments on aggregation in accounting. Abdel-khalik asked respondents to estimate the probability of loan default by a hypothetical firm and to estimate the subjective probability of its being a good credit risk within the next three years. Ronen and Falk report the results of three laboratory experiments designed to probe the relationship between entropy and the expected value of information.

A third approach that has been used to study the usefulness of financial statement data has been to try to measure the effectiveness of the communication of these data. One way of measuring effectiveness has been to apply readability formulas to disclosures in samples of financial statements. Soper and Dolphin (1964) and Smith and Smith (1971) used this approach to measure objectively the comprehension ease level of financial statement disclosure. Another way of measuring communication effectiveness is to measure the meaning assigned to accounting terms by various interest groups. Haried (1972, 1973) and Oliver (1974) each developed semantic differentials for selected accounting concepts and terms and then sampled groups with different backgrounds and professional affiliations to measure and compare the meanings these groups assigned to those concepts and terms.

The overall conclusion that emerges from this research is that financial statements appear to be, at best, of limited value in making investment decisions. First, investors and analysts tend to consider nonfinancial statement factors to be relatively more important in making investment decisions. Investors consider factors concerned primarily with expectations to be relatively more important than financial statement data in making these decisions. Moreover, they tend to rely on stockbrokers and advisory services for their investment information and to attach only minor importance to financial statements as a source of information. Similarly, analysts tend to consider data about the general economy and the industry within which a company operates to be relatively more important than the reported financial statement data.[5] However, it appears that the perceived value of financial statement data may be affected by the perceived riskiness of an investment. Falk and Ophir (1973a, 1973b) found that use of financial statement data was highest for securities not guaranteed by the government and not traded on the stock exchange and lowest for securities traded on the stock exchange with government guarantee. In addition, it appears that income statement items are considered to be relatively more important than balance sheet items in making investment decisions.

Second, it is not clear that the use of financial statements leads to either better forecasts or better decisions. It appears that analysts want some kinds of financial statement data to the extent that they are willing to pay

5. Horngren (1957) found that there was widespread agreement among security analysts that the company annual report served as the springboard for their review. He concluded that, although the annual report was not always the most important source of information, in terms of universal usage it belonged in first place among the sources.

for them, and that their use of these data can in some instances result in slightly better forecasts of stock prices on average than if these data had not been used. However, it is not clear that these better forecasts necessarily resulted in better decisions—e.g., choosing portfolios.

There are several reasons why financial statement data might not be useful to investors and analysts. One reason may be that generally accepted accounting principles and generally accepted auditing standards reduce the usefulness of financial statement data by reducing the extent to which subjective, not easily auditable judgments are reflected in those data.[6] Another reason may be that the information content of financial statement data is known by the time the statements are available to the public. Yet, financial statement data might be useful to investors and analysts by providing them with a reasonably good (or at least better than random) history of the economic status and progress of the company. If it were not for published financial statements, some financial data might not be available during the year or at year-end. In addition, some financial data may be communicated more efficiently (in a cost-benefit sense) by using financial statements than by using other sources. Year-end financial statements also may merely confirm information otherwise obtained during the year. Investors receive information from analysts, brokers, or company officials and may tend to rely on this information because at year-end an accounting will be available in the form of audited financial statements. In this way, financial statement data may provide a useful check on the accuracy of data received from nonfinancial statement sources. However, within this context, investors' expectations about financial statement data must be specified in some way, otherwise one cannot interpret the extent to which these data tend to confirm or disconfirm their expectations.

2.3. Attitudes about Corporate Reporting Practices. Even though the development and reformulation of accounting principles has been a slow and often controversial process, the last decade has brought about many significant changes in corporate accounting and disclosure policies. Studies that have focused on the attitudes of various interest groups about current and proposed corporate reporting practices include Nelson and

6. Schneider (1972), for example, wants the SEC to remove its prohibition against issuers' including "soft" information, such as sales and earnings forecasts and appraisals, in prospectuses. As he puts it, "SEC filings generally have an artificial or unreal quality. They purport to be full disclosure documents but, as a matter of convention, they exclude important types of information investors consider relevant, and stress much information investors consider irrelevant or relatively unimportant."

Strawser (1970), Brenner and Shuey (1972), Carpenter and Strawser (1972), Copeland, Francia and Strawser (1973), and Godwin (1975).

Some of these studies have focused on preferences for alternative methods of accounting for specific transactions or events. The approach used in these studies has been to develop a questionnaire describing a transaction or event and alternative methods of accounting for it. Respondents are then asked to indicate their preferences for one of the alternative methods described. Often one of the alternative methods described has been one suggested by an accounting policy-making group (e.g., APB) in an exposure draft. Nelson and Strawser (1970) surveyed members of the Institute of Chartered Financial Analysts, the AICPA, and the American Accounting Association (AAA) to determine which of three methods of accounting for business combinations they preferred. In a follow-up study, Brenner and Shuey (1972) surveyed controllers, CFAs, and CPAs about the use of the purchase and pooling-of-interest methods of accounting for business combinations. Similarly, Carpenter and Strawser (1972) surveyed controllers, CFAs, AAA members, and CPAs about methods of reporting accounting changes.

Other studies have focused on more general reporting issues. The approach used in these studies has been to develop a questionnaire consisting of several items and to ask respondents to indicate (usually on a five- or seven-point scale) how much information they feel is available now to users of financial statements, how much information they feel should be available to these users, and how important the item is, in their opinion. Mean responses to the question of how much information is available now are used as measures of the respondent's perceptions of the present state of the art and mean responses to the question of how much information should be available are used as measures of the respondent's attitudes about what the state of the art should be. The difference between what "should be" and what "is" provides a measure of perceived information deficiency (if positive) or fulfillment (if negative). Mean responses to the question of how important the item is provide indications of relative importance. Copeland, Francia and Strawser (1973) used a questionnaire consisting of 27 items to survey the attitudes of accounting students, controllers, CPAs, CFAs, and AAA members about financial reporting practices. Mean responses for each item were analyzed by group and compared across groups. Using a slightly different approach, Godwin (1975) surveyed CPAs about the feasibility of auditing certain items and their willingness to audit 25 proposed SEC disclosures, and surveyed financial analysts and stockholders about the usefulness of these disclosures and their current accessibility to these disclosures.

The studies focusing on preferences for alternative methods of accounting for specific transactions or events have provided useful data about several controversial accounting issues. In particular, these studies have provided data about the extent to which these preferences have been consistent with those of the APB, at least for specific (though often limited) samples of CPAs and others. Yet, it appears that in evaluating these studies, it is important to consider carefully the exact wording used to obtain attitudinal data. Nelson and Strawser (1970) asked respondents to indicate which of three methods of accounting for business combinations they preferred and found that the majority of the respondents favored alternatives other than the one selected by the APB. Brenner and Shuey (1972) asked respondents about the extent to which they believed the purchase method and pooling-of-interest method were alternatives for a single business combination and the extent to which the choice of a specific method depended on the circumstances surrounding the combination. They concluded that respondents were in general agreement with the conditions set forth by the APB.

The studies focusing on more general reporting issues suggest that there are apparent intergroup attitudinal differences between students, controllers, CPAs, CFAs, and AAA members. However, it is impossible to assess the importance of these apparent attitudinal differences without some insight into how these attitudes were formed, how strongly they are held, or how they are related to behavior.

2.4. Materiality Judgments. Research on financial statement disclosure and use has also focused on materiality judgments that affect financial reporting. These judgments concern either the collection, classification, and summarization of data about the results of a company's economic activities or the presentation of these data and related disclosure in financial statements. Research on materiality judgments has generally focused on what factors influence these judgments and on what people consider material. Studies that have focused on these topics include Woolsey (1954a, 1954b, 1973), Dyer (1973), Boatsman and Robertson (1974), Pattillo (1975), Pattilo and Siebel (1973, 1974), Rose et al. (1970), and Dickhaut and Eggleton (1975).

Research on what factors influence materiality judgments has typically involved the development of a questionnaire that consists of hypothetical cases containing a common set of situational variables and asks respondents to make materiality judgments for each case. This approach was first used by Woolsey (1954), who developed a set of ten questionnaire cases, each of which set forth specific circumstances using six different sets of figures. He then asked samples of preparers, auditors, and users of financial statements to make materiality judgments for each of the six sets of figures for each case. In a more recent study, Woolsey (1973), used a single questionnaire case involving an error found in the examination of the cost of goods sold account of a hypothetical manufacturing company to obtain materiality judgments from various groups, Similarly, Pattillo (1975) used six sets of questionnaire cases that focused on a variety of items, including extraordinary items, contingencies, accounting changes, segment reporting, interim reports, and groups of these items, to obtain materiality judgments from preparers and users of financial statements, CPAs, and educators. Both Woolsey and Pattillo focused on the amounts or range of amounts at which items were considered to be material and on the factors respondents indicated as influencing their judgments.

Boatsman and Robertson (1974) presented a sample of CPAs and a sample of security analysts with 30 hypothetical cases containing a common set of eight variables. Subjects were asked to sort the 30 cases into one of three categories according to how they believed the cases *should* be disclosed, without regard for how the cases *might* be disclosed under current practice. Boatsman and Robertson used multiple discriminant analysis to model the composite judgments of the subjects, stepwise discriminant analysis to develop separate models for the CPAs and the security analysts, and evaluated the use of a simple percent of net income rule to distinguish material from immaterial judgments.

Research on what people consider material has sought to determine how much of a difference in an accounting datum is required for a judgment of a difference and whether that difference is a constant function of the amount of the item presented. Rose et al. (1970) conducted a laboratory experiment to determine the magnitude of the percentage change in earnings per share (EPS) required before a subject would perceive a difference. On two occasions subjects were presented with pairs of EPS figures in the format of an abbreviated financial statement for a single company and asked to provide judgments about whether a share of the company's stock should be selling for essentially more, essentially the same, or essentially less from one year to another. The hypothesis was that the change in magnitude required before it could be detected was a constant function of the amount presented (Weber's Law). In a more recent study, Dickhaut and Eggleton (1975) sought to test the strength of Weber's Law over manipulations of the setting in which judgments were made, the sequence of data presentation, and the format in which standards and comparison stimuli were presented.

The overall conclusion that emerges from research on materiality judgments is that several factors, either individually or in combination, appear to influence these judgments. The relationship of an item to current year's income appears to be an important factor influencing these judgments. However, this factor also appears to combine with other factors, such as the nature of the item and characteristics of the company and its management, in influencing these judgments. Because of the simultaneous influences of these and other factors, people tend to differ somewhat in their materiality judgments, even though many of the observed differences do not appear to be statistically significant. In addition, people appear to be indifferent between footnote and line item disclosure, indicating that the decision of where to disclose may not be as difficult or as important as the decision of whether to disclose. Finally, it appears that the use of a quantitative criterion such as a simple percent of net income may err on the side of underdisclosure.

Even though both Rose et al. and Dickhaut and Eggleton found that their results were generally consistent with the predictions of Weber's Law, the implicit psychological process that underlies this law may not be useful in determining what is material for numerical data. The fundamental proposition underlying Weber's Law is that some distortion of a physical continuum occurs on a subject's psychological continuum such that the subject is an imperfect measurement device. Because there is greater measurement error at higher levels of the physical continuum, the stimuli become more indistinguishable and the just noticeable differences surrounding a particular standard increase. Weber's Law suggests a specific form the distortion will take and suggests that the relationship between a just noticeable difference and a standard will be a constant one. Yet, it is not clear that people assimilate numerical stimuli in the same manner they assimilate physical stimuli or that a similar distortion of an individual's psychological continuum is likely to result.

3. Accounting Principles and Models

This section reviews experimental and survey research into the general principles of financial accounting and into various alternative financial accounting models. The number of studies included in this section is not large, for two reasons. First, much of the research done has been oriented to particular financial disclosure or use issues and therefore is covered in sections 2 and 4. Second, there has been a paucity of empirical research into the fundamental nature of financial accounting information. Such research has not begun to keep up with nor to deal adequately with the large volume of theoretical writing on financial accounting models and measurement.

The discussion below will consider four not entirely unrelated areas of research: (1) general views about accounting principles; (2) "de facto" application of accounting principles; (3) price-level adjusted and current-value accounting proposals; and (4) probabilistic financial statements and allied proposals.

3.1. General Views of Accounting Principles. This has been a popular area for researchers, especially in recent years. Research reviewed here includes Carsberg, Hope and Scapens (1974), Copeland, Francia and Strawser (1973), Fisher (1974), Flynn (1965), Francia and Strawser (1972, 1971a and 1971b), Hay (1955), Mautz (1972), Morton (1974), and Piaker and Dalberth (1973). In addition to these studies, professional journals and business publications have frequently carried reports of similar questionnaire or interview-based solicitations of views.

Letters, questionnaires, or interviews provide useful devices for "taking the pulse" of various constituencies about accounting matters. Such solicitations can be used to demonstrate readily enough both that someone "out there" cares about the various issues the researcher chooses to ask about, and that a diversity of opinion exists on the issue. Yet, such conclusions often are obvious in advance. In addition, these conclusions can be challenged on the basis of nonresponse rate, potential response bias due to the questions' context, difficulty of wording questions unambiguously, lack of connection of answers to respondents' actual behavior, and possible arbitrariness in selecting questions to ask. Nonetheless, a carefully designed questionnaire (e.g., Hay, 1955) can provide useful data on people's thoughts about the objectives and the content of accounting reports.

Several approaches have been used to try to get beyond the compilation of views and to provide a systematic structure to the research. One approach, used by Carsberg, Hope, and Scapens (1974), has been to send identical questionnaires to members of different groups and to compare the groups' positions on each question. The research method itself cannot illuminate the reasons for any reported differences, but such findings provide possible hypotheses for more intensive follow-up research. Unfortunately, since no such follow-up research seems to have been done, any statements which go beyond the listing of differences remain speculative. A refinement of this approach has been used by Copeland, et al. (1973), and Francia and Strawser (1972, 1971a and 1971b). As we noted in Section 2.3, these studies, by using a questionnaire technique that, it was hoped, would reduce response biases, attempted to detect differences not only in direction but also in the importance of views held. This method expanded the dimensions on which differences were displayed but still provided no explanations for observed differences. However, some of the differences were intriguing. For example, Copeland, et al. (1973) asked students and accounting educators eight identical questions about proposals for improving financial reporting. The two groups differed significantly on all eight questions about deficiencies in information now available, but on only one concerning the importance of the deficiencies. Students' attitudes differed from those of analysts on all of the seven questions about information available on certain financial reporting objectives, but on only one of the seven about the importance of the information. Such tidbits are tantalizing; it is unfortunate that we are given no further insights.

Another approach, used by Mautz (1972), has been to send letters soliciting illustrative examples of circumstances that would lead to departures from usual accounting treatments to provide a focus for later seminars on the issues and for the development of a survey questionnaire. The eventual survey questions as well as the answers were empirically derived and the conclusions rooted in a context that had some applied meaning. In addition, the letters, seminars, and questionnaire responses provide varying vantage points for triangulating on the issues. For example, the importance of the context in which accounting choices are made, and their impact on the uniformity versus flexibility issue, were illuminated in useful and different ways by the various data sources.

Another approach has been to turn to the theoretical issues behind an accounting principle in designing the questionnaire and to relate the results to the theoretical questions. Morton (1974) tested specific hypotheses concerning the survey respondents' perceived relationships among relevance, understandability and bearing (direction of effect on investment decisions) of footnote disclosure and found a significant positive correlation between each pair of the three concepts. However, his study did not explore the reasons for, or causal structure underlying, the observed correlations.

3.2. "De facto" Accounting Principles. Research in this area has consisted of mailing brief situational descriptions to CPAs and asking respondents to report how they would account for the item described. McDonald (1968) provides an early example, followed by Sterling and Radosevich (1969), Sterling (1969) and Sterling, Tollefson and Flaherty (1972).

Large variations in reported outcomes were observed, resulting apparently from differences in choice of accounting method and calculation parameters (e.g., asset life) and from incomplete accounting rules (such as for barters). The findings suggest that financial accounting measurement may not be objective; however, we have two serious reservations. First, because the situational descriptions provided were terse, practicing accountants may have had to make assumptions to fit these descriptions into their usual decision rules, and such assumptions could easily have produced large variations in reported outcomes. Second, the questionnaire approach allowed no consultation with others, nor other actions that might be usual in reaching actual accounting decisions. Hence, the results may not reflect "de facto" accounting in any real sense. However, such difficulties with validity are not unique to this kind of research.

3.3. Price-level and Current-value Accounting Proposals. Survey and interview-based studies in this area include American Institute of CPAs' Technical Services Division (1958), Backer (1973, 1970), Brenner (1970), Estes (1968), Garner (1972), Hanna (1974 and 1972), Horngren (1955) and Rosen (1972). Experimental studies include Dyckman (1969), Heintz (1973), and McIntyre (1973).

The survey and interview-based studies were intended to examine the ultimate usefulness of price-level adjusted cost or current-value financial information. Opinions were sought primarily from presumed users of financial statements, especially analysts and bankers who were interviewed to explore their perceptions of the usefulness of various alternatives to the historical cost model. In general, three conclusions seem to emerge. First, no interest was found in replacing historical cost statements with current-value statements or with price-level adjusted historical cost statements. These alternatives have been perceived as being useful but only as supplements to the historical cost statements. Second, there was stronger interest in current-value information than in price-level adjusted historical cost information. This result apparently was due more to a lack of interest in the latter, even as supplementary information, rather than to any very great interest in the former. Third, there appears to be some confusion in the minds of survey respondents about the difference between the current-value and price-level proposals, suggesting that much of the scattered support for the latter may have been due to respondents' thinking the former was meant. Rosen (1972, p. 10) observed, "A very small number in the Canadian business community seem to understand well the difference in effect between a price-level restatement of historical cost and replacement cost or reproduction cost. The belief that a price-level restatement equals current value must be overcome if any progress is to be made on the subject of this study." This point also applies to the interpretation of research results, because it is not always evident that the research questionnaire made clear the distinction between price-level adjustments and replacement cost or explained how such information would have impact on the financial statements. Copeland, et al. (1973, p. 368) asked respondents to rate "the effects of price-level changes" in terms of how much information "is now available to the users of financial statements" and "should be available to the users of financial statements." The respondent might well be uncertain as to whether general or specific price-level changes were meant and whether provision of such information in the body of the statements was implied. Such uncertainty might increase with the sophistication of the respondent.

These uncertainties and ambiguities are a major barrier to interpreting the results of the nonexperimental studies in this group. The studies varied widely in the wording of questions and the conduct of the interviews. The results from four studies illustrate these variations. AICPA (1958) asked respondents, by mail, whether they were in favor of "disclosing current dollar cost of depreciation"; 74% were in favor. Estes (1968) asked respondents, by mail, whether they considered various kinds of information "useful"; 81% thought current-value information was useful, 70% thought price-level adjusted cost information was useful. Garner's (1972) respondents, also obtained by mail, were asked about "need" for current-value or price-level adjusted information; only 28% of the respondents saw a need for current-value information, and only 26% for price-level adjusted information. Hanna (1974, 1972) asked 30 analysts, in an interview setting, to "rank alternative sets of statements (prepared by him) in terms of usefulness." There were four choices: historical cost only; current-value only; price-level adjusted only; and a combination of current-value and price-level adjusted. Twenty-eight analysts ranked historical cost first, all 30 ranked current value second or third, and 28 ranked price-level adjusted cost last. How much impact on the results the nature of the illustrative statements may have had was not measured, though it may have been a crucial factor. In general, these studies suggest that price-level adjusted information is not highly valued by those queried. Definite conclusions, however, remain elusive because of the ambiguities and variations referred to above.

Differences in results and methodology were just as prominent in the experimental studies as they were in the nonexperimental studies. Dyckman (1969) mailed questionnaires to analysts, while Heintz (1973) and McIntyre (1973) conducted their studies at universities, using students as subjects. Heintz's subjects made a sequence of decisions over several simulated time periods; Dyckman's and McIntyre's made decisions or evaluations once, without replication. Even though both Heintz and Dyckman used price-level adjusted statements, Heintz relied on interviews and visits with companies having experience in such adjustments to help him develop such statements, while Dyckman relied on "reasonable assumptions" to make his adjustments. McIntyre made both current-cost and price-level adjustments in developing his statements. In all cases, subjects were asked to make simulated investment decisions using controlled information (traditional historical cost information or proposed revised information or both) and the apparent impact of the various kinds of information on their decisions and judgments was observed. Dyckman's analysts, however, were asked to select the better investment for a described client, while Heintz's and McIntyre's students were asked to make specific forecasts. In addition to expertise differences, the analysts and students differed on task familiarity, task performance, prior expectations and viewpoints.

Suppose for a moment that the results of the three studies had shown a statistically strong preference for one of the proposed alternative accounting methods. Generalizing from such experiments nevertheless to actual decision-making contexts would still be risky. In particular, it is not clear that the information used in the manipulation contained all that is used by "real" decision-makers, nor that the contextual simulation was sufficient, nor that the subjects brought an appropriate degree of motivation to the task, nor that subjects (especially, but not exclusively, the students) knew how to make investment decisions.

Subject to such external validity caveats, however, the results of the three published experiments are not encouraging with respect to the alternative accounting methods. McIntyre found no statistically significant effects of using his price-level and current-value adjusted statements. Heintz found few effects, generally nonsignificant, of using price-level adjusted information. Dyckman found some significant effects of using price-level adjusted information, but the relationships found were not strong (statistical significance is partly a function of sample size, and Dyckman's sample was quite large). And in a critical behavioral measure of information impact, the per-share evaluation assigned by the analyst subject to the hypothetical company, no significant differences were found.

From an overall market point of view, the efficient market literature would suggest that general as well as specific price-index measures of inflation are already common knowledge. Hence, it is only to the extent that certain financial information (e.g., the age of an organization's assets) is not generally known that such information, if reported, could influence the relative structure of security prices. Thus, the conclusion would appear to be that simple disclosure of such data would be sufficient for decision-making. Moreover, for our purposes, the results suggest the difficulty of attempting to establish conclusions in behavioral studies of inflation adjustments when subjects are prevented access to other sources of information normally available (or which could be made available). This issue restricts the scope of conclusions which can be drawn from studies dealing with the impact on decision-making of inflation-adjusted data, and hence on an evaluation of the formation content of inflation-adjusted data.

3.4. Probabilistic Financial Statements and Allied Proposals. Oliver (1972) is the only published study included in this section, although there have been a number of recent dissertations in this area.[7] Oliver used an experiment to investigate the effect of "confidence interval" financial statements that put specific confidence bands around the reported numbers on the hypothetical lending decisions of bankers. No judgment was made

7. See, for example, K. K. Chen (1974), Danos (1974), Hawkins (1974) and King (1973) in the dissertation bibliography.

about the quality of any decisions; rather, the study tried to detect any perturbations from the use of such altered statements. Further analysis in this area awaits a critical mass of published research efforts.

The research reviewed in this section has been successful in displaying wide ranges of opinions on issues of financial accounting principles. For example, the issue perhaps of most interest to practitioners now—the use of price-level adjusted historical cost information—has found, at most, lukewarm support. Few of the research efforts reviewed in this section have been methodologically or theoretically rigorous. The most popular kind of research has been the exploratory survey or interview but without more rigorous or more specific follow-up investigation. There has been no research to speak of on the fundamental purposes of financial accounting, and much more investigation of proposed alternative bases of financial accounting is needed before it could be said that such bases have received serious empirical investigation. More consideration is needed of the place of financial accounting information in users' decision models, and of the assumptions made by researchers about what that place is. People may not use the information in the way the experimenter thinks they do, they may not even use it in the way *they* think they do. For example, individuals may not use it if other sources are available or cheaper. They may not use it at all.

4. Special Topics

Several studies have focused on issues of what and when to report and the effects of alternate reporting methods on individual decisions within the context of special topic areas. In this section, we focus on the following five special topic areas: (1) segment and subsidiary reporting; (2) interperiod reporting; (3) forecast reporting; (4) decision effects of alternate reporting methods; and (5) effecting changes in reporting practice.

One interesting observation can be made before we begin. The behavioral research methods used by the respective researchers can be classified by the type of question addressed. The questions of what and when to report have been investigated almost exclusively by using survey research methods, interviews and questionnaires, and these methods have provided considerable data. Respondents often have been asked to identify the critical reporting issues relevant to the topic under investigation. Users of financial reports have provided information about their desires for specific information and the uses to which such information might be put. Although sometimes respondents have been asked what they would do with a specific bit of information, the responses have represented at most the stated opinions, beliefs and attitudes of those answering the question. Respondents have never been asked, however, to make either a real decision using the data involved, or to pay for the data requested.

Two other types of data occasionally have been obtained by using survey research methods. First, problems likely to be encountered in the implementation of new reporting requirements have been suggested by those who were either to provide or certify the new requirements. In rare cases information has been solicited from those who have already implemented or tried to implement a new reporting technique. Once again the data have expressed only the attitudes, opinions, and, occasionally, the recollections of the respondents.

Issues involving the effects of alternative reporting methods on user decisions have generally been studied by designing experiments. Researchers have attempted to control the setting in which subjects respond to the data presented, hoping in this way to minimize the effects of extraneous variables which tend to confound the decision results and make interpretation difficult, if not impossible. The objective was to make inferential statements concerning cause and effect or, alternatively, associations among the variables studied.

Because many of these studies have used student subjects, extrapolation of the results to the target populations is tenuous at best. Moreover, in most of these studies it is not clear that the researcher has been able to reproduce the decision environment, and this raises questions about the validity of the responses obtained. For these and other reasons to be discussed briefly in the subsequent methods section, there typically remain at the conclusion of each separate study several contending explanatory hypotheses. The emergence of a dominant hypothesis will require a substantial number of studies designed to eliminate competing explanations. The recent work of Dopuch and Ronen (1973) provides a good example.

4.1. Segment and Subsidiary Reporting. In one respect, research on segment and subsidiary reporting extends analysis of disclosure issues to further breakdowns of the activities of an organization. The area is a timely one, given the recent (September 30, 1975) issuance of the FASB's Exposure Draft on *Financial Reporting for Segments of a Business Enterprise.* If the draft is adopted in its present form, business enterprises would be required to report their activities in different industries and their major customers, as well as other activities. Of particular importance to us is the required disclosure of segment revenues, profitability and identifiable assets.

The research summarized in this section includes the following studies: Backer and McFarland (1968); Cramer (1968); Mautz (1968); Martin, Laiken and Haslam (1969); Stallman (1969); Backer (1970); Dascher and Copeland (1971); Crumbley and Strawser (1974); and Ortman (1975).

Supporters of segment reporting have argued for some time that the separate segments of a business are usually subject to different economic conditions, degrees of risk, and exhibit different rates of growth. A single all-inclusive report tends to average and thereby obscure these factors. The research on user attitudes suggests that the primary value of segment reporting would be to display the effects of growth, risk and economic conditions on the activities of the enterprise. With this information, analysts believe they could make better investment analyses and improve investment decisions and recommendations to individual investors. Those involved in merger and acquisition activities suggest that they could do a better job of identifying merger candidates and of appraising an acquisition decision. Bankers point out that their loan decisions would be facilitated; a bank typically has no recourse to a subsidiary's assets if it forecloses on a loan, netted payables and receivables cloud the financial position of the potential loanee, and the earnings strength of a company is more clearly suggested by separate reporting of both subsidiary and segment earnings and sales data.

Research on segment reporting suggests that extensive practical problems are likely to impede implementation. These problems, and the uses described in the previous paragraph could be deduced by logical analysis, but it is useful to discover central issues which the "experts" agree must be addressed when solutions are offered.

An initial issue requiring resolution is the definition of product lines and segments. The research indicates that this definition may be company specific, and that a more general (perhaps industry) approach may be necessary if comparability among companies is to be maintained.

A second issue is that of just when an event occurs which affects segment reporting. These events could well differ from those affecting the overall company's report. Certain cost allocations have been mentioned as particularly difficult examples. Since there is no one correct way to allocate common and joint costs, problems which influenced the firm's reported profits over time would now affect the reported segment's profits within that time period.

Even if the technical issues could be resolved, the research suggests that management may be reluctant to disclose segment earnings for competitive reasons. Even though financial executives tend to recognize that segment data may be useful to investors, they have expressed concern that investors might be confused by such data. Analysts, as might be expected, strongly favor such reporting.

The problems and attitudes discussed above, when taken together, explain why the reporting of sales by segments is common practice while separate segment income statements are rare among surveyed firms.

Segment-reporting problems are in part a result of business combinations involving diverse activities. In a study by Martin, Laiken and Haslam (1969), the authors examined reporting practices in Canada for business combinations. This extensive survey describes the accounting approach used and the reporting problems encountered by a substantial set of firms traded on the Toronto Stock Exchange. The authors conclude that in Canada there has been a rather liberal interpretation of the standards used for deciding whether a combination qualified as a pooling of interest, despite the fact that only about 5% of all combinations were accounted for as poolings. The study reveals that two of the three allowed methods of accounting for purchases resulted in roughly the same balance sheet presentation for the purchase transaction as if it had been treated as a pooling. This fact could account for the relatively infrequent use of the pooling technique in Canada. In over 50% of the cases treated as purchases, no portion of the excess over book value paid was charged against income. As the authors conclude, "The implication is clear that comparability of earnings data among these companies was difficult, if not impossible, to determine since in most cases the information concerning disposition of (the) excess was not clearly spelled out (disclosed) in published annual reports."[8]

All but three of the studies in this area were based on data obtained from interviews and questionnaires. The response rates ranged from 22% to 50% with little, if any, attempt to examine possible nonresponse biases. In evaluating these studies, particular attention must also be paid to the populations sampled. In general, many of those surveyed (including businessmen) could be expected to be opposed to segment reporting. On the

8. In this regard, it is interesting to note that the FASB is presently gathering data on the problems experienced by U.S. firms in accounting for business combinations under the relevant APB opinions.

other hand, analysts will nearly always prefer more data, especially if the data are offered for free. High quality experimental work in this topic area would be welcome.

One experimental study on the disclosure of divisional data on investment evaluations has been attempted (Stallman, 1969). The reactions of sophisticated investors to additional disclosure were examined by focusing on their judgments of a stock's "intrinsic" or long-run value in the presence of manipulated price data together with the disclosure differences. The statistical finding that the analyst adjustments were less affected by the manipulation of price data when in the presence of the additional disclosure is cited as evidence of the value (but not the net value considering disclosure cost) of segment reporting for multi-industry companies.[9]

A related study requiring operating decisions was conducted by Dascher using less sophisticated students as subjects. The results are reported in Dascher and Copeland (1971). No statistically significant decision effects were found; yet it should be emphasized that this study differed in both the sophistication of the subjects (analysts versus students) and task (investment valuations versus operations decisions). Hence, the results should not be taken as *necessarily* conflicting.[10] Moreover, we observe that many of the difficult issues involved in segment reporting (e.g., the allocation of joint costs) are substantially reduced for consolidated firms. This was the type of disclosure involved in both of these experiments.

In a recent study by Ortman (1975), a field experiment using financial analysts was "conducted to determine the effects on investment analysis of the presence of segment data in financial statements of diversified firms." Subjects were divided into two groups, with one group receiving the additional segment data. Ortman found that "the introduction of segmented data significantly reversed the analysts' evaluations of the diversified firms presented," in the direction of what was expected, given the situation. As in similar studies, the response rate was quite low (about 25%) and there is no way of knowing if subjects acted toward the experimental situation as they would have acted toward a real one.

4.2 Interperiod Reporting. The question of what to report has been expanded recently to deal with when to report. Specifically, should firms

9. For detailed critiques of the study see the comments of McDonald and Kleinman which immediately follow Stallman's paper, and Dascher and Copeland (1971).
10. We note that precisely this error is often made by competent researchers. As an example, Dopuch and Ronen (1973) fall into this error in evaluating the conclusions of several behavioral studies involving investment versus managerial operating decisions. See in particular their claim of "inconsistent results" on page 192.

report on an interim basis, normally within the year, on their operations? Several studies have addressed this issue, including Bird (1969), Edwards, Dominiak and Hedges (1972), Lipay (1972), Bollom (1973) and Nickerson, Pointer and Strawser (1975). The recently adopted amendments to SEC Regulation S-X and to Form 10-Q, which significantly increase quarterly reporting requirements and expand the auditor's involvement therein, highlight the importance of this area.

The importance of interim reports is related to the intensity of analysis on the part of the user. The kaleidoscope of analysis intensity varies from the mere tracking of investments to intensive evaluation. For those in this latter category, interim reports are seen as providing the basis of short- and long-run growth predictions, estimations of sales and earnings variability, and the revision or modification of estimates, predictions and trends.

One of the major results of the attitude studies in this area is the apparent consensus about the type of data users want. As is usual with this type of research, the opinions have been expressed without concern for cost of the data and nearly always without any indication of the specific use to which the information would be put. Moreover, no attempt has been made to monitor requests coincident with decisions.

Users and potential users both appear to want more frequent reporting of two particular types of data: income data, particularly before taxes and extraordinary items; and product-line breakdowns. The tie-in with segment reporting is clear. Simultaneously and perhaps surprisingly, given the importance attached to audited yearly statements, there appears to be little enthusiasm either for seasonal adjustments to reports covering less than one year or for attestation of interim reports by independent auditors. The most general summary of what the unspecified user apparently desires is simply unaudited company reports concerning the status of those items reported annually. This is precisely what many companies are presently reporting.

Preparers have expressed little opposition to providing such interim reports, since many, if not most, of the publicly held companies are already providing much of what users appear to want reported on an interim basis. However, preparers have expressed a preference for allocations while analysts and others desire actual figures (e.g., costs). Preparers stress the relevance of allocations to long-term investors, but it is likely that a more parochial interest supports their position on this issue.

The studies reviewed indicate that, even several years ago, over 80% of the publicly held firms were reporting sales, net income before extraordinary items, and earnings per share on an interim basis. However, less than 10% were reporting even major items from the balance sheet. Quarterly reporting appears to have been the dominant form of interim-report accounting for over 90% of company-reporting practice in this area.

Only one study, Bollom (1973), was of an experimental nature. Students in a business-game setting made investment-type valuations of a seasonal business using interim vs. yearly reports under several alternative reporting techniques. The research did not find any statistically significant decision-related differences, although results cannot be generalized because of the nature of the sample involved, the experimental environment simulated and the content of the reports presented.

We have made the point here and elsewhere that obtaining the views of preparers and users is a valuable input to the policy-decision process. Yet, two warnings should be made. First, we need to be concerned with consequences. Research on what may and, where possible, what does happen when a particular proposed policy is implemented is essential to the policy decision-maker. Too little attention has been given to date by policy-makers (and researchers) to consequences, and too much to prior attitudes. Second, the information which, in users' opinions, will optimize performance may not actually do so when supplied. This substantial leap of faith is much too tenuous to support the present reliance of policy-makers on opinion research. Empirical behavioral research is needed on this point.

4.3. Forecast Reporting. One of the more recent and more hotly contested reporting questions has been whether forecasts should become an integral element of the financial statements or of the annual report. Several recent behavioral studies have looked at this issue, including Daily (1971), Asebrook and Carmichael (1973), Carmichael (1973), Financial Executives Research Foundation (1973), Benjamin and Strawser (1974), Corless and Norgaard (1974), and Nickerson, Pointer and Strawser (1974).

Studies of the impact of reporting forecasts again have been primarily of the attitude variety. The users studied, namely investors and analysts, appeared to favor the reporting of forecasts, as would be expected given a cost-free choice. The user groups surveyed did not indicate that such forecasts should be mandated, but indicated that any forecast made should be attested to by the CPA and some estimate of the error associated with a given forecast should be provided.

Initial and fragmentary evidence has failed to show any increase in the confidence users place in a forecast when attested to by the auditor. On the other hand, more accurate forecasts, indicated by a lower error measure, did influence earnings-per-share predictions in one study (Benjamin and Strawser, 1974), and greater accuracy was associated with greater reliance on the forecast.

Stockholders surveyed indicated they considered forecasting to be part of management's job and believed it appropriate for them to be provided with management's forecasts. They assumed that the auditors would at least review the essential assumptions and verify the underlying computations, even though they were less certain about whether the historical data and the statistical methods used would be covered as part of the attest function.

Providers of forecast data—financial executives and certified public accountants—are generally against providing audited forecast data to the public. The Financial Executives Research Foundation (1973) found that 65% of the financial managers it surveyed stated they believed the financial community was doing a good job projecting the earnings of their companies. Auditors argue that they are not trained to evaluate forecast techniques and they cite a lack of the knowledge prerequisite to evaluating management's projections. Providers appear to be very concerned about the loss of independence that they believe could follow attestation as auditors become concerned with, and perhaps even responsible for, attaining the forecasted results. The specter of the auditor's legal liability for attaining the forecast is cited as a potentially reinforcing argument for their concern about the possible loss of independence.

Finally, providers appear to be uneasy about the ability of investors and potential investors intelligently to digest forecast data. One study (Nickerson, Pointer and Strawser, 1974) found that investors expected forecast errors of 10% to be maximum for any company, which suggests that the difficulty of forecasting is not affected by type of industry, product line, or other salient business characteristics. It was also noted that this particular set of users expected sales and income forecasts to be done with equivalent preciseness. Using actual company data, the Financial Executives Research Foundation (1973) found substantive differences in the accuracy of sales, expense and corporate earnings forecasts.[11]

One of the more valuable contributions to research on forecasts has been the interview study by Carmichael (1973) of the English experience. This

11. The concern here is with information processing at the individual level and hence cannot be directly extrapolated to support a position of inefficiency in the market for securities.

study points to the need to educate potential consumers to the meaning of, and particularly the uncertainty inherent in, forecasts. This will not be an easy task. For example, the possible range of a forecast was not found to be at least in England, an adequate measure of uncertainty.

This study also points to the need to clarify the paramount issue of legal responsibility associated with the attest function. Questions such as the allowable variability, and the permissibility of expost facto explanations, and the importance of fraud and intent in determining legal liability must be resolved prior to the reporting of forecasts. This research suggests that we may be able to avoid unfortunate consequences and perhaps make more effective and efficient decisions by careful analysis of the experience of other countries.

In terms of present practice, only 3% of companies now indicate that they are providing forecasts to the public although 95% of the firms in the Financial Executives Research Foundation study (1973) prepare such forecasts for internal use. These forecasts are not audited. Criteria for judging forecast accuracy have not been established nor have the factors affecting forecast accuracy been researched.[12]

4.4. Decision Effects from Using Alternate Accounting Procedures. Some of the more interesting behavioral research has been done in the area of reporting effects on individual decision-making. This was one of the earlier subject areas to be investigated using experimental methods. The studies influencing our review include Horngren (1959), Dyckman (1964), Dyckman (1966), Jensen (1966), Livingston (1967), Khemakhem (1968), Barrett (1971), Elias (1972), Hofstedt (1972a), Hofstedt (1972b), Dopuch and Ronen (1973), Hawkins and Wehle (1973), Libby (1975), and Ortman (1975). These studies do not neatly fit into the previous subject areas examined. Many of them were of an experimental nature and nonstudent subjects were commonly employed.

These studies support the contention that alternative reporting procedures can influence individual evaluations. This phenomenon has been observed among students, stockholders, potential individual investors, analysts, bank loan officers, certified public accountants and financial

12. A study by Daily (1971) suggests that firm size may not be an important factor. The Financial Executives study (1973), on the other hand, finds larger variances for smaller companies. This study found no significant effects due to type of industry, the existence of written instructions, or the use of a range presentation format.

executives as subjects. However, the extent or importance of the influence has often been less than expected.

The extent of the influence appears to depend, in part, on the nature of the particular decision and decision-maker as well as the alternate reporting techniques investigated. The different effects of alternate reporting can be mitigated by the inclusion of supplementary information in the form of schedules, footnotes or narrative form which facilitate comparability, unless the added data, whether in numerical or narrative form, conflicts with that originally supplied. Cost-benefit tradeoffs, as they relate to disclosure, have not been investigated by these studies.

The impact of alternate reporting methods also appears to be related to the characteristics of the users. More sophisticated users, in terms of their understanding and appreciation of accounting data, tend to rely more heavily on the accounting data supplied to them in financial reports, rather than on the nonaccounting portions of such reports. Unsophisticated users, on the other hand, rely more on the nonaccounting data in the financial reports. Sophisticated users are more likely to be able to perceive economic realities underlying alternative reporting methods. These user characteristics are job-related and are probably related to the user's experience as well. Therefore, the effect of alternative reporting practices is likely to be influenced by the same factors.

The nature of the experimental environment (as well as the experimental parameters) appears to influence decisions. Hence, the access to expert technical assistance will likely influence the experimental results obtained. This possibility is typically ignored in most experimental situations. The experimental environment, and hence the validity of extrapolating the results obtained, is also affected by motivation, a realistic time-decision framework, and task-familiarity. The results of the experiment (or interviews) will depend on just how these factors are controlled; whether valid generalizations can be drawn will depend on the effectiveness of the experimental environment in inducing behavior reflective of what would have been done in actual decision situations. For example, one of these studies involved (either directly or indirectly) the allocation of the subject's capital with real rewards and penalties.[13]

It should be emphasized that although the use of alternative reporting methods may result in individuals' making different investment decisions, these differences do not necessarily imply inefficiencies in the market.

13. In some cases, payoffs to the subjects are included, but they are not the rewards earned from operating in the market.

The presence of sufficient arbitrage activity will dampen and can even remove these effects from the market.[14]

A study by Libby (1975) extended the predictability work on firm failure begun by Beaver (1966), by trying to determine whether bank loan officers could distinguish between failed and nonfailed firms in a reporting population in which 50% of the firms failed within a short period. The research indicated that "a small empirically derived set of accounting ratios allowed bankers ranging widely in backgrounds to make highly accurate and reliable predictions of business failure." Limitations of subjects (and the reality of the task) caused Libby to raise the usual cautions about generalization.

Although the research examined in this review is, by nature of this conference, restricted to financial accounting and disclosure, we cannot totally overlook the somewhat overlapping boundaries of financial reporting and managerial decisions. Khemakhem (1968) offers the observation based on his research that managerial decisions may be influenced by goals different from maximizing reported income. These could include the concern for competitive position (including survival and market share), funds (or cash) flow, and others. There can exist in some firms an interdependence among certain managerial decisions and a concern for what will be reported in the company's financial reports, known to the operation-research analyst as constrained optimization and to the behavioral scientist as "satisficing" behavior. We also note that the flow of information reaching the manager and the investor (beyond that contained in financial statements) is extensive and often heavily relied on in the making of decisions, including investment evaluations.

4.5. Effecting Changes in Reporting Practice. Our knowledge of what may affect the decision-making process, together with what we know about efficient capital markets, is a necessary input to accounting policy. Yet, it is not sufficient to indicate which accounting policies should be adopted. The research problems in this area have been immense, and little substantive progress has been made on them to date. Behavioral studies have, however, leap-frogged this issue and have begun to examine how changes in accounting practice can be achieved. Studies addressing this issue include Sorter and Becker (1964), Sorter, Becker, Archibald and Beaver (1966), Comiskey and Groves (1971), Copeland and

14. See Dyckman (1964), p. 286, footnote 5, for an early recognition of this fact.

Shank (1971), Rakes and Shenkir (1972), Piaker and Dalberth (1973), and Ritts (1974).

Research to date suggests that the learning-set corporate-personality characterization of companies appears to be superior to diffusion theory in explaining innovation. The characteristics of the innovation appear to be less important than the behavior set of the firm affected by it. (See also Shank and Copeland [1973].) Acceptance of this viewpoint implies that a learning set can be created by starting with easily implementable and noncontroversial reporting changes. As experience with the new reporting techniques is obtained, the approach (if not the solution) becomes transferable. The theory may suggest likely industries or companies where specific reporting changes might be implemented.

Some research also has focused on just when attitude changes related to accounting policy-board pronouncements actually take place. Psychological studies suggest that behavioral changes may precede attitude changes. Certified public accountants, for example, appear to believe that APB opinions lead ultimately to forced compliance. It may well be that the forced compliance results in the eventual acceptance of the accounting procedure as the appropriate one. The method advocated by the opinion, then, becomes the accepted norm to be defended.

The policy of the FASB in issuing exposure drafts may be a critical step in the development of attitudes supportive to the change.[15] Research suggests that major attitude changes can occur when an exposure draft is released as well as when the final opinion or standard is issued. This appears to reflect the belief that the final opinion will mirror the exposure draft. If so, then it is important that any substantive research be accomplished prior to the issuing of such drafts.

The research just reviewed points to a noticeable gap in our knowledge. To date there has been almost no research done on how companies make accounting choices. The studies of corporate personality, Sorter et al. (1964 and 1966), provide the best attempts of which we are aware, but they do not deal with the essence of the issues involved.

5. Evaluation of Research Methods

The previous sections of this paper have provided considerable evidence of the empirical vigor of experimental and survey research in finan-

15. The point also applies to SEC releases.

cial accounting. In the last decade, over 100 experimental and survey studies have been conducted and published, and the rate of production has increased dramatically in recent years. But the increasing volume of research activity has not resulted in a dramatic increase in our body of knowledge, partly because the empirical evidence has not been obtained in a form that allows it to be integrated with prior evidence. The accumulation of knowledge requires more than an increasing literature.

Our review of experimental and survey research in financial accounting has provided us with a relatively broad perspective. Several features of this research are evident from this perspective and we will now attempt to describe these features and some of their consequences for the accumulation of knowledge.

Based on general impressions gained from our review, the "typical" study in this area was done by an academic, often as part of a Ph.D. dissertation, with little, if any, nonuniversity financial support. The study was done in isolation from others, at a relatively rapid pace, and often published in one or more condensed versions. It made only passing reference to the work of others and provided little, if any, theoretical formulation of the problem or of the hypotheses to be tested. It usually described data-collection and data-analysis procedures in somewhat more detail; there has been, nevertheless, considerable variation in both the sophistication and rigor employed by these researchers. In presenting results, conclusions usually have been limited to those justified by statistical inference, although the discussion of these results often has gone beyond the data, implying both stronger and less equivocal results than can be justified by the research. Finally, the need for research that replicates the findings and explores the variables further has been strongly urged.

This characterization is, of course, an oversimplification and an overgeneralization. It is a composite of a number of features, each of which occurs frequently although not necessarily together in any one study. The point of the characterization is not that all of the studies reviewed have all of these features; rather, the point is that lack of theoretical emphasis, lack of ties to the work of others, and lack of rigor all are very general problems in the research reviewed and that these problems have implications for the accumulation of knowledge.

5.1. Lack of a Theoretical Emphasis. A theory provides a guide that tells a researcher where to look for what is to be observed. Ideally, a theory hypothesizes specific outcomes under specified conditions in terms that both make it possible to test the prediction and anchor the hypotheses into a broader context of assumptions. Most of the research reviewed here has been done (or at least reported) without explicit formulation of theory. Surveys of attitudes of preparers, auditors, and users of financial statements have been done without benefit of a theory of attitude formation, of attitude change, or of the relationship between attitudes and behavior.[16] In addition, most experiments on the usefulness of financial statement data or on the effects of alternative accounting methods on decision behavior have been done without benefit of a theory of information processing or of decision-making. This lack of emphasis on theory effectively has limited data analyses in these studies to tests for differences (and occasionally to measures of the strength of relationships), even though it has been difficult, if not impossible, to interpret meaningfully the differences observed without a theory of why they might exist or what their direction might be.

As reflected in our review, experimental and survey research has been conducted in a large number of areas and has focused on a wide variety of topics and issues. But there have been relatively few areas in which a critical mass of studies has emerged. Consequently, many studies have been in areas so little studied that researchers have had to choose between the alternatives of collecting data with little theory to guide them in its interpretation or of pausing to build the requisite theory while having little evidence to give them confidence that they were building something useful. Given such a choice, many researchers have chosen the first alternative, perhaps because it may have been the less frustrating one, or maybe the only practical one.

An alternative to building theory is to use theory previously developed in other fields and disciplines. Recent experimental research in financial accounting has reflected an increased use of this alternative. For example, Abdel-khalik (1973, 1974) and Ronen and Falk (1973) have used entropy concepts to study aggregation in accounting; Rose et al. (1970) and Dickhaut and Eggleton (1975) have used Weber's Law from psychophysics to study judgments of numerical data; Boatsman and Robertson (1974) and Libby (1975a, 1975b) have used the Brunswik Lens model (Brunswik, 1952, 1956) to study judgment formation, and Ritts (1974) has used dissonance theory to explain compliance with APB Opinions.

16. The conduct of many studies in this area has left the typical respondents (e.g., financial analysts) less than enthusiastic about further participation. We, like the economy, may well have used up a substantial portion of a scarce resource with relatively poorly-structured research instruments.

The use of theories developed elsewhere is a convenient way to formulate testable hypotheses in a financial accounting context. Whether these theories are likely to contribute to our body of knowledge will depend in part on how well they are (or can be) integrated into accounting contexts. Often the process of integrating theories developed elsewhere is as difficult and frustrating as the process of building theories. Theories which are adapted from one field to another often carry with them a type of thinking and some of the concepts of their area of origin which are not always appropriate to their application in an accounting context.

We believe that knowledge will accumulate more rapidly if researchers conducting experiments and surveys in financial accounting use theory to guide their choices of where to look for what they want to observe. We are more concerned about the use of more and better theories than we are about whether these theories are developed within an accounting context.

5.2. Lack of Ties to the Work of Others. Independent researchers conducting studies unknown to each other usually do not design their studies to facilitate later comparisons. Researchers sometimes claim a theoretical connection to earlier studies through one or more variables common to their studies and earlier studies. Yet, they rarely detail differences in their measures of those variables and the measures used in earlier studies. For example even though several studies used indices of disclosure to measure the extent to which companies differed in disclosure, these studies differed dramatically in the specific items included in these indices. Similarly, surveys of attitudes of various individuals about corporate reporting practices used different questionnaire items to obtain measures of these attitudes.

Studies differ dramatically in the specific actors, behaviors, objects, and context of focus. Despite these differences however, researchers seldom specify how the various aspects in their studies compare with those in earlier studies. Indices of disclosure have been applied to very different samples of corporate annual reports; attitude surveys have obtained data from very different samples of users, preparers, auditors, students and academics; and experiments on the usefulness of financial statement data and on the effects of alternative accounting methods have been conducted in very different decision-making contexts and have used very different subjects. Few of these studies have attempted to compare precisely these differences and to assess their implications.

We believe that knowledge will accumulate more rapidly if researchers do not leave the task of comparing and integrating their studies with past efforts entirely to future researchers. Researchers should deliberately design their studies to dovetail in useful ways with other studies and should attempt to specify the limits and aspects of their studies with precision. In addition, future research should deliberately undertake the task of comparing two or more studies to the end of drawing new conclusions.

5.3 Lack of Rigor. Over 75% of the studies reviewed were done in natural rather than contrived settings. Of these studies, about 60% were based on mail surveys and another 18% were experiments based on mail questionnaires. This preponderance of studies done in natural settings and relying on survey research methods is somewhat surprising in view of the academic affiliations of most of the researchers. The preference for these settings and methods probably stems from many sources, including the fact that mail survey studies can be done rapidly, at relatively low cost, can be easily adapted to current issues or topics, and so forth. However, a major consequence of the extensive use of natural settings and survey methods is the general lack of rigor. Studies conducted in natural settings and based on survey methods tend to maximize opportunities for realism and external validity or generalizability, but they run the risk of less precision and control and thereby typically exhibit low internal validity.

A natural inclination is to call for more extensive use of the laboratory method. After all, the laboratory method represents the quintessence of science, regardless of the substantive problem involved. The use of this method can improve control and precision relative to that possible in natural settings. Yet, there is no reason to expect that the heavy reliance on natural settings and survey research methods will diminish. Therefore, it may be more useful to note some ways in which researchers can increase precision and control in conducting survey studies or survey-based experiments.

The research strategy used in surveys or survey-based experiments is the "sample survey" (Runkel and McGrath, 1972). The key attributes of this strategy are that the behaviors of interest are elicited (1) in response to predetermined stimulus inputs such as questions, presentations and instructions controlled by the researcher, and (2) in settings to which the respondents are indigenous. The typical survey is generally concerned with generalizability over respondents and therefore samples respondents from the populations to which the results are intended to be generalized. In surveys used as a basis for experiments, the concern is not only with generalizability over respondents, but also with generalizability over stimuli, and these studies usually focus as well on sampling stimulus properties that are of interest.

The sample survey provides for control by the researcher over stimulus *inputs*. However, it does not provide for control by the researcher over stimulus *conditions*. Researchers usually assume that the effects of the behavioral setting either are muted or neutralized by its being a natural one, or that these effects are extraneous to the behavior being studied rather than being important determinants of that behavior. For example, one's preference for one method of accounting over another or one's evaluation of a hypothetical company's prospects presumably may be unaffected by when and where one answers the question. However, some features of the behavioral setting may distract or distort a subject's responses. For example, responses may be deliberately or unwittingly distorted by social pressures, or judgment errors may occur due to physical distractions peculiar to the setting.

In using the sample-survey research strategy, a researcher should take advantage of the opportunities that exist to control stimulus inputs and sample selection. The researcher should specify the populations to be sampled, should randomly draw respondents to be included, and should standardize the instructions, presentations and the phrasing of questions. The broadest sampling base possible should be used. The initial set-up cost for a sample survey is relatively high, but the cost of additional observations is relatively low. A researcher should be constantly aware of his inability to control the setting and should attempt to obtain information about it if there is reason to believe that responses may be influenced or biased by the setting and therefore not generalizable over a wide range of settings. In this regard, and for purposes of checking responses, a post-experiment questionnaire is useful. Few studies employed such a device.

Most of the surveys and all of the survey-based experiments used a "static group comparison" research design (Campbell and Stanley, 1963). In pure form, this research design includes one group which is measured after exposure to an experimental treatment and a different group which is measured without exposure to the experimental treatment. Most of the studies reviewed were similar to this design only in that group comparisons were based on postexposure tests only. Rather than use a control group that received no experimental manipulation, most studies used several experimental groups.

The group comparison research design is vulnerable to two confounding factors. The first factor is selection. There is no assurance that the groups being compared started from equivalent levels, especially if entry into either group was voluntary or was affected by administrative or logistic convenience. Any observed differences between the groups could have come about through differential recruitment. The second factor is sampling mortality. Observed differences between groups could have come about through differential drop-out from the groups. For example, mortality may result from feelings about the experimental treatments: subjects who do not like the treatments may be more likely to drop out than subjects who like the treatments. Such differential mortality, interacting with experimental treatments, can account for differences observed between comparison groups.

True experimental designs usually control for selection biases by providing for the random assignment of subjects to experimental and control groups from a common pool of subjects. Random assignment will not always insure subgroup equivalence, but it is more likely to result in the averaging out of individual biases. However, it is difficult to use randomization when groups are not being selected from a common pool of subjects. Here, sampling procedures have to be relied upon to generate equivalent subgroups. Sampling procedures, however, cannot be relied upon to generate subgroup equivalence when response rates are low, and low response rates have been reported in almost all of the surveys and survey-based experiments reviewed. Too many studies have had more nonrespondents than respondents, and this raises questions about external validity—whether respondents are representative of the populations from which they were drawn. In addition, too many studies have reported differential response rates for comparison groups, and this raises questions about internal validity—whether experimental treatments or differential mortality rates explain observed differences between groups.

Researchers using survey research methods simply must deal with the nonresponse problem. Several practical approaches exist. First, the researcher should try to compare the characteristics and backgrounds of respondents with those of the population from which the respondents were drawn. In addition, the researcher should attempt to compare the responses of early respondents with those of late respondents as another means of testing for a response bias. A trend suggests nonrespondents might have attitudes similar to late respondents and, hence, not like the average reply. Finally, in situations where a researcher is sampling subgroups from different populations, these comparisons should be made within as well as between subgroups.

Two other technical problems pervade the analysis of differences between groups. The first is the use of multiple variables in making group comparisons. Most survey studies have dealt with a relatively large number of dependent variables. For example, some of the survey questionnaires used in these studies have included up to 50 items. Analyses of questionnaire items typically have focused on mean differences between groups on each item. Yet researchers using questionnaires with multiple items should worry about possible intercorrelations and patterns of intercorrelations between responses on these items. Our suspicion is that many of these items are intercorrelated and that researchers should try to reduce the number of dependent variables through factor analysis (or some other multivariate technique) to a smaller set of orthogonal dimensions. Comparisons between groups could then be made on the basis of mean factor scores on these dimensions. The second problem is the use of multiple t tests to make pairwise comparisons between groups. Performing multiple t tests to make these comparisons overstates the probability of finding significant differences and overutilizes the sample data. Researchers interested in making multiple comparisons should consider the alternative of using a one-way analysis of variance (F test) followed by one of several procedures for examining pairwise differences between groups.[17]

Often it is more useful to measure the strength and hence the importance of the relationship rather than simply to test for significance. Significance does not necessarily imply an important relationship. The hypothesis-testing (significance-testing) procedure used by most authors is essentially a question of whether the sample size is sufficiently large to show the differences that must inevitably exist between different groups. The fact that the groups differ is trivial. This is why some indication of the strength of the relationship found is of more interest.[18]

An additional set of problems concerns surrogation of task and subject.

17. See Winer (1971) or Morrison (1967) for a discussion of methods developed by Scheffe, Tukey, or by Newman and Keuls for examining pairwise differences between groups.
18. A lack of significance is a good indication of an unimportant relationship. Unfortunately, the converse does not follow.

Most, if not all, of the experiments reviewed in this paper are open to the criticism that we cannot be certain of adequate task surrogation. Does the subject treat the experimental task in a way that mirrors actual decision-making behavior? Among other problems here are the effects of alternate information sources normally available but excluded from the experiment of similar task interest, of task familiarity of the effect of learning and of a representative reward system. The problems suggest the value of a laboratory study using the appropriate subjects. The goal is not to obtain realism per se, but rather to induce the relevant behavioral set and task characteristics. If this can be done in a simple and controlled setting, so much the better.

Finally, we observe that about 14% of the studies reviewed were experiments in which students were used as subjects, and for those that were purely experimental, students were used in more than 50%. Several critics have either raised or discussed the question of using students as subjects in experiments.[19] We do not intend to repeat that discussion here. Simply put, the issue typically raised in these discussions is whether student subjects are "good" surrogates for "real" decision-makers. In addition, we believe that the issue of rigor in laboratory methods should be raised.

In a laboratory experiment, a researcher not only manipulates variables of interest; he also creates a behavioral setting within which observations are to be made. The purpose of this behavioral setting should not be simply to mirror some naturally occurring behavioral system, but rather to highlight selected behavioral processes and certain conditions related to those processes. The laboratory experiment is not concerned only with generalizing over subjects but also over settings. Ideally speaking, if a laboratory experiment is well-conceived and well-designed to capture the intended behavioral processes, one subject should be interchangeable with another, and different subjects would be used only in the interest of replication and reliability. This, in contrast with our earlier discussion of sample surveys, leaves the generalizability over subjects as a separable issue. Surveys deal with behavior elicited in response to stimuli in settings to which the subjects are indigenous but the stimuli are not. Laboratory experiments, on the other hand, deal with behavior emitted in response to a setting to which the stimuli are indigenous but the subjects are not. Differences observed between students and other groups in surveys should, then, raise questions about generalizability over respondents. Differences

19. See Birnberg and Nath (1967), Hofstedt (1972a), Copeland, Francia and Strawser (1973), Watson (1974), Copeland, Francia and Strawser (1974), and Abdel-khalik (1974b).

observed between students and others in laboratory experiments should raise questions about the reliability and replicability of responses to stimuli in the setting created.

6. An Evaluation of Research Impact

The impact of behavioral research on accounting practice has been almost nonexistent. While the pronouncements of the APB and now the FASB may have reflected behavioral considerations, there is no clear tie-in to the behavioral research we have examined. The changes we have seen in recent years and those being considered by policy makers at this time do not reflect the findings of behavioral research nor do the official pronouncements indicate any reliance on the existing behavioral literature. The thinking of senior and influential practitioners as expressed in their writings and speeches gives little evidence of a behavioral research impact. Operating rules and requirements of major government bureaus and organizations involved with accounting reports also do not appear to reflect any behavioral research findings. We believe there are several reasons why this is the case.

First, most professionals and those in policy-making positions are not trained in behavioral science and the research they rely on is often of an interview or questionnaire variety rather than experimental.[20] Hence, they are not ideally trained by education or experience to evaluate the existing behavioral research. Yet this is critical in determining and evaluating what has been achieved, to integrate one study with others, and relate it to policy issues.

Secondly, behavioral research is of relatively recent vintage and has had little time to have an impact on policy-makers. The communication of research results from academic researcher to practicing accountants has not been adequate. The academic typically writes for other academics. The better experimental studies in accounting tend to be published in the *Journal of Accounting Research* and *The Accounting Review.* These journals are not the prime reading material of the practicing accountant or the policy maker. Perhaps through review and summary papers, such as those presented at this symposium, research results can be communicated to practitioners.

In addition, behavioral research is costly both in terms of time and out-

20. We note some changes here as the FASB has done a semi-behavioral study in conjunction with its study of business combinations.

of-pocket costs. Much of the research we have reviewed is the outgrowth of doctoral dissertations. While doctoral students typically spend a year or so on this requirement for their degree, such research studies, particularly if they are of the experimental variety and done in the field, may need a longer time to do them justice. Limited funds often limit samples to students or artificial groupings of practitioners (e.g., executive development programs). Doctoral students are novices at doing research and are perhaps the least competent to draw policy conclusions from their work, although they are typically asked to do so, often with unfortunate results.

Junior faculty also can neither afford the time nor command the resources for such studies. The requisites for promotion and tenure promote an interest in short-term, low-risk research endeavors. By the time a track record has been established, such that resources can be commanded and tenure attained, and longer-run research becomes appealing, the competent researcher is often entangled in the administrative jungle. Sometimes those academics in the best position to understand practice and adopt the proper research perspective are either not able to conduct the appropriate research or lack the time or inclination to do the research. On the other hand, practitioners either do not have the training, the time, or the inclination to engage in other than opinion research. Some reasons for this situation are supplied in the paragraphs that follow. Perhaps it would be useful to encourage junior faculty with research expertise to work more closely with practitioners who possess the resources, including data access, to secure potentially useful research. We note, however, that such apparent opportunities have remained unexploited for some time.

Third, those doing research must remember that formulating accounting policy is essentially a political process. The "art of the possible" plays a paramount role in the determination of what gets adopted. It may be partly for this reason that policy bodies including the FASB place so much weight on opinion research. But, as we noted earlier, this focus misses several potential benefits of research and ignores the consequences of policy decisions.[21] Research about these consequences prior to major policy decisions would make it possible to improve our knowledge of the cost-benefit tradeoffs of a proposed course of action. There is also a tendency for policy-makers to accept users' opinions concerning the optimal information set despite the shortcomings of this research approach.

21. The investment credit issue provides an excellent example of what happens when consequences are not given sufficient attention.

The question should be addressed empirically. Hawkins and Wehle (1973) note, for example, that "empirical (opinion) data alone does not lead to a resolution of the lease accounting controversy." We know of no empirical research in accounting supportive of this behavior on the part of policy-makers, and at least one study which questions it (Libby, 1975).

But the above represents only the top of the iceberg. Of more importance in our minds is the failure of researchers to define and follow through on a logical, well-conceived plan of research. Until they do, they should not expect practitioners and policy-makers to pay much attention to them. Let us be more specific on this point.

The selection of research topics by academic researchers has been haphazard at best. In part, this reflects the failure to tie in our research with the questions of professional concern. Often research is undertaken after a position has been adopted rather than when the results could be of assistance to policy formulation. The issue here is one of timing. And, given the extensive time required for certain types of behavioral studies, adequate communication at an early stage of problem analysis is critical. If the key issue is to affect policy, then more attention must be given to the policy issues of concern and less to the investigation of intellectually satisfying issues. Further, the early identification of policy issues becomes paramount.[22]

Basic research also needs more attention. First and foremost, some theory, some model of the decision process is needed to support the empirical results found and to suggest reasonable and useful research projects. Without theory, the research becomes like the nautical derelict, merely an aimless wandering. Whether such a theory is developed from psychology (information-processing models, conflict and dissonance theory, attitude formation and change models) or from economics (information economics, market choice and marginal analysis, capital asset pricing) is not the critical issue. Indeed, separate theories may all prove productive.

Yet, even with (or without) an adequate theory, proper attention must be given to the experimental design. Studies to date have not always (or even usually) done a satisfactory job of assuring internal validity. Re-

22. Since some research will require longer lead time than we can expect, research of a basic nature unrelated to current policy issues must continue. In this way, a fund of relevant data may already exist when a policy issue arises. (We speak only of a reordering of priorities and do not wish to imply that basic research should cease.)

searchers need better training in the techniques of behavioral experimentation. The fact that most of the studies suffer from important omissions
in this area makes the sum total of the research on any given issue tenuous
at best. The concern is one of critical mass; in most areas, we simply
have not accumulated sufficient data. Failure to achieve internal validity
makes it hard to evaluate the confidence a reader should place in a study
and also helps explain the minimal impact achieved by behavioral research
to date. Indeed, the difficulty of evaluating a given study and the knowledge that shortcomings are almost sure to exist may cause the reader to
totally reject this type of research. The very integrity of the researcher
may have contributed to the lack of impact. Some researchers carefully
document the limitations of their studies, but if they overlook even a
minor limitation found or expected by a reader, the reader may reject
the study.

Behavioral research and research in general appears to suffer from a
lack of credibility with the profession, a feeling that may have been partly
reinforced by what the profession viewed as unsatisfactory experiences
with professionally oriented research commissioned by the AICPA and by
the perceived lack of interest of academicians in researching real problems
and communicating the results.

A final reason for the lack of impact of behavioral research appears to
be the failure of nearly every study to consider explicitly the cost-benefit
tradeoffs. Investors and analysts, when asked whether additional disclosure
is useful, will almost always answer in the affirmative if the information
is free. While it may not be easy to quantify these aspects, it is critical
that their order of magnitude be estimated before effective policy decisions can be made, keeping in mind that the learning phenomenon may
drastically alter any initial relationships. Researchers have been remiss
in not explicitly recognizing cost-benefit tradeoffs in their research and
recommendations.

Bibliograpy I. Annotated Bibliography of Published Experimental, Survey and Interview Research in Financial Accounting

Each entry in this bibliography is followed by information classifying it
on three dimensions:

  (a) the section(s) and subsection(s) of the paper in which the study is
      reviewed;

(b) the research methodology used;

(c) the kind of subjects, participants or respondents involved.

Abdel-khalik, A. Rashad. "The Effect of Aggregating Accounting Reports on the Lending Decision: An Empirical Investigation." *Journal of Accounting Research Supplement* to Volume 12, 1973. (2.2; experiment by mail; bank loan officers.)

―――. "The Entropy Law, Accounting Data and Relevance to Decision-Making." *Accounting Review* (April 1974a): 271–83. (2.2; experiment by mail; bank loan officers.)

―――. "On the Efficiency of Subject Surrogation in Accounting Research." *Accounting Review* (October 1974b): 743–50. (2.2; experiment by mail using bank loan officers and "take home" experiment using MBA students.)

American Institute of C.P.A.'s Technical Services Division. "Opinion Survey on Price-Level Adjustment of Depreciation." *Journal of Accountancy* (April 1958): 36–42. (3.3; mail survey; businessmen, analysts and educators.)

Asebrook, R. J., and D. R. Carmichael. "Reporting on Forecasts: A Survey of Attitudes." *Journal of Accountancy.* (August 1973): 38–48. (4.3; mail survey; CPAs, financial executives, analysts.)

Backer, Morton. *Financial Reporting for Security Investment and Credit Decisions.* National Association of Accountants, New York, 1970. (3.3, 4.1; interviews; analysts, bankers, executives.)

―――. *Current Value Accounting.* Financial Executives Research Foundation, New York, November 1973. See also report on this research in Morton Backer, "A Model for Current Value Reporting," *The CPA Journal* (February 1974): 27–33. (3.3; interviews; analysts, bankers, CPAs.)

―――, and Walter B. McFarland. *External Reporting for Segments of a Business.* National Association of Accountants, 1968. (4.1; interviews; analysts, commercial bankers and executives.)

Baker, M. Kent, and John A. Haslem. "Information Needs of Individual Investors." *Journal of Accountancy* (November 1973): 64–69. (2.2; mail questionnaire; investors in the Washington, D.C. area.)

Barrett, M. Edgar. "Accounting for Intercorporate Investments: A Behavioral Field Experiment." *Journal of Accounting Research Supplement* to Volume 9, 1971, pp. 50–92. (Pages include discussion comments.) (4.4; experiment by mail; analysts.)

Benjamin, James J., and Robert H. Strawser. "The Publication of Forecasts: An Experiment." *Abacus* (December 1974): 138–46. (4.3; experimental simulation; students.)

Bird, Francis A. "Interperiod Comparability in Financial Reporting." *Journal of Accountancy* (June 1969): 56–56. (4.2; mail survey, analysts.)

Boatsman, James R., and Jack C. Robertson. "Policy-capturing on Selected Materiality Judgments." *Accounting Review* (April 1974): 342–52. (2.4; on-site experiment; analysts and CPAs.)

Bollom, William J. "Toward a Theory of Interim Reporting for a Seasonal

Business: A Behavioral Approach." *Accounting Review* (January 1973): 12–22. (4.2; business game experiment; students.) .

Bradish, Richard D. "Corporate Reporting and the Financial Analyst." *Accounting Review* (October 1965): 757–66. (2.1; interviews; analysts.)

Brenner, Vincent C. "Financial Statement Users' Views of the Desirability of Reporting Current Cost Information." *Journal of Accounting Research* (Autumn 1970): 159–66. (3.3; mail survey; stockholders, bankers, analysts.)

———, and Ronald E. Shuey. "An Empirical Study of Support for APB Opinion No. 16." *Journal of Accounting Research* (Spring 1972): 200–208. 2.3; mail survey; analysts, CPAs, controllers.)

Buzby, Stephen L. "Selected Items for Information and Their Disclosure in Annual Reports." *Accounting Review* (July 1974): 423–35. (2.1; mail survey; analysts.)

Carmichael, D. R. "Reporting on Forecasts: A U.K. Perspective." *Journal of Accountancy* (January 1973): 36–47. (4.3; interviews; United Kingdom Accountants.)

Carpenter, Charles G., and Robert H. Strawser. "Disclosure of Changes in Accounting Methods." *Journal of Accounting Research* (Spring 1972): 209–16. (2.3; mail survey; controllers, accounting educators, analysts, CPAs.)

Carsberg, Bryon, Anthony A. Hope, and R. W. Scapens. "The Objectives of Published Accounting Reports." *Accounting and Business Research* (Summer 1974): 162–73. See also K. V. Peasnell, "The Objectives of Published Accounting Reports: A Comment," *Accounting and Business Research* (Winter 1974): 71–76, and Carsberg, et al., "The Objectives of Published Accounting Reports: Reply to a Comment," *Accounting and Business Research* (Spring 1975): 152–56. (3.1; interviews and mail questionnaires; United Kingdom accountants.)

Cerf, Alan R. *Corporate Reporting and Investment Decisions.* Institute of Business and Economic Research, Berkeley, California, 1961. (2.1; interviews, mail survey; analysts.)

Chandra, Gyan. "A Study of the Consensus on Disclosure among Public Accountants and Security Analysts." *Accounting Review* (October 1974): 733–42. (2.2; mail survey; CPAs and analysts.)

Comiskey, E. E., and R. E. V. Groves. "The Adoption and Diffusion of an Accounting Innovation." *Accounting and Business Research* (Winter 1971): 67–75. (4.5; mail survey; company officers.)

Copeland, Ronald M., Arthur J. Francis, and Robert H. Strawser. "Students as Subjects in Behavioral Business Research." *Accounting Review* (April 1973): 365–72. See also David J. H. Watson, "Students as Surrogates in Behavioral Business Research: Some Comments," and Copeland et al., "Further Comments on Students as Subjects in Behavioral Business Research," both in *Accounting Review* (July 1974): 530–33 and 534–37 respectively. (2.3, 3.1; mail survey; controllers, CPAs, analysts, accounting educators.)

Copeland, Ronald M., and John K. Shank. "LIFO and the Diffusion of Innovation," *Journal of Accounting Research Supplement* to Volume 9, 1971, pp. 196–230. (Pages include discussion comments.) (4.5; mail survey; company officers.)

Corless, John C., and Corine T. Norgaard. "User Reactions to CPA Reports on Forecasts." *Journal of Accountancy* (August 1974): 46–54. (4.3; mail survey of analysts and classroom questionnaire of MBA students.)

Cramer, Joe J., Jr. "Income Reporting by Conglomerates—Views of American Businessmen." *Abacus* (August 1968): 17–26. (4.1; mail survey; business executives.)

Crumbley, D. Larry, and Robert H. Strawser. "Allocation of Income Taxes in Segmented Financial Statements." *The CPA Journal* (July 1974): 35–38. (4.1; mail survey; management accountants.)

Daily, R. Austin. "The Feasibility of Reporting Forecasted Information." *Accounting Review* (October 1971): 686–92. (4.3; interviews; company executives.)

Dascher, Paul, and Ronald M. Copeland. "Some Further Evidence on 'Criteria for Judging Disclosure Improvement.' " *Journal of Accounting Research* (Spring 1971): 32–39. (4.1; experiment; students.)

Dickhaut, John W., and Ian R. C. Eggleton. "An Examination of the Processes Underlying Comparative Judgments of Numerical Stimuli." *Journal of Accounting Research* (Spring 1975): 38–72. (2.4; classroom experiment; MBA students.)

Dopuch, Nicholas, and Joshua Ronen. "The Effects of Alternative Inventory Valuation Methods—An Experimental Study." *Journal of Accounting Research* (Autumn 1973): 191–211. (4.4; classroom experiment; MBA students.)

Dyckman, Thomas R. "On the Investment Decision." *Accounting Review* (April 1964): 285–95. (4.4; classroom experiment; students.)

———. "On the Effects of Earnings—Trend, Size and Inventory Valuation Procedures in Evaluating a Business Firm." In Jaedicke et al. (ed.) *Research in Accounting Measurement,* American Accounting Association, 1966, pp. 175–85. (4.4; classroom experiment; students and business executives.)

———. *Investment Analysis and General Price-Level Adjustments: A Behavioral Study,* AAA Accounting Research Study #1, American Accounting Association, 1969. (3.3; experiment by mail; analysts.)

Ecton, William W. "Communication through Accounting—Bankers' Views." *Journal of Accountancy* (August 1969): 79–81. (2.1; mail survey; bankers.)

Edwards, James W., Geraldine F. Dominiak, and Thomas V. Hedges. *Interim Financial Reporting.* National Association of Accountants, New York, 1972. (4.2; interviews; analysts, bankers, executives.)

Elias, Nabil. "The Effects of Human Asset Statements on the Investment Decision: An Experiment," *Journal of Accounting Research Supplement* to Volume 10, 1972, pp. 215–40. (Pages include discussion comments.) (4.4; mail experiment using analysts and classroom experiment using students.)

Estes, Ralph W. "An Assessment of the Usefulness of Current Cost and Price-

Level Information by Financial Statement Users." *Journal of Accounting Research* (Autumn 1968): 200–207. (3.3; mail survey; analysts, bank loan officers and credit men, financial executives.)

Falk, Haim. "Financial Statements and Personal Characteristics in Investment Decision Making." *Accounting and Business Research* (Summer 1972): 209–22. (2.2; field investigation; bankers.)

―――. and Tsvi Ophir. "The Influence of Differences in Accounting Policies on Investment Decisions." *Journal of Accounting Research* (Spring 1973a): 108–16. (2.2; interview-based simulation; bankers.)

―――. and Tsvi Ophir. "The Effect of Risk on the Use of Financial Statements by Investment Decision-Makers: A Case Study," *Accounting Review* (April 1973b): 323–38. (2.2; interview-based simulation; bankers.)

Financial Executives Research Foundation. "How Accurate are Forecasts?" *Financial Executive* (March 1973): 26–32. (4.3; mail survey; financial managers.)

Fisher, J. "Financial Information and the Accounting Standards Steering Committee." *Accounting and Business Research* (Autumn 1974): 275–85. See also critical comments on this research, T. A. Lee, "Empirical Research into Information Utility and Acceptability," *Accounting and Business Research* (Spring 1975): 140–44. (3.1; interviews and mail survey; wide variety of United Kingdom, North American and European bankers, practicing accountants and others.)

Flynn, Thomas D. "Corporate Executives View Accounting Principles." *Journal of Accountancy* (June 1965): 31–36. (3.1; letter to heads of business firms.)

Francia, Arthur J., and Robert H. Strawser. "Perceptions of Financial Reporting Practices by Accounting Educators: An Empirical Study." *Accounting Review* (April 1971a): 380–84. (2.3, 3.1; mail survey; accounting educators.)

―――. "Perceptions of Financial Reporting Practices by CPAs." *Journal of Accountancy* (December 1971b): 84–86. (2.3, 3.1; mail survey; CPAs.)

―――. "Attitudes of Management Accountants on the State of the Art." *Management Accounting* (May 1972): 21–24. (2.3, 3.1; mail survey; controllers.)

Garner, Don E. "The Need for Price-Level and Replacement Value Data." *Journal of Accountancy* (September 1972): 94–98. (3.3; mail survey; analysts, bankers, accountants, businessmen.)

Godwin, Larry B. "CPA and User Opinions on Increased Corporate Disclosure." *The CPA* (July 1975): 31–35. (2.3; mail survey; CPAs, analysts, investors.)

Hanna, John R. "An Application and Evaluation of Selected Alternative Accounting Income Models." *The International Journal of Accounting Education and Research* (Fall 1972): 135–67. (3.3; interviews; Canadian analysts.)

―――. *Accounting Income Models: An Application and Evaluation.* Special

Study No. 8, The Society of Industrial Accountants, Hamilton, Ontario, 1974. (3.3; interviews; Canadian analysts.)

Haried, Andrew A. "The Semantic Dimensions of Financial Statements." *Journal of Accounting Research* (Autumn 1972): 376–91. (2.2; factor analysis of sementic differential scales; students, some CPAs.)

————. "Measurement of Meaning in Financial Reports." *Journal of Accounting Research* (Spring 1973): 117–45. (2.2; mail and group administered questionnaire; CPAs, analysts, attorneys, investment club members, students.)

Hawkins, David F., and Mary M. Wehle. *Accounting for Leases.* Financial Executives Research Foundation, New York, 1973). (4.4; interviews and mail survey; financial executives.)

Hay, Robert D. "Management Thinking Concerning Corporate Annual Reports." *Accounting Review* (July 1955): 444–50. (3.1; mail survey; company officers.)

Heintz, James A. "Price-Level Restated Financial Statements and Investment Decision Making." *Accounting Review* (October 1973): 679–89. (3.3; laboratory experiment; students.)

Hofstedt, Thomas R. "Some Behavioral Parameters of Financial Analysis." *Accounting Review* (October 1972a): 679–92. (4.4; classroom experiment; MBA students and business executives.)

————. "The Processing of Accounting Information: Perceptual Biases." *Behavioral Experiments in Accounting,* ed. Thomas J. Burns, Ohio State University, 1972b, pp. 285–315. (Pages include discussion comments.) (4.4; classroom experiment; MBA students.)

Horngren, Charles T. "Security Analysts and the Price Level." *Accounting Review* (October 1955): 575–81. (2.1, 3.3; interviews; analysts.)

————. "The Funds Statement and Its Use by Analysts." *Journal of Accountancy* (January 1956): 55–59. (2.1; interviews and examination of reports; analysts.)

————. "Disclosure: 1957." *Accounting Review* (October 1957): 598–604. (2.1; interviews; analysts.)

————. "Increasing the Utility of Financial Statements." *Journal of Accountancy* (July 1959): 39–46. (4.4; mail survey; analysts.)

Jensen, Robert E. "An Experimental Design for Study of Effects of Accounting Variations in Decision Making." *Journal of Accounting Research* (Autumn 1966): 224–38. See also Thomas R. Dyckman, "Observations on Jensen's Experimental Design for Study of Effects of Accounting Variations in Decision Making" and Robert E. Jensen, "A Rejoinder," both in *Journal of Accounting Research* (Autumn 1967): 221–29 and 230–261 respectively. (4.4; experiment by mail; analysts.)

Khemakhem, Abdellatif. "A Simulation of Management-Decision Behavior: 'Funds' and Income." *Accounting Review* (July 1968): 522–34. (4.4; business game experiment; analysts and students.)

Libby, Robert. "The Use of Simulated Decision Makers in Information Evalua-

tion." *Accounting Review* (July 1975a): 475–89. (4.4; information processing analysis; bankers.)

————. "Accounting Ratios and the Prediction of Failure: Some Behavioral
Evidence." *Journal of Accounting Research* (Spring 1975b): 150–61. (4.4;
information processing analysis; bankers.)

Lipay, Raymond J. "What's Happening with Interim Financial Reporting."
Financial Executive (October 1972): 28–34. (4.2; mail survey; company
executives.)

Livingstone, John L. "A Behavioral Study of Tax Allocation in Electric
Utility Regulations." *Accounting Review* (July 1967): 544–52. (4.4; published data used to make behavioral inferences.)

Martin, Samuel A., Stanley N. Laiken, and Douglas F. Haslam. *Business Combinations in the '60s: A Canadian Profile.* Toronto and London Ont.:
Canadian Institute of Chartered Accountants and The School of Business
Administration, University of Western Ontario, 1969. (4.1; questionnaires
and interviews; executives.)

Mautz, Robert K. *Financial Reporting by Diversified Companies.* Financial
Executives Institute, 1968. (4.1; mail survey; business executives, investors.)

————. *Effect of Circumstances on the Application of Accounting Principles.*
Financial Executives Research Foundation, N.Y., 1972. See also report on
this research, Robert K. Mautz, "Uniformity or Flexibility in Accounting,"
Financial Executive (August 1973): 26–30. (3.1; letters, seminars, questionnaires; executives, financial executives, analysts, CPAs.)

McDonald, Daniel L. "A Test Application of the Feasibility of Market Based
Measures in Accounting." *Journal of Accounting Research* (Spring 1968):
38–49. (3.2; experiment by mail; CPAs.)

McIntyre, Edward V. "Current-Cost Financial Statements and Common-Stock
Investments Decisions." *Accounting Review* (July 1973): 575–85. (3.3;
laboratory experiment; students and some business executives.)

Morton, James R. "Qualitative Objectives of Financial Accounting: A Comment on Relevance and Understandability." *Journal of Accounting Research*
(Autumn 1974): 288–98. (3.1; mail survey; auditors, financial executives,
security and credit analysts.)

Nelson, Kenneth, and Robert H. Strawser. "A Note on APB Opinion No. 16."
Journal of Accounting Research (Autumn 1970): 284–89. (2.3; mail
survey; analysts, CPAs, accounting educators.)

Nickerson, Charles A., Larry B. Pointer, and Robert H. Strawser. "Attitudes
of Financial Executives toward Interim Financial Statements." *The CPA
Journal* (March 1975): 21–24. (4.2; mail survey; financial executives.)

————. "Published Forecasts—Choice or Obligation?" *Financial Executive*
(February 1974): 70–73. (4.3; mail survey; stockholders of a single
company.)

Oliver, Bruce L. "A Study of Confidence Interval Financial Statements."
Journal of Accounting Research (Spring 1972): 154–66. (3.4; classroom
experiment; bankers.)

————. "The Semantic Differential: A Device for Measuring the Interprofessional Communication of Selected Accounting Concepts." *Journal of Accounting Research* (Autumn 1974): 299–316. (2.2; factor analysis of semantic differential scores obtained by mail; CPAs, accounting educators, analysts, security dealers, financial executives, bankers, investment bankers.)

Opinion Research Corporation. *Public Accounting in Transition.* Arthur Andersen and Company, 1974. (2.1; telephone survey of shareowners, interviews of chief executive and chief financial officers, interviews of "key public" including professors, portfolio managers, analysts, brokers, lawyers, accountants, government officals, business press and corporate social activists.)

Ortman, Richard F. "The Effects on Investment Analysis of Alternative Reporting Procedure for Diversified Firms." *Accounting Review* (April 1974): 298–304. (4.1 and 4.4; experiment by mail; Canadian analysts.)

Pankoff, Lyn D., and Robert L. Virgil. "Some Preliminary Findings from a Laboratory Experiment on the Usefulness of Financial Accounting Information to Security Analysts." *Journal of Accounting Research Supplement* to Volume 8, 1970, pp. 1–61. (Pages include discussion comments.) See also Lyn D. Pankoff and Robert L. Virgil, "On the Usefulness of Financial Statement Information: A Suggested Research Approach," *Accounting Review* (April 1970): 269–79. (2.2; laboratory experiment; analysts.)

Pattillo, James W. "Materiality: The (Formerly) Elusive Standard." *Financial Executive* (August 1975): 20–27. (2.4; mail questionnaire; preparers, users and auditors of financial statements.)

Pattillo, James W., and Jerry D. Siebel. "Materiality in Financial Reporting." *Financial Executive* (October 1973): 27–38. (2.4; mail survey; preparers users and auditors of financial statements.)

———. "Factors Affecting the Materiality Judgment." *The CPA Journal* (July 1974): 39–44. (2.4; mail questionnaire; business executives, CPAs.)

Piaker, Philip M., and James Dalberth. "Acceptance of Changes Among Accountants: An Examination of Attitudes Toward Current Controversies." *The CPA Journal* (February 1973): 132–38. (3.1, 4.5; mail survey; CPA practitioners, accounting educators.)

Rakes, Ganas K., and William B. Shenkir. "User Responses to APB Opinion No. 19." *Journal of Accountancy* (September 1972): 91–94. (4.5; mail survey; analysts.)

Ritts, Blaine A. "A Study of the Impact of APB Opinions on Practicing CPAs." *Journal of Accounting Research* (Spring 1974): 93–111. (4.5; experiment by mail; CPAs.)

Ronen, Joshua, and Gideon Falk. "Accounting Data and the Entropy Measure: An Experimental Approach." *Accounting Review* (October 1973): 696–717. 2.2; classroom experiments; MBA students.)

Roper, Elmo. *A Report on What Information People Want About Policies and Financial Conditions of Corporations.* Controllers' Institute Foundation, New York, 1948, Vols. 1 and 2. (2.1; mail survey; investors.)

Rose, Jerry, William Beaver, Selwyn Becker, and George Sorter. "Toward an

Empirical Measure of Materiality." *Journal of Accounting Research Supplement* to Volume 8, 1970, pp. 138–56. (Pages include discussion comments.) (2.4; classroom experiments; students.)

Rosen, Lawrence S. *Current Value Accounting and Price-Level Restatements.* Canadian Institute of Chartered Accountants, Toronto, 1972. (3.3; interviews, variety of Canadian accountants, executives, analysts.)

Sanders, Thomas H. *Company Annual Reports to Stockholders, Employees and the Public.* Andover, Mass.: Andover Press, 1948. (2.1; interviews, questionnaires; financial executives, analysts and stockholders.)

Shank, John K., and Ronald M. Copeland. "Corporate Personality Theory and Changes in Accounting Methods—an Empirical Test." *Accounting Review* (July 1973): 494–501. (4.5; published data used to infer corporate personality.)

Singhvi, Surendra S., and Harsha B. Desai. "An Empirical Analysis of the Quality of Corporate Financial Disclosure." *Accounting Review* (January 1971): 129–38. (2.1; interviews; analysts.)

Smith, James E., and Nora P. Smith. "Readability: A Measure of the Performance of the Communication Function of Financial Reporting." *Accounting Review* (July 1971): 552–61. (212; readability analysis.)

Soper, Fred J., and Robert Dolphin, Jr. "Readability and Corporate Annual Reports." *Accounting Review* (April 1964): 358–62. (2.2; readability analysis plus judges of readability.)

Sorter, George H., and Selwyn W. Becker, with the assistance of T. R. Archibald and W. Beaver. "Corporate Personality as Reflected in Accounting Decisions: Some Preliminary Findings." *Journal of Accounting Research* (Autumn 1964): 183–96. (4.5; field study; business managers plus behavioral inferences from published data.)

————, Selwyn W. Becker, Ross Archibald, and William H. Beaver. "Accounting and Financial Measures as Indicators of Corporate Personality—Some Empirical Findings." In Jaedicke et al. (eds.), *Research in Accounting Measurement,* American Accounting Association, 1966, pp. 200–10. (4.5; field study; business managers plus behavioral inferences from published data.)

Stallman, James C. "Toward Experimental Criteria for Judging Disclosure Improvement." *Journal of Accounting Research Supplement* to Volume 7, 1969, pp. 29–54. (Pages include discussion comments.) (4.1; experiment; analysts.)

Sterling, Robert R. "A Test of the Uniformity Hypothesis," *Abacus* (September 1969): 37–47. (3.2; mail questionnaire; CPAs.)

————, and Raymond Radosevich. "A Valuation Experiment." *Journal of Accounting Research* (Spring 1969): 90–95. (3.2; mail questionnaire; CPAs.)

————, John O. Tollefson, and Richard E. Flaherty. "Exchange Valuation: An Empirical Test." *Accounting Review* (October 1972): 709–821. (3.2; experiment by mail; CPAs.)

Woolsey, Samuel M. "Development of Criteria to Guide the Accountant in

Judging Materiality." *Journal of Accountancy* (February 1954a): 167–73. (2.4; mail survey, preparers, auditors and users of financial statements.)

———. "Judging Materiality in Determining Requirements for Full Disclosure," *Journal of Accountancy* (December 1954b): 745–50. (2.4; mail survey; preparers, auditors and users of financial statements.)

———. "Materiality Survey." *Journal of Accountancy* (September 1973): 91–92. (2.4; mail survey; preparers, auditors and users of financial statement.)

Bibliography II. Annotated Bibliography of Some Recent Unpublished Doctoral Dissertations in Financial Accounting That Used Experimental, Survey or Interview Methods

Dissertations, the *empirical* parts of which have been published are included in the separate bibliography of published research, and are not listed here.

Each entry in this bibliography is followed by information (taken from the abstract) classifying it on two dimensions:

(a) the research methodology used;

(b) the kind of subjects, participants or respondents involved.

Acland, C. Derek. "The Effect of Human Resource Information on Investment Decision Making: An Accounting Experimental Study." University of North Carolina, Chapel Hill, 1973. (Experiment by mail; Canadian analysts.)

Arnold, Donald F., Sr. "The Feasibility of Measuring Income Concepts Defined by 'Alternative' Accounting Principles." SUNY Buffalo, 1972. (Test application of revised acounting reports following alternative principles; practicing accountants.)

Bacon, Leonard A. "An Exploratory Study of the Role of Financial Disclosure of Accounting Data in the Development of the Stock Exchange and Capital Growth in Mexico City." University of Mississippi, 1973. (Interviews; various Mexican officials.)

Bariff, Martin L. "A Study of the Impact of Replacement Cost Data on Individual Investment Behavior." University of Illinois, 1973. (Laboratory and mail experiment; businessmen and analysts.)

Beard, Larry Holden. "The Effect on Projections of Alternative Disclosures of an Accounting Change: A Behavioral Investigation." University of Georgia, 1974. (Experiment; accountants, financial executives, analysts.)

Belkaoui, Ahmed. "The Impact of the Disclosure of 'Pollution Control' Information on the Investors: A Behavioral Field Experiment and a Market Reaction Investigation." Syracuse University, 1972. (Experiment; subjects unknown.)

Brandon, C. H. "The Disclosure of Forecasts in Annual Reports." University of Georgia, 1972. (Experiment; students.)

Brennan, W. John. "Investment Analysis and Generally Accepted Accounting Principles." University of Michigan, 1972. (Experiment; apparently analysts.)

Bullara, Ruth M. "The Effect of Accounting for Combinations on Investor Decisions." University of Texas at Austin, 1973. (Mail survey; analysts.)

Cadenhead, Gary M. "Circumstantial Variables in Accounting for Inventories." Stanford University, 1969. (Questionnaires and interviews; company officers, etc.)

Carter, Clairmont P., Jr. "Sources of Substantial Authoritative Support for Accounting Principles: A Theoretical and Empirical Investigation." Kent State University, 1971. (Mail questionnaire; analysts, financial executives, CPAs, accounting educators.)

Cattanach, Richard L. "An Inquiry into the Informational Needs of Stockholders and Potential Investors." Arizona State University, 1972. (Mail survey; analysts.)

Chen, Kung-Kong. "Removing the Appearance of Certainty from Accounting Information: A Behavioral Experiment." University of Texas at Austin, 1974. (Classroom experiment; MBA students.)

Chen, Rosita S. C. "The Behavioral Implications of the Stewardship Concept and Its Effects on Financial Reporting." University of Illinois, 1973. A portion of the dissertation, without the empirical results, appears in Rosita S. C. Chen, "Social and Financial Stewardship," *Accounting Review* (July 1974): 533–43. (Mail survey; apparently accountants.)

Clay, Raymond J., Jr. "An Analysis of Selected Annual Reports as an Input into the Investment Decision Process of Bank Trust Investment Officers." University of Kentucky, 1974. (Questionnaires and interviews; bankers.)

Crooch, Gary M. "An Investigation of Investors' Financial Statement Knowledge." Michigan State University, 1970. (Mail survey; stockholders.)

Cumming, John, Jr. "An Empirical Evaluation of Possible Explanations for the Differing Treatment of Apparently Similar Unusual Events." University of Illinois, 1972. (Mail questionnaire; company officers.)

Custer, Henry L., Jr. "The Courts' Concepts of Accounting Principles as Revealed by Court Decisions." University of Alabama, 1970. (Search of court records for accounting interpretations.)

Danos, Paul Peter. "Confirmability Level Financial Statements: A Theoretical and Empirical Assessment." University of Texas at Austin, 1974. (Mail survey; CPA firm partners, analysts.)

Dascher, Paul E. "The Behavioral Impact and Implications of Varying Approaches to Market Segment Reporting: An Empirical Study." Pennsylvania State University, 1969. (Experiment; students.)

Davidson, Lewis F. "Impact of Various Forms of Accounting Statement Presentation and Disclosure on Decision Making Behavior: An Empirical Study in Communication and Information Theory." Pennsylvania State University, 1968.

Deakin, Edward B., III. "On the Usefulness of Annual Report Information for Common Stock Investment Decisions." University of Illinois, 1972. (Experiment and interviews; bankers.)

Denham, Ross A. "A Theoretical and Empirical Study of Net Income Normalized as Earnings Per Share Data." University of Minnesota, 1972. (Apparently mail survey; CPAs, analysts.)

Durham, Winferd. "Ratings of Accounting Concepts by Businessmen." University of Northern Colorado, 1973. (Survey; businessmen.)

Dyer, Jack Lawson. "Search for Objective Materiality Norms in Accounting and Auditing." University of Kentucky, Lexington, 1973. (Questionnaire; auditors.)

Estes, Thomas G., Jr. "An Investigation of Compliance with Desirability of Depreciation Disclosure Requirements in Accounting Principles Board Opinion Number 12." University of Arkansas, 1971. (Mail survey; analysts.)

Etnier, Donald E. "The Switch from LIFO: Disclosure Methods and Their Effect upon Investors' Decisions." University of Minnesota, 1973. (Mail experiment; analysts.)

Fetters, Michael L. "Accounting for Extraordinary Gains and Losses: An Empirical Analysis of the Behavioral Consequences." University of Wisconsin, 1973. (Mail experiment; analysts.)

Gleim, Irvin N. "The Content of Broker-Dealer Research Reports Prepared for Institutional Investors and Their Implications for Corporate Financial Reporting." University of Illinois, 1971. (Analysis of brokers' actual research reports.)

Harvey, David W. "A Test of the Usefulness of Financial Statements Prepared with a Communication-Theory-Derived Aggregation Criterion." University of Minnesota, 1972. (Mail experiment; analysts.)

Hawkins, Ennis M. "A Study of the Probabilistic Nature of Financial Statements." Texas Technological University, 1972. (Mail experiment; analysts.)

Hendricks, James A. "Human Asset Accounting and Its Relation to Stock Investment Decisions: An Empirical Study." University of Illinois, 1974. (Experiment; subjects unknown.)

Henderson, Murray Scott. "Some Factors Influencing the Annual Reports of North American Corporations." University of California, Los Angeles, 1969. (Questionnaires and interviews; apparently company officers.)

Hofstedt, Thomas R. "Some Behavioral Implications of Aggregation in Accounting Reports." Stanford University, 1970. (Experiment; students.)

Jain, Tribhowan N. "A Study of the Effects of Alternative Methods of Accounting for Income Taxes on Term Loan Decisions." Michigan State University, 1970. (On-site experiment; bankers.)

Karadbil, Laura L. "On the Disclosure Function of Financial Reporting for Intercorporate Investments in Controlled Corporations." The American University, 1971. (Mail survey; company officers.)

Keller, Robert J. "Disclosure of Projected Financial Information in Corporate Annual Reports." Louisiana State University, 1973. (Mail survey; analysts, CPAs, English chartered accountants.)

Kennedy, Henry A. "A Behavioral Study of the Usefulness of Financial Ratios." University of Washington, 1971. (Simulation study; bank loan officers, analysts.)

Kinard, James C. "The Effect of Variations in the Timing and Ordering of Presentation of Otherwise Identical Information on Expectations." Stanford University, 1969. (Laboratory experiment; students.)

King, Thomas E. "The Information Content of Accounting Reports as a Criterion for Selecting from among Alternative Accounting Methods." University of California, Los Angeles, 1973. (Laboratory experiment; apparently students.)

Kretschmar, Carl G. "Annual Financial Reporting Requirements: A Critical Analysis of Sensitivity to Investor Desires." Indiana University, 1969. (Interviews; analysts, CPAs.)

Kroener, Peter M. "The Effects of the Unattested Part of the Annual Report on the Evaluation of the Company—an Empirical Study." Indiana University, 1973. (Classroom experiment; apparently students.)

Ladley, Herbert Vern. "A Business Simulation Study of the Behavioral Implications of Price Level Adjustments to Financial Statements." George Washington University, 1970. (Simulation experiment; students.)

Landry, Maurice. "Circumstantial Variables in Accounting for the Pre-computed Income of Finance Companies." University of California, Los Angeles, 1970. (Questionnaires and interviews; company officers.)

Liao, Shu Sheng. "An Empirical Investigation of the Behavioral Assumptions of the Entity Concept: A Study of Management's Perceptions of the Business Firm." University of Illinois, 1971. (Questionnaires; business managers.)

McCabe, Robert K. "Communication and Accounting: An Empirical Investigation into the Level of Language Complexity, Meaning Compatibility and the Attitudes of Analysts Toward the Usefulness of External Financial Reports, Management Credibility and Auditor Credibility." University of Colorado, 1973. (Mail questionnaire; analysts.)

McGillivray, Robert E. "Income concepts Used by Bank Loan Officers in a Metropolitan Environment." North Texas State University, 1974. (Simulation; bankers.)

Miller, Thomas I. "An Inquiry into the Feasibility of External Reporting of Forecasted Financial Information." University of Arkansas, 1973. (Mail survey analysts, CPAs, controllers.)

Min, Han Ki. "A Theoretical and Empirical Investigation into Publication of Forecasts." University of Oklahoma, 1974. (Mail survey; analysts, CPAs, managers.)

Moore, Charles K. "The Impact of Alternative Presentations of Income Tax Expense on Selected Decision Behavior—an Empirical Study." Texas Technological University, 1973. (Mail experiment; business executives, bankers, analysts.)

Neyhart, Charles A., Jr. "Treatment of Accounting Changes: An Attitudinal

Investigation." Pennsylvania State University, 1973. (Mail questionnaires; bank loan officers, analysts, financial executives.)

Pearl, Daniel. "User Information in Corporate Reports: An Examination of the Availability of User Information in Corporate Reports Prepared for the Primary and Secondary Markets." University of Minnesota, 1969. (Mail survey, analysts.)

Petro, Freddie A. "A Study of Accounting for Long Term Leases in the Financial Statements of the Lessee and the Lessor." University of Arkansas, 1973. (Mail survey; CPAs, analysts, accounting educators.)

Pratt, James W. "Extending the Certified Public Accountants' Attest Function to Quarterly Financial Reports of Publicly Owned Companies." University of Southern California, 1972. (Mail survey; analysts, CPAs.)

Radebaugh, Lee H. "Accounting for Price Level and Exchange Rate Changes of U.S. Firms with Manufacturing Subsidiaries in Brazil." Indiana University, 1972. (Interviews and questionnaires; company officers.)

Rao, Kailas J. "An Evaluation and Empirical Study of the Disclosure of Accounting Policies in Published Financial Statements." Unversity of Oklahoma, 1974. (Mail survey; analysts.)

Reinoso, Ricardo C. "The User Assumptions Underlying Generally Accepted Accounting Principles: An Empirical Study of a Credit Grantor as a User of Financial Statements." University of North Carolina, Chapel Hill, 1971. (Observational study of the use of financial statements by the commercial lending operation of one large bank.)

Ronen, Joshua. "Some Effects of Sequential Aggregation in Accounting on Decision-Making Behavior." Stanford University, 1970. (Experiment; students, business executives.)

Sadhwani, Arjan. "Acounting for Land Development." Michigan State University, 1972. (Questionnaires, interviews; apparently company officers.)

Salzarulo, William P. "The Use of a Policy Capturing Approach to Assess the Relevance of Non-Financial Statement Information in Investment Decisions." University of Colorado, 1973. (Information processing analysis; analysts.)

Schmidt, Lester L., Jr. "An Evaluation of the Entity Theory as a Partial Solution to the Non-Comparability Enigma of Inter-Firm Income Statement Analysis." University of Arkansas, 1971. (Questionnaires; analysts, CPAs.)

Schwan, Edward S. "A Study of the Effects of Human Resource Data on Bankers' Decisions about a Firm." University of Colorado, 1973. (Experiment by questionnaire; bankers.)

Smith, James E. "A Critical Analysis of the Application of Communication Theory to Accounting Communications with Published Financial Statements." University of Arizona, 1972. (Interviews, questionnaires; CPAs, analysts.)

Stark, Maurice E. "Accounting for Initial Franchise Fees." University of Missouri, 1972. (Mail experiment; analysts, CPAs, accounting educators.)

Strawser, Robert H. "An Inquiry into the Financial Reporting Practices of Commercial Banks." University of Maryland, 1969. (Mail survey; bankers, CPAs, analysts.)

Thompson, John Allen. "An Inquiry into the Nature of Earnings Per Share with Emphasis on the Usefulness and Predictive Ability of Primary and Fully Diluted Earnings Per Share Concepts." University of Arkansas, 1974. (Mail survey; CPAs, analysts.)

Uecker, Wilfrid C. "Unattested Management Representations in the Annual Report: A Potential Source of Bias in the Evaluation of the Firm?" University of Texas at Austin, 1973. (Classroom experiments; students.)

Waters, Edwin D. "Some Criteria for Materiality Decisions in Financial Reporting for Small Businesses." University of Alabama, 1971. (Interviews; CPAs.)

Warren, Robert L. "A Critical Examination of External Reporting of Changes in Financial Position with Emphasis on the Impact of Accounting Principles Board Opinion No. 19 and on the Usefulness of 'Fund Flow' Information." University of Arkansas, 1973. (Mail survey; controllers, analysts, bankers.)

Zehms, Karl M. "Municipal Finance Reporting." University of Wisconsin, 1970. (Interviews, mail questionnaires; municipal financial officers.)

Bibliography III. Other References

Beaver, William. "Financial Ratios as Predictors of Failure." *Journal of Accounting Research Supplement* to vol. 4, 1966, pp. 71–127. (Pages include discussion comments.)

Birnberg, Jacob C., and Raghu Nath. "Implications of Behavioral Science for Managerial Accounting." *Accounting Review* (July 1967): 468–79.

Brunswik, E. *The Conceptual Framework of Psychology.* Chicago: The University of Chicago Press, 1952.

———. *Perception and the Representative Design of Experiments.* Berkeley, Calif: University of California Press, 1956.

Campbell, Donald T., and Julian C. Stanley. *Experimental and Quasi-Experimental Designs for Research.* Chicago: Rand McNally & Co., 1963.

Committee on Behavioral Science Content of the Accounting Curriculum. "Report of the Committee," Supplement to vol. 46 of the *Accounting Review,* American Accounting Association, 1972, pp. 247–85.

Financial Accounting Standards Board. Exposure draft of proposed statement of financial accounting standards: *Financial Reporting for Segments of a Business Enterprise.* Stamford, Connecticut: Financial Accounting Standards Board, September 30, 1975.

Gonedes, Nicholas J., and Nicholas Dopuch. "Capital Market Equilibrium, Information Production, and Selecting Accounting Techniques: Theoretical Framework and Review of Empirical Work." *Journal of Accounting Research Supplement* to vol. 12, 1974, pp. 48–169. (Pages include discussion comments.)

Green, David O. "Behavioral Science and Accounting Research," in Nicholas Dopuch and Lawrence Revsine (eds.), *Accounting Research 1960–1970: A Critical Evaluation*. Urbana, Ill.: University of Illinois, 1973, pp. 93–134. (Pages include discussion comments.)

Hofstedt, Thomas. "A State of the Art Analysis of Behavioral Accounting Research," Stanford Working Paper, October 1975.

———, and James C. Kinard. "A Strategy for Behavioral Accounting Research." *The Accounting Review* (January 1970): 38–54.

Morrison, D. F. *Multivariate Statistical Methods*. New York: McGraw-Hill, 1967.

Rhode, John Grant. "Behavioral Science Methodologies with Applications for Accounting Research: References and Source Materials," in Committee on Research Methodology in Accounting, "Report of the Committee," Supplement to vol. 47 of the *Accounting Review,* American Accounting Association, 1972, pp. 494–504.

Runkel, Philip J., and Joseph E. McGrath. *Research on Human Behavior: A Systematic Guide to Method*. New York: Holt, Rinehart and Winston, Inc., 1972.

Schneider, Carl W. "Nits, Grits, and Soft Information in SEC Filings." *University of Pennsylvania Law Review,* vol. 121, 1972, pp. 254–305.

Watson, David J. H. "Students as Surrogates in Behavioral Business Research: Some Comments." *Accounting Review* (July 1974): 530–33. (See also the Copeland, Francia and Strawser listing in Bibliography I.)

Winer, B. J. *Statistical Principles in Experimental Design,* Second Edition, New York: McGraw-Hill, 1971.

Discussion

Kenneth P. Johnson and Felix Pomeranz

I am honored to present this paper on behalf of my distinguished colleague, Kenneth P. Johnson. I shall endeavor to reflect his views fully, with additional comments of my own.

We agree with the major conclusion of the authors—that certain financial accounting research has not been accepted because the studies do not sufficiently bridge the gap between the results of the research and their application in practice. However, the authors have drawn an overly bleak picture, and they have put a disproportionate part of the blame on research methodology. We believe that there are other significant causes of the shortcomings in financial accounting research. I plan to discuss these and also to suggest possible approaches to closer collaboration between academics and practitioners, each of whom could bring unique credentials to a combined effort.

Given the tender age of our profession, its struggle to develop rules and theory is not unusual; the struggle simply reflects the course of human history. This point was made by the German philosopher Georg Hegel, whose students published his lectures posthumously in 1832 under the title *The Philosophy of History*. I believe one of Hegel's observations is singularly pertinent: "The adoption of rules (by a government) must be preceded by a long struggle to understand, before what is really appropriate can be discovered. Reason governs the world and, consequently, has governed history."

We should note, by way of introduction, that in the foregoing paper the authors have not—at least in my view—defined their terms of reference, i.e., "experimental and survey research." Consequently, I had difficulty integrating their observations into my background. I am more familiar with terms such as "pure research," "product development," and "applied research"—the classical terms commonly used.

I will use the practitioner's frame of reference in discussing the reasons for the nonacceptance of research. Essentially these reasons relate to: (1) communication, (2) the state of accounting theory, and (3) political decision processes.

Communication. Experimental and survey research in financial accounting can have an impact on accounting practice only to the extent that the results reach and influence accountants in policy-making positions. The great majority of practicing accountants have little interest in behavioral research findings, because (1) they lack time to ponder the findings; (2) their efforts would be unrewarding, because most research does not relate to their everyday concerns of solving problems and serving clients; and (3) the larger issues are beyond their sphere of influence.

On the other hand, the smaller number of accountants responsible for technical policy—in their own organizations or on policy-making boards —represent the focal points of accounting power. Their work is to weigh, consider, debate, and finally to pronounce policy. In academic terms, their work is "theory construction." Experimental and survey research results that would contribute to the process of theory construction could be useful, but, as Messrs. Dyckman, Gibbins and Swieringa have pointed out, such research has not had an impact on policy decisions, for reasons that can be identified.

One of the most significant reasons is that a majority of the policy-makers cannot decipher researchers' reports. The authors have accurately pointed out that academic researchers report primarily to an academic audience. Consequently, their reports typically contain lengthy descriptions of research methodology and statistical analyses of data, which serve the purposes of informing other academics that the author is accomplished in methodology and of facilitating an evaluation of the significance of the findings. But the simple fact is that this type of content gets in the way of conclusions and their relevance to practice.

If researchers truly expected to reach the policy-makers, they would prepare a summary of the objective and the results of their research, without lengthy methodological descriptions, and transmit it directly to influential persons. The fact that the results were published in a learned journal (with full methodological description), and were available for further perusal, would add weight to the summary by inference of its having passed an editorial referee.

Our comments elaborating on some of the authors' other reasons will be organized around certain concepts of theory construction and verification—with which many of you are intimately familiar.

The State of Accounting Theory. With some risk of oversimplification, it may be said that present accounting purports to be analytical—consisting of a logical construction of arithmetical measurement rules that prescribe acceptable inputs, the operations performed on them, and the resultant outputs in the form of balances and flows presented in financial statements. Accountants ask others (e.g., users) to accept this construction of principles because of its analytical properties. Users, however, are not inclined to be so kind to accountancy; they prefer to look upon accounting as empirical and seek to accommodate accounting results to observable economic phenomena.

Accounting policy-makers have not succeeded in "selling" accounting as an analytically valid system, and apparently they are unwilling or unable to settle upon a proper balance of the empirical with the analytical that might achieve greater acceptance by users. For example, one could point to the fact that the APB never fulfilled its charge to develop a basic theory of accounting, and that the FASB's conceptual-basis project has not yet emerged.

All this is to say that there is little or no substantive theory to support experimental and survey research. The authors have correctly pointed out that the research they reviewed exhibited very little development of theory that could serve as a foundation for meaningful results.

We should not be surprised at this lack—theory development would be an immense undertaking in itself. Practical constraints of the academic environment make such efforts costly and basically unproductive for the researcher. Furthermore, to expect useful development would be to expect more from an individual or small team than we have gotten from well-funded organizations that have been charged with the development of theory.

The practice of borrowing from other disciplines also has its limitations. Borrowed hypotheses must be reinterpreted, often in complex ways, to fit the accounting frame of reference. Such adaptations may be tortured to the point of being far removed from the original discipline, and still bear little resemblance to accounting problems. The net result is that the communication difficulties are compounded, and researchers adopting this line of attack have a long way to go before their findings are understandable to policy-makers.

The state of accounting theory, therefore, creates a barrier. Lacking a fundamental basis for the research in the first place, researchers are hard put to relate their results meaningfully to problems faced by policy-makers. As a consequence, their research is often viewed as having no pragmatic goal or purpose, and thus is given little or no attention.

Political Decision Processes. The authors have properly identified accounting policy-making as a "political" process. This notion of "political" should be understood as a combination of several factors. The accounting "political process" is influenced by the following factors.

1. *Countervailing forces:* Producers (clients), processors (accountants-auditors), and users (e.g., analysts) of information all have competing interests. It is no accident that accountants are listed here "in the middle."
2. *Resistance to change:* Accounting policy still depends on the long-standing concept of "general acceptance." In fact, the requirement of general acceptance places significant limits on the extent of change in accounting policy.
3. *The art of the possible:* Accounting policy is effective only when it is accepted by the countervailing forces. We have no coercive power, only the power of persuasion.
4. *Cost and benefit:* We cannot remove our own function from the economic framework and act as though the laws of supply and demand are repealed for us.

These four factors are powerful in the arena of accounting policy-making, where the pressures are intense. Even if we were convinced of the soundness of a particular analytical-empirical formulation for accounting, and endeavored to legislate it, we would still have to contend with this political process. Messrs. Dyckman, Gibbins, and Swieringa have dealt briefly with these issues in the final section of their paper; in our opinion, these are the weightiest issues.

Research that ignores or suppresses consideration of substantive countervailing forces and vested interests will founder, sunk by the weight of criticism. Some behavioral survey research merely sketches the viewpoints of competing interests; for example, surveys show that users desire more forecast information, producers are reluctant to change the status quo, and accountants are generally in between. Accounting policy-makers are aware of these differing views without a researcher's survey. Some relationships are intuitively obvious. Research that reports the obvious is usually dismissed as trivial, and research that contradicts intuition is hard to believe, and is thus dismissed on some other grounds (e.g., lack of rigor, experimental design deficiencies). Unfortunately, the researcher may be playing a no-win game.

Research itself cannot cope with the fact of life that we have termed "resistance to change." In our opinion, such resistance is a desirable feature in the current environment, because it helps keep the rate of change within the capacity of preparers and users of financial statements to assimilate and understand. The authors have referred to this point, but we wish to emphasize that the accounting profession cannot lead the way with radical changes if recipient-users lag behind in understanding and action. We suppose that these views characterize us as "evolutionist" rather than "revolutionist."

In the halls of the accounting legislature, the art of the possible is the art of persuasion. Arguments pro and con on an issue are weighed on several grounds, not the least of which is the source of the argument. It would be naive to pretend that policy-makers give equal weight to arguments advanced by eager junior faculty members and those offered by executives of long acquaintance. Never mind that the former may be well equipped to argue on a scientific and objective basis and that the arguments of the latter may be "intuitive." As the authors have pointed out, the academic world has its practical constraints which force persons with few resources to the forefront to offer policy recommendations that ultimately carry little weight and exert even less influence.

The same academic constraints prevent many senior people from engaging in substantive research projects, with the result that very few academic personalities are forceful in the legislative process. (Then they are removed from academia when they join a CPA firm!) The so-called "opportunity" to join forces with knowledgeable practitioners is all but nonexistent. Practitioners seldom seek out younger, unproved members of the academic set; and CPA firms are generally unable to accommodate the number of academics who would like to have access to data. Any change in this condition would itself involve a significant cost-benefit relationship, in which the CPA firms would perhaps bear most of the initial cost.

In another context, as the authors have noted, costs and benefits are generally not considered in experimental and survey research. This is indeed a serious omission since cost is always a factor in accounting policy decisions. To have an impact on practice, research studies must give the cost factor the consideration it deserves.

We are acquainted with a current research document on the subject of accounting for business combinations. It is large—to suit the magnitude of the subject—and is in fact a compendium of prior and current research. The lengthiest portions report the results of two surveys; only time will tell whether they can achieve a significant impact on the current situation. The document is illustrative in two respects: (1) it reflects a massive effort involving FASB members, a task force of the advisory council, a staff project director and a task force member, cooperation of the Financial Executives Institute, and many man hours in interviews, questionnaire preparation, and data summarization; and (2) it contains a minimum of methodological description and a maximum of findings. This document suffers from the intrinsic problems of all questionnaire surveys, but other features set it apart from most research produced on campus. First, it commanded researchers, and second, it was written for a public audience; hence, its minimization of methodological description. If this effort has no discernible impact, then there is little hope for questionnaires produced under less favorable auspices.

Conclusion. Many of our comments may appear to be hypercritical. Messrs. Dyckman, Gibbins, and Swieringa have concluded that, for the most part, experimental and survey research has had little impact and at times has been counterproductive. Unhappily we must agree, while wishing that it were not so. Accounting policy-makers could benefit from the results of research if it were aligned with their needs, and we have touched on several areas of need that are not presently being met.

Progress is not served merely by criticism. There are avenues of research that might lead to influence on accounting policy; some of these are suited to experimental and survey designs. One particular current problem, which is mentioned on page 74 of the paper, relates to questions about auditors' independence once they become involved with financial forecasts. Since the issue involves how issuers and users of financial information perceive independence, it seems to us that a properly conducted survey could shed considerable light on the subject, perhaps even to the point of settling the issue (on grounds of independence) of whether auditors should be associated with forecasts. If such objectives can be satisfied, the future may be brighter.

Improved definition of research objectives, stated in terms of detailed specifications, accompanied by measurement criteria, and subject to monitoring and appraisal, would significantly enhance research productivity. Further, evaluation of resource application in terms of benefits gained would be facilitated. And, project staffing could be on a task-force basis, allowing us to take advantage both of practitioners' knowledge of auditing techniques and of academics' knowledge of research methodology.

Discussion

Robert S. Kay

1. Some Preliminary Remarks

In an anecdote in the October 1975 issue of *The Accounting Review,* Robert E. Jensen talked about truth versus ΦΙΚΤΙΟΝ versus something. The purpose of his good-natured polemic was to underscore the conviction with which certain parties staunchly support exit values, value estimates, and historical costs. It seems to me that the proponents of differing valuation bases have considerable "research" to support the primacy of their views. At least some of the research so used has been obtained via experimental and survey research. This raises a considerable question as to the efficacy of such methods if they result, in the words of the authors, in "paddling powerfully towards the White Cliffs of the obvious."

The authors list the following as the subject matter of their paper, and for ease in addressing it, I will summarize their topics:

1. A review and evaluation of recently published experimental and survey literature in financial accounting, in an effort to "examine the benefits of recent accounting research . . . and to provide guidelines for future research." In undertaking this subject, the authors examine alternative reporting models and disclosure practice to observe choices and possible improvements.
2. A review of research that has focused on financial statement disclosure and use.
3. A review of research that has focused on accounting principles and alternative accounting models.
4. An examination of research that has focused on several special topic areas not included above.
5. An evaluation of certain aspects of the research methods.
6. An evaluation of the relevance and impact of experimental and survey research on financial accounting practice.

At the outset, the authors summarize their belief: "That the data support the contention that experimental and survey research has made, at best, a modest contribution to the resolution of reporting and disclosure issues. Moreover, the results may even have been counterproductive in several instances."

Before discussing the authors' views, it is important to understand that my perspective is that of a practicing accountant and not that of an academic (nor even one with an academic bent) involved in formal research. However, a practicing CPA often finds it necessary to perform survey research of a sort—certainly not in any attempt to evaluate an entire universe—in order to observe what precedents may have been created with respect to a particular accounting or disclosure problem he has under consideration. It would be overharsh to refer to this kind of research as a "lowest common denominator" determination, but it would be too pious to suggest that each accountant makes his decision in an uncharted area completely oblivious of the conclusions already reached by others similarly situated.

Another dimension affecting the practicing CPA, perhaps more incisively than it affects the academician (who is, after all, the primary research unit) is the on-going activity of the Financial Accounting Standards Board and the Securities and Exchange Commission. A few comments about these very imposing facts of life are in order.

Financial Accounting Standards Board. The research program of the Accounting Principles Board, the forerunner of the FASB, was probably reasonably conceived, but resulted in much too little production much too late. As reported in the publication, "Establishing Financial Accounting Standards," (the Wheat Committee Report which gave birth to the FASB) there were no new studies after August 1967, and of 24 studies authorized, only 11 resulted in publication through 1971. (Since that date 3 others have been released.) Many of these published studies took more than four years to complete. An explanation of the undue delays included the fact that much of the research was not assigned under contract and did not require the researcher to devote his full time to the work. If that requirement had been made, the Wheat Committee editorialized that ordinarily one year—in exceptional cases two years—would have been sufficient to complete a research study. The Wheat Committee came to the conclusion that "Full-time research should . . . be the normal pattern for the future."

For those research studies completed under the auspices of the Accounting Research Division of the AICPA, the Accounting Principles Board generally followed quite promptly—within two years—in issuing an Opinion. It was therefore hypothesized that if more research had come out of the ARD, the APB effectiveness might have been greater. The Wheat Committee could not resist giving the impression "that research projects have not always been initiated with a clear statement of the issues before the Board and an indication of the types of evidence that the Board would consider persuasive in formulating an accounting standard. . . . We come to the inescapable conclusion that much of the work of the Accounting Research Division has not been related closely enough to the needs of the Board."

In suggesting the proper base of research for the Financial Accounting Standards Board, the Wheat Committee, taking note of the "abundance of published research prepared by academics, professional and business associations, and the like," stated its view that "research performed by the Standards Board should be analytical, empirical, evaluative, and directed toward systematically dealing with the topics before the Board." For example, it should deal with such questions as: What are the issues? What are the alternatives? What theoretical and practical support exists for alternative solutions? What are the practical effects and implications of the alternatives? "We do not believe that the Board's staff should be expected to conduct a broad, fundamental research program dealing with basic concepts on an ongoing basis, since we believe that this type of research is best left to those in the academic field."

As finally constituted, the bylaws of the Financial Accounting Foundation provide that: "The Chairman of the FASB shall provide for such research as he may deem necessary or desirable in the circumstances in connection with the preparation of Statements of Financial Accounting Standards or Interpretations of such Statements. Research may be conducted by the FASB's staff or by consultants or independent contractors appointed by its Chairman." But the FASB is not obligated to perform formal research with respect to matters under consideration.

Finally, the rules of procedure of the Financial Accounting Standards Board provide that proposals for research can come from any place, but those undertaken at the direction of the FASB Chairman will be directed to specific issues associated with the Standards Board projects. More important, "the research will have a problem-solving orientation and will be directed to providing information about specific questions and the impact of alternative solutions. The general character of the research will be of an empirical type. Theoretical and conceptual research may also be deemed necessary."

Securities and Exchange Commission. The SEC is not in the research business per se. However, as indicated in Accounting Series Release No. 150, in fulfilling its "responsibility to assure that investors are furnished with information necessary for informed investment decisions," it will continue to specify what information is needed in addition to that included in financial statements conforming to generally accepted accounting principles.

There seems to be a distinct difference between the amount of "conceptualizing" which has occurred at the SEC in recent years, as compared with earlier years. A priori, this suggests that the present Chief Accountant, who as an academician performed some notable research studies, believes that some academic approaches are very helpful in resolving contemporary issues.

ASR 150, in endorsing the Financial Accounting Standards Board, points out that "the Board would provide an institutional framework which will permit prompt and responsible actions flowing from research and consideration of varying viewpoints."

Let me comment on the foregoing mixture of fact and supposition. The Financial Accounting Standards Board has not, to my knowledge, engaged in any extensive amount of outside contracted research. Basically, the FASB relies on its staff, on its discussion memoranda task forces, and on the voluminous input from respondents to both discussion memoranda and exposure drafts. In a sense, the combination of in-house staff and experienced task-force members does seem to accomplish the "problem-solving orientation" and "empirical type" of research specified in the FASB's rules of procedure.

Frankly, at a time when the Financial Accounting Standards Board has not put to rest numerous complaints about its alleged lethargy in the resolution of burning practice questions, the Board can ill afford, it seems to me, a great deal in the way of protracted research. Of the numerous issues currently on the Board's agenda, perhaps only two would be likely candidates for extensive research: objectives of financial statements; and accounting for interest costs. With respect to each of these, an incredible amount of research or quasi research has already been performed. Accordingly, it would seem appropriate that the Board assimilate what it already has, and not place itself in the shoulder-shrugging position of having to wait for what could be the "White Cliffs of the obvious."

As far as the SEC is concerned, its impact on financial accounting comes, quite clearly, from a perspective other than research (although, as indicated above, there is some vestige of academia showing through in a few releases). It should not be the function of the SEC to commission or perform research, but it may, through a moratorium device (such as ASR 163, freezing capitalization of interest policies) stimulate the resolution of current accounting problems whether through research or otherwise (such as by FASB fiat).

It is interesting to note that, by and large, FASB discussion memoranda make considerable use of existing research. Their bibliographies are replete with citations of notable, as well as some obscure, researchers. As a member of two FASB task forces (Business Combinations and Interest Costs) I am satisfied that the FASB is commissioning academic research with considerable discretion—stated differently, it is not calling for much of it, because of the short time frame in which resolutions are required. However, I do believe the FASB staff does perform a thorough survey of available research, and to the extent that the FASB staff is influenced by such research, there is also the broad perspective of the task force which acts as a sounding board with respect to the staff's selections of applicable research.

It is not too soon, in this discussion paper, to point out that the authors have omitted reference to what, perhaps, has been one of the most significant research efforts in the history of accounting—that undertaken by the Accounting Objectives Study Group in calling for written position papers, in holding interviews with financial statement users, and in holding public hearings—all directed to the ultimate publication of the Trueblood Report. I assume the authors do not consider this kind of endeavor to be "research based on experimental data." If so, then they would likewise not consider the discussion memoranda, responses thereto, public hearings, exposure drafts, and exposure draft responses (all related to the FASB) to constitute this type of research. Admittedly, such endeavors are not rigorously structured, in the sense that the responses can be tallied as in a referendum. (However, in a virtually self-contained issue, such as oil- and gas-tax allocation, it can almost be assumed that all affected parties are responding—namely the members of the oil- and gas-production industry; although I'm not sure anyone has tried to tabulate who did and who did not respond, I have a feeling that the industry was very well represented in casting its "votes.")

2. Financial Statement Disclosure and Use

My approach in commenting on this and the following two sections will be, basically, to give my impressions of the results of the research cited. I recognize that, simply because I may express views different from the researcher's conclusions, it would appear that I am elevating my a priori judgment over the empirical results obtained by the researchers. Nonetheless, it is my intention to provide the viewpoint of the practicing CPA; it may well be that intuitive reaction to research results is something researchers ought to consider before finalizing their positions.

2.1. Adequacy of Disclosure. I do not find it surprising that an overall conclusion of research on the adequacy of disclosure is "that there does not appear to be a burning desire for drastic revisions or changes in the form and content of financial statements." The fact that this conclusion is unchanged, as the authors point out, in over 25 years strongly suggests that users of financial statements are unable to articulate the fundamental approach they desire. Whenever there is a contemporary concern about a particular issue, the user almost automatically answers that he desires more disclosure on that subject—but disclosures are like barnacles; once attached, they are very difficult to remove.

And the barnacles proliferate. The SEC considers disclosure as its primary obligation—to provide investors and potential investors with adequate information on which to base investment decisions. We all know how difficult it is to eliminate a disclosure once specified in the authoritative accounting literature—and how much more so to remove one from SEC requirements.

If it were natural for financial statement users to articulate the basic information they need for economic decision-making, there would have been no need for the Trueblood Study Group Report. Even the Financial Accounting Standards Board, without acute focusing on the subject, cannot expect to arrive at a conclusion on the objectives of financial statements. Under these circumstances it is no surprise that the FASB finds it necessary to release statements and interpretations which beg the question of what accounting model is being or will eventually be followed, and that the SEC is now involved in a broad spectrum of "what if" disclosures. Examples are plentiful; the FASB's objectives project on price-level accounting was undertaken well before any real establishment of broad qualitative standards for the project. That the SEC may view price-level accounting as an albatross is also not surprising, in view of the SEC's release of a proposal on replacement cost accounting. In the SEC "what if" arena, additional disclosures on leases (ASR 147) and interest capitalized (ASR 163) are good examples.

A second conclusion indicated by the authors is that, apparently, "most readers of financial statements have relatively little difficulty understanding these statements, and that the investing public generally is not very critical of the complexity of these statements." I find that very hard to believe. Perhaps this conclusion is a function of which financial statements were presented to research participants, but if financial statements are not overly complicated, what is the source of the oft-heard complaint about "the fine print in the footnotes"? Surely we have all seen relatively brief basic financial statements followed by many, many pages of hypercomplex disclosures seemingly calculated to baffle even the expert accountant. We have all heard of, if not felt, litigation about the lack of clarity in financial presentations, and we have cringed at judicial homilies concerning the need for financial statements to communicate to the average man. Even the SEC adds fuel to this fire with its concept of differential disclosure—certain disclosures are necessary in the basic financial statements because they would be meaningful to the average investor, whereas other data only need be included in the 10-K annual report because such information would be of interest only to the sophisticated investor (e.g., the analyst). I submit that any conclusion indicating that substantially all readers of financial statements do understand them either sampled a faulty universe or caught the research participants at a time when the market was on the upswing.

The third conclusion, concerning more disclosure by large firms audited by large CPA firms, is a rather bland, and almost self-justifying, result. As the authors suggest, the large enterprises are required by regulation to report much more, and their size and often diversity of business practice would spawn disclosures simply not needed in smaller enterprises. In sum, it seems to me that the three foregoing conclusions from all the research indicated by the authors as having been performed, are trite, still highly debatable, and finally, meager in relation to the effort apparently extended.

2.2. Usefulness of Financial Statement Data. One of the approaches cited as having been used is to list information and ask financial statement users to indicate relative importance of the items, usually on a five-point scale. I often receive questionnaires of this nature and have completed several quite recently. Whenever I answer one of these "relative importance" questionnaires, I am relieved that I have to classify my responses into only five categories, finding that task rather simple, especially when dealing with what is not, at least to me, a real-life situation. How much more complex is "live-case" decision-making than a five-point scale!

One particular approach cited (Libby) was an experiment to investigate the use of financial statement data (e.g., accounting ratios) by loan officers to predict business failure. While I have not gone back to review Libby's research, I submit that this particular experiment is misclassified: it does not deal with "usefulness of financial statement data," but rather with whether financial statement data have been usefully manipulated. Loan officers, investors, and even public accountants have had the ability to draw off telling ratios. In recent years, with high inflation, tight money, and the resulting liquidity crunch, it is my understanding that many CPAs are observing, often with the help of computer software programs, significant financial ratios to look for possible future liquidity problems.

Again, I am troubled, but certainly not surprised, by the overall conclusions emerging from this batch of research. If investors in fact consider nonfinancial statement factors relatively more important in making investment decisions than the financial statements, we must express dismay at the overwhelming significance attached to financial statements when an enterprise is in distress. To put it more colloquially, the "insurance policy" provided by the CPA firm's attest attaches to the financial statements, whereas the data that should truly be backed up by someone—the nonfinancial statement factors—are subject to considerably less rigor. Going on further in this analysis, it is believable that investors tend to rely on stockbrokers and advisory services for their investment information, and that analysts tend to consider general economic and industry data more than they do the financial statement information. (I am not sure these conclusions, however, are fully supported by the indicated research.) Do not these conclusions suggest some reassessment of whether research should be directed to financial statements? Should it not be addressed to the "soft data" surrounding, but excluded from, the financial statements? Recognizing that there has been much research on the question of what "moves the market," and that this research certainly has included nonfinancial data, I am surprised that there has not been greater clamor for a formal attest (i.e., "certification") of these data.

I tend to agree with the authors' suggestion that financial statement data might not be useful to investors and analysts because the constraints of generally accepted accounting principles and generally accepted auditing standards reduce usefulness by limiting the extent to which subjective, not easily auditable judgments, are reflected in those data. However, it seems inevitable, at least to me, that financial disclosures will in the near future expand to include much more "soft" information, such as sales and earnings forecasts, and appraisals. Furthermore, we are going to see a considerably greater experimentation with value-based accounting (however defined) along with some appropriate attestation by the CPA; and I would intuitively expect considerably more attention being paid to such data having a future cash-flow orientation than is now given to historical cost-based financial statements.

2.3. Attitudes About Corporate Reporting Practices. I believe the authors should have given more information concerning not only the problem of "the exact wording used to obtain attitudinal data," but also to the issue of how to factor into the results the differences in accounting-model conception which certainly exists among those surveyed. In other words, if academics disagree on the appropriate accounting model, so do financial statement users, preparers, and attestors; the only difference between the latter group and academics is that the academics recognize their debate while it is often merely latent in the latter group. This problem is underscored by the conflicting results the authors indicate with respect to business-combination accounting.

2.4. Materiality Judgments. The debate on what is material will not end even when the FASB releases a Statement of Financial Accounting Standards on the Materiality. Originally scheduled for the fall of 1975, the public hearing and the due date for responses to the FASB Discussion Memorandum on Materiality were postponed until the spring of 1976. Much research is cited in the Discussion Memorandum, but in the end, the result will have to be somewhat of a "political compromise."

Researchers on the subject of materiality fail to take into account, I think, the dimension of judicial interpretation of materiality (for example, the case of Escott versus BarChris Construction Company) in which the court's opinion on what was or was not material to the financial statement users defies complete understanding to this day.

I have attempted to fill out a great many questionnaires on materiality, and even to provide "cassettes" for researchers to cut their materiality teeth on. I have always felt uncomfortable in responding to these questionnaires, both for the reason that it is physically impossible to capture all the circumstances involved in making a materiality decision (at least in a questionnaire—though we as practicing accountants believe we can capture these factors in our file documentation of a decision once made), and because the qualitative factors affecting materiality seem to change before the ink on the researchers' questionnaires has dried. Witness the current debate over what constitutes a material illegal, or possibly illegal, payment. Payments in five figures have been called material with respect to companies whose earnings may approach the nine figure category and whose revenues exceed a billion dollars.

Although the FASB had a reasonable rationale for postponing the materiality project (to give respondents more time to consider the subject— very few responses had been received at the time the due dates were extended) I cannot help believing that the Board felt frustration at the probability of being unable to deal with qualitative data in the absence of some greater specification of the objectives of financial statements. In response to the FASB discussion memorandum, I was prepared to urge that, for the time being, only quantitative measures should be specified, and that later on the Board should tackle qualitative measures. By postponement, perhaps the Board will be in a position to deal with both, but I somewhat doubt any financial accounting standard on materiality can answer the "really tough ones."

3. Accounting Principles and Models

I am somewhat impressed with the Mautz technique of soliciting illustrative examples to provide a focus for later seminars on the issues, and for developments of survey questionnaires on these topics. We have participated in such research in the past, and it gives us the opportunity to describe those factors, within one of our own real-life cases, which we felt had the most significance. While this method seems to have considerable appeal to the person who provides the case, we do wonder, however, whether others who may be asked to comment on a questionnaire derived from the case may not have the same "sterility" questions we do when responding on someone else's case. Perhaps seminars are as far as these kinds of research-captured data can be taken. In general, I must admit some considerable concern about the validity of questionnaires as a research technique with respect to accounting principles and models.

3.1. "De Facto" Accounting Principles. The kind of research here described bears little discussion. It falls under the weight of the "serious limitations" addressed by the authors.

This is quite close to the "consensus" or "referendum" establishment of accounting principle I alluded to earlier. In addition to ignoring the serious limitations addressed by the authors, what the researchers failed to do was to consider the "minimum qualifications" respondents ought to have. This may be a failing in much accounting research—and it is as fundamental as the proposition that "all CPAs are equal." This is patently untrue, despite the protestations of the AICPA. Putting aside variation from person to person in the relative quantity of "gray matter," experience, environment, training, and temperament all contribute to the uneven responses obtained from CPAs. The problem is aggravated with financial statement users, but researchers at least profess to have considered this factor.

3.2. Price-Level and Current-Value Accounting Proposals. The authors list a number of survey- and interview-based studies in this area, but have certainly left out the most prominent of these, simply because it did not bear a label supporting either "price-level" or "current-value" accounting. I am again referring to the Report of Study Group on Objectives of Financial Statements (the Trueblood Report) which certainly was a very heavily interview-based research project. Despite the lack of a label, and despite some compromise conclusions, the Trueblood Report, in establishing the primacy of utility for the purpose of making economic decisions, certainly did adopt a future cash-flow orientation as its theme. Admittedly, it left implementation questions to others, including the question of what to do with historical cost, but no one could accuse the Trueblood Study Group Report of constituting a defense of exclusively historical cost-based accounting. Furthermore, its use to support general price-level adusted financial information has been somewhat minimal, because it takes a great deal of stretching to draw that conclusion out of it.

Intuitively I would object to the conclusion that "no interest has been found in replacing historical cost statements with current-value statements," though I do not doubt that price-level adjusted historical cost statements certainly would come out a loser in any referendum. On the contrary, we find more than a few clients interested in some form of current-value accounting, considering it presently as something possibly supplemental, with historical cost being retained at least for the stewardship function. Ultimately, however, these clients see no reason why value-based financial statements should not be the primary statements.

We still believe that many financial statement users will not understand the difference between price-level adjusted financial information and value-based information, and for this reason, among many others, price-level information should be down-played, at best optional, or possibly even proscribed.

The research described by the authors certainly seems undisciplined in the sense that respondents might all have attached different meanings to the same questions. I would also question using students as subjects, though admittedly my bias in this regard should not, perhaps, be any greater than that applicable to poststudents.

The final paragraph of this section refers to "certain financial information" which, if reported, could influence the relative structure of security prices. A very fundamental contemporary concern is that of liquidity. It is doubtful that price-level adjusted financial statements favorably contribute to liquidity assessments (actually, they may conceal significant liquidity problems); but there is a chance that value-based data, particularly if they have some exit value or short-term "cash out" attributes, could be very helpful in assessing liquidity.

3.3. Probablistic Financial Statements and Allied Proposals. While the authors indicate that there is only one published study on this subject, I submit that the "confidence interval" in hypothetical lending decisions of bankers is, at least formalistically, applied in almost all loan agreements. By this I mean that, via covenants dealing with financial statement ratios and balances, the bankers have indicated their "pain level," though I would not accuse most bankers of scientifically determining what these figures ought to be. Often times, such figures represent a "floor" of recent achievement by the company, and in order to assure a reasonable level of credibility in management's optimistic generalizations as to the future, such minimum-level covenants are installed.

I would object to the statement that "there has been no research to speak of on the fundamental purposes of financial accounting"; I need merely refer the authors to the work of the Trueblood Study Group. I do agree that "much more investigation of proposed alternative bases of financial accounting is needed. . . ."

4. Special Topics

The topics selected by the authors in this area are quite interesting; they all represent contemporary issues, though some of them have been around for quite a while. If it can be accepted that there is "no fundamental truth in accounting," but only consensus—or better yet, pragmatic convention (and I certainly believe that), then survey techniques may be the appropriate manner of gathering information. I do not believe that asking a respondent whether he would pay for the data requested is an essential characteristic of this type of research. Frankly, neither the surveyors nor the respondents have a good handle on what it would cost. However, the data are probably attainable at some price, or they would not be the subject of a survey in the first place.

As to the question of "certification" of new information or new reporting requirements, surveys on these topics are more or less destined to failure because the frame of reference of the respondent is basically status quo. The AICPA is moving ever so slowly to acknowledge the probability that the CPA's attest—in whatever appropriate form—will have to be extended to much more information, some of it much "softer" than what we now address (the report of the AICPA Committee on Scope and Structure, for example). The SEC has likewise not been particularly impressed with the "uncertifiability" of certain materials such as interim financial statement data, although it has not required attestation of this information in its recent releases on the inclusion of interim financial data in annual reports. This may be as much derived from an appreciation of the infirmities of the Securities Acts provisions as it is from clamor by CPAs about the inability to accomplish some form of attestation. (It should be noted, however, that time and cost constraints do effectively preclude certification of quarterly results in the sense of annual audit certification. I am confident we will yet see some form of publicized attest with respect to timely reported quarterly data, and this will convey a lesser degree of assurance, and hopefully commensurately less responsibility, than attaches to an annual audit.)

4.1. Segment and Subsidiary Reporting. I have what is perhaps an unkind reaction to this entire section. Much research is cited in the area of segment reporting needs, but I believe that the respondents in any surveys are preconditioned to the idea that "more disclosure is better disclosure." Specifically, one has to wonder whether the FASB's proposal on segmented reporting represents the FASB's conclusions as a result of surveying all the research done, or whether, despite the research, it is a foregone conclusion because of the SEC's earlier requirement that such data be included in reports and filings of registrants. I recognize that the FASB carefully studies what it should require, but the basic thrust— whether the information is to be provided—seems to be a foregone conclusion. (It will be interesting to note whether the FASB releases a requirement regarding issuance of general purchasing power financial statements; the SEC has been almost derisive on this topic, and has counter-proposed another variety. This phenomenon is the opposite of what has occurred in the segment situation.) I must admit, for the record, that I am not personally against providing segmented data; I am only commenting on the way this accounting change is being brought about.

4.2. Interperiod Reporting. The subject of interim financial reporting has also been catalyzed (that may be too mild a term) by the SEC. The Accounting Principles Board took a quantum leap in the issuance of Opinion 28, which, with all its infirmities, was joyfully welcomed, considering the dearth of information on appropriate interim-reporting standards. As with other subjects, however, the foundation in Opinion 28 has not been adequate to deal with many interim-reporting questions turning up, particularly in view of SEC requirements (ASR 177) which caused both preparers of financial statements and associated independent CPAs to be much more punctilious after December 26, 1975.

Recently, the Financial Accounting Standards Board has been provided with numerous questions relating to interim financial reporting, some of which concern the underlying philosophy of Opinion 28—e.g., is an interim period indeed a portion of a fiscal year (the basic reporting unit), as opposed to a discrete reporting period in itself? Resolution of this question in the latter fashion could produce significantly different interim-reporting results than heretofore.

It is interesting to note the authors' conclusion: "It is not at all clear that the information which, in users' opinions, will optimize performance actually does so when supplied." The SEC, in requiring the inclusion of summarized data for the last eight quarters in an unaudited footnote accompanying the annual financial statements, seems to have made the "tenuous" and "substantial leap of faith" in assuming that the marshaling of all this data (already available in form 10-Q) will actually optimize investor performance.

4.3. Forecast Reporting. There is little I can add to the authors' indications of research on this topic. However, attempting to determine attitudes toward forecasting is, in my opinion, an exercise in futility unless one postulates an unchanging historical cost accounting model. Should a value orientation be adopted—and we are creeping toward this—the place of forecasting will certainly change.

Consider the recent activities of AICPA Committees. The Management Advisory Services Executive Committee issued a publication on necessary attributes of a good forecasting system. The Accounting Standards Executive Committee has released a statement of position on what forecasts should look like when presented. And finally, the Auditing Standards Executive Committee has debated, for a couple of years, the question of the CPA's appropriate relationship to published forecasts.

Again, not an insignificant factor in this debate, although not the cause of the foregoing AICPA activities, has been the SEC's proposal for a formal system for the dissemination of forecasting information within the framework of the Federal Securities Laws. It is problematic whether the Auditing Standards Executive Committee will act on this subject in advance of further activity by the SEC; some feel that as long as the SEC proposal is left on the back burner, other more important items remain to be dealt with. Without detracting from the truthfulness of that statement, there is some question as to whether academic research or Columbian (District of, or University, as you prefer) a priori research will govern.

4.4 Decision Effects of Alternate Reporting Methods. As the authors indicate, user characteristics represent the predominant factor in this research. The likely influence of "access to expert technical assistance" on the experimental results strongly suggests that there should be careful control of study participants. This raises a concern as to whether research should be directed toward obtaining a view of what the "average" reaction might be, when in fact the important reactions—those that will be controlling as to future information-dissemination—might well be at some level of sophistication well above the "average."

4.5 Effecting Changes in Reporting Practice. It has always been our understanding that the Financial Accounting Standards Board does the pertinent research prior to the issuance of the exposure draft. With one exception, final pronouncements have mirrored exposure drafts (the one exception being oil- and gas-tax allocation). Accordingly, and I believe the Board has stated this, substantive remarks concerning the direction the Board should take should be provided at the discussion-memorandum stage, so that when the exposure draft is to be commented on, we may hope that we are down to a process of fine tuning.

5. Evaluation of Research Method

Describing experimental and survey research in financial accounting as having had considerable vigor in the past decade seems to amount to a violent yawn. Simply tabulating the amount of activity which has occurred says nothing for the subject matter or the results. Further, research efforts boiled up out of the huge academic cauldron to come to the attention of the authors is undoubtedly only a fraction of much similar activity that does not proceed beyond the doctoral dissertation stage, if it gets that far. I have to ask the question, therefore, as to whether any of the experimental and survey research is effective. As the authors point out, we have not experienced a dramatic increase in our body of knowledge because the evidence gathered by research is not in a form which allows it to be integrated with prior evidence. Thus, we have much more knowledge, but it is lacking interconnection.

Of significant note is the authors' description of the "typical" research study environment. Considering that most of the work is done for doctoral dissertations, it may not be an overstatement that the perceived contribution to professional knowledge might not be the uppermost factor in the researchers' mind.

5.1. Lack of a Theoretical Emphasis. I certainly would like to be included in the group of "typical respondents (who are) less than enthusiastic about further participation." In my present position, I receive numerous questionnaires, and not more than once or twice a year can I honestly state that I have received one which I felt was well enough designed to allow me expeditiously to indicate my views. Even recently, when I received a questionnaire I thought was very well done, I had to point out to the researcher that a threshold question attempting to compartmentalize respondents was not all-inclusive, and would have caused at least a small number of respondents, including myself, to skip over to another section of the questionnaire, thus eliminating the possible input I might have been able to give in earlier parts of the questionnaire. More specifically, this asked me to classify myself according to the nature of my *present* clientele. Because of National Office position, I do not have any clients for which I assume any direct responsibility, although I do have consultative responsibilities. The questionnaire might have asked about my present and recent past experiences. There were other problems with this bifurcation—it assumed that responding CPAs all had the same firm policies as to classification of one partner as a partner in charge of an engagement.

In this area, the authors express their belief that surveys in financial accounting must use theory to underlay surveys and experiments. I am inclined to agree. Random attitude surveys, without either postulating a theory or clearly obtaining the respondent's theory perspective, are bound to provide random answers.

5.2. Lack of Ties to the Work of Others. It is my understanding that the American Accounting Association Committee on Research Activities has a project designed to disseminate broadly, within that organization, research efforts underway, and to attempt to dovetail the various elements of research in a useful way. I think this is certainly a necessary ingredient if future research is to be more productive than past research. There is much to be studied in financial accounting, but the relatively small segments selected by a single researcher often do not self-contain sufficient nutrition to keep them from withering.

5.3. Lack of Rigor. Conducting surveys and experiments by mail, with nothing more, places a great deal of blind faith in the competence of the respondents—i.e., those who choose to respond. It seems to me that, as a minimum, there should be some attempted corroboration by interviews with selected respondents whose competence is known or can at least be evaluated during the course of the interview. I know in my case that my responses are often deliberately slanted to express a company view, or that I may do a hasty job because I am distracted by other matters. Yet I have participated in interview surveys, knowing in advance what the questions will be, and I find it much easier to express my views in a manner to which

I am accustomed, letting the researchers translate my responses into the measurements necessary for their survey.

Another question that should be raised is whether survey results are affected by the stature of the researchers. I think a question can be raised as to whether doctoral students can obtain the necessary attention from prospective respondents. On the other hand, a sufficient number of established academic names, on the right kinds of letterheads, will produce a better response rate.

6. Evaluation of Research Impact

I must agree that "the academic typically writes for other academics." Accordingly, communication of the results of behavioral research to practicing accountants cannot be adequate. On the other hand, I believe the Financial Accounting Standards Board makes it its business to translate applicable academic research; to that extent, the practicing accountant is now receiving some benefit as a result of the FASB's having considered the appropriate input.

The question of how shortage of funds often restricts research to students or artificial groupings of practitioners is something that must be addressed. It certainly raises an argument for a more comprehensive institutional approach to research. Finally, doctoral students, who will continue to be the major source of accounting research, will have to team up with practicing professionals in order to draw more useful conclusions from their work.

I have a number of overall conclusions that dance across the entire paper, and perhaps draw upon other papers being presented at this conference.

Experimental and survey research in financial accounting has not had much of an impact. Frankly, I do not think it ever will. In my opinion, a priori and theoretical research will continue to be the most notable research force in accounting.

I have, however, some concerns about the extent to which research is able truly to have impact on accounting. In large measure, because accounting is represented by conventions designed to serve an objective (which is still officially ill-defined), much of accounting regulation is a political process. It is political in the sense that the SEC, CASB, the Stock Exchanges, the Internal Revenue Service, Congress, various regulatory agencies, the International Accounting Standards Committee, and on and on, are able, on the basis of perceived effects of a particular accounting standard, to exert a significant influence on both whether a standard will be issued, and what it will say. I have already spoken about the SEC; we should not overlook Congress in its action on the investment tax credit (and in the fact that constituents have asked their duly elected representatives to intervene on the question of lease accounting). Also do not forget the Internal Revenue Service, which has been operating at a generally low-visibility level on the question of conformity of tax and financial accounting, but every now and then a clamor erupts; witness the debates on LIFO disclosures and on changes in the composition of overheads included in inventories. It must be remembered that in many countries financial accounting and income tax accounting are inextricably intertwined.

Apart from the FASB and to some extent the SEC, the practicing CPA is certainly an a priori researcher. Practice questions come to him and require a resolution. Even if his subject is included in the professional literature, rarely is that source sufficiently case-specific to permit an immediate transfer of solution. Instead, he must reason from abstract literature, or he must deduce by comparison with treatments he believes similar, to arrive at a satisfactory conclusion for his specific case. Currently, he is fortified by much more information than has been available in the recent past. Most notably, he has the national automated accounting research system (NAARS) to permit him to discern whether publicly held companies may have had to account for or disclose a situation of the nature he is considering. Whether NAARS will ultimately turn out to be a boon or a bane is problematic; it has often been accused of stimulating "lowest common denominator" practices. I believe that NAARS is useful in a more professional way—the practicing accountant does need a knowledge of the environment (i.e., others faced with similar situations) before he can make an informed decision as to his own particular case. I would not expect most accountants honestly to believe that whatever they find in NAARS is a justification for a practice they may have had good reason to be skeptical about prior to pressing the magic button.

We are, of course, operating under an ill-defined concept of the objectives of financial statements. I realize many will argue with me on this point, but having had available the results of the Trueblood Study Group for over two years, creates, at a minimum, some uneasiness about whether historical cost accounting might be a terminal case. Furthermore, financial accounting standards released in recent years, including a few from the Accounting Principles Board, have made some notable incursions in what may be called value accounting; it certainly takes a great deal of elasticity to define them as fully supported by the historical cost model.

The future of research in accounting—whatever form it may take— is bound to be considerably enhanced when the Financial Accounting Standards Board establishes, with at least some degree of specificity, the objectives of financial statements. Even if the Board were to specify that historical cost is *it,* that could put to rest much of the survey techniques which consciously or unconsciously are designed to adapt to the respondents' perception of financial statement objectives. (Frankly, if the Board were to specify historical cost, I doubt that the current thrust of research would change, because researchers would continue looking for something different. Intuitively, I feel that if something "more advanced" than historical cost accounting were specified, researchers would not look "backwards" to reminisce about historical bases.)

Finally, too much experimental and survey research designed to ascertain what a consensus might be as to a given issue, as the authors point out, lacks a theoretical foundation. If we are to establish accounting principles via consensus or referendum, without regard to theory, we will end up describing "the usually fragrant, multipetaled flower of a plant characteristically having prickly stems and many stamens" as a weed.

PART III

The Impact of Empirical Research

The Information Content of Financial Accounting Numbers: A Survey of Empirical Evidence

Robert S. Kaplan

1. Introduction

When I was first asked to do a paper surveying empirical research in accounting, I found it difficult to believe that the world needed yet another survey on this topic. I sometimes think that there are more surveys on empirical research than there are papers to be surveyed. Nevertheless, the theme of this conference is the relevance of recent research to practice (some cynics may argue that this should guarantee both short papers and a brief conference) and most previous surveys of empirical research have been addressed more to academicians than to practitioners (see Beaver [1973] for an exception). I could thus see at least a tiny niche in which this paper might fit without flagrantly duplicating previous efforts.

It seems only prudent for me to acknowledge other survey papers and admit that I have both read and been influenced by the views in these sources. Therefore, any similarity between the views expressed here and the evaluations in these other papers could hardly be considered accidental Among these other sources of surveys are Beaver (1972), (1973), (1974b), (1975), Gonedes and Dopuch (1974; Section 8), Hakansson (1971), and Lev (1974). Of these, Lev (1974) is a particularly comprehensive treatment which should be readable by many practitioners.

I have decided to classify the empirical papers into five principal subject areas: (1) information content of annual accounting numbers; (2) information content of interim earnings reports and corporate forecasts; (3) time-series properties of accounting income numbers; (4) effect of accounting alternatives on common stock prices; and (5) predicting bankruptcy with accounting data. A separate section will be devoted to each of these subject areas.

Much of the literature on the above topics builds upon extensive developments in the finance literature studying and documenting the efficiency of capital markets. We have obtained significant insights into the speed and effectiveness of capital markets in responding to information, into appropriate definitions of risk, and into methodology for testing hypotheses about various aspects of information processing and risk-and-return relationships in capital markets. Before moving to a survey of the accounting literature, I must initially summarize some important concepts in this efficient markets literature which form the basis of many of the accounting studies.

Even before that, however, I must issue a disclaimer as to what I will *not* be doing in this survey. As previously mentioned, I *am* attempting to relate the significance of recent academic research to practitioners. Consequently, I will *not* be discussing methodological details or criticizing the methodology used in the various studies. This should not be construed as tacit approval of the methodology used in each case. In fact, I have yet to read an empirical study whose methodology was beyond criticism. It does, however, represent my judgment that the surveyed papers were done in a reasonable fashion and that there is a distinct possibility that the authors' conclusions would still follow even had somewhat different procedures been used in the papers.

With this background, we are ready to start.

2. Efficient Capital Markets and the Market Model

Over the last fifteen years, a considerable amount of theoretical and empirical analysis has pointed to the conclusion that, as a good working approximation, the securities markets in which common stocks of U.S. corporations are traded are efficient with respect to publicly available information (a feature sometimes called semi-strong efficiency). We mean by this that the current price incorporates all publicly available information including the entire sequence of past prices, annual reports, accounting income numbers and ratios, macroeconomic variables such as monetary and fiscal policies, and a variety of other industry-specific and firm-specific information. The fact that this information is "included" in the current price implies that trading strategies based on such information will not yield a profit, on average, after paying transactions costs and controlling for the risk of the trading strategy. In particular, technical analysis, which is the arcane study (not unlike astrology) of past sequences of stock prices in order to predict future prices will not, on average, be a profitable way of spending one's time, unless one prefers such graphical activities for recreational or psychological reasons. Also, it is suggested that detailed perusals of annual reports, SEC filings, Alan Abelson's weekly Barron's column, or any of Professor Abraham Briloff's critical "exposés" of the frailties of the accounting profession will not yield special returns to the informed reader.

These ideas were in conflict with much prevailing Wall Street wisdom and naturally have not been widely accepted by financial analysts and many other practitioner groups, including public accountants and SEC regulators. For example, the public-accounting profession is constantly in contact with presumably financially knowledgeable individuals who show a disconcerting amount of ignorance about the assumptions under which financial reports are prepared. It is therefore hard to believe that any degree of market efficiency and rationality can exist in such a sea of ignorance and chaos. Nevertheless, the literature on this question is both lengthy and basically supportive of market efficiency. The technically inclined reader is referred to Fama (1970) and Jensen (1972) for extensive surveys of this literature, but these papers do assume a fair amount of mathematical and economic sophistication on the part of the reader. Lorie and Hamilton (1973) provide, perhaps, the most accessible discussion of the theory and evidence of efficient capital markets (see especially Chapters 4, 5, 10, 11, 12).

Some evidence in conflict with the efficiency of markets has been reported by Black (1973), Jaffe (1974), and Downes and Dyckman (1973). Despite these latter sources, most academics who have studied the evidence now accept as a highly reasonable first approximation that the market is efficient with respect to publicly available information; i.e., new information is processed rapidly and unbiasedly into security prices and no important dependencies exist which allow one to make superior predictions about future stock prices on the basis of past prices or previously available information.

The other important result that we will need from the finance literature is a concept of risk in securities markets. It is reasonable to assume that risk has something to do with possible variation of the actual return of a security or portfolio from its expected return; e.g., a 30-day government note (the U.S. government, not New York City) is considered as close as one can get to a risk-free security (it would be even better if the return were adjusted for increases in the price level over the 30-day period). Again, as a first and reasonable approximation, researchers have found that stock-price returns are normally distributed, so that the statistical variance of the actual return distribution is a reasonable measure of variation about the expected return.

Modern finance theory, however, indicates that it is incorrect to estimate the risk of individual stocks considered in isolation. Sensible risk-averse investors hold diversified portfolios of securities. Therefore, the riskiness of an individual security is judged by its effect on the riskiness of a well-diversified portfolio, how much the stock contributes to the variance of a diversified portfolio. This effect is measured by a quantity known as a stock's *beta* (β) which is a measure of the sensitivity of the stock's (or other asset's) return to general movements in the market.

The market, as a whole, has a β equal to 1. High-risk stocks ($\beta = 1.5$ or above) tend to increase in price faster than the market when the market is rising and to go down in price faster than the market when the market is falling (the so called go-go funds which came into prominence during the later 1960s, and some of which are still around, provide excellent illustrations of high-risk portfolios). Conversely, low-risk securities tend to increase in value slower than the market during rising markets but tend to fall less in value when the market is declining. Gold stocks and utilities are usually considered low beta securities. This relationship is summarized by the following "market model":

$$R_{it} = \alpha_i + \beta_i R_{Mt} + \epsilon_{it} \tag{1}$$

where R_{it} is the rate of return of security i in period t, the rate by definition being equal to $(P_{it} + D_{it})/(P_{it-1})$,

with P_{it} = price of security i at the end of period t

P_{it-1} = price of security i at the end of period t-1 (or the beginning of period t)

D_{it} = dividend paid by security i during period t.

The length of the period can be a week, a month, three months, etc.

R_{Mt} is the rate of return on the market portfolio sometimes measured by Standard and Poor's Composite Index of 500 Stocks or the New York Stock Exchange Index (some other indices have also been developed for empirical studies).

Equation (1) implies that there is a linear relationship between the return on a security and the return on the market. The coefficient β_i indicates how strong the relationship is, as mentioned before. A security with β_i equal to one rises or falls, by definition, on average, about as fast as the market as a whole. The error term, ϵ_{it}, indicates that many factors affect the return on a particular security other than overall market movements.

With weekly data, the linear dependence on the market explains about 15% of the return of an average security. With monthly data, the linear dependence can explain 30–40% of a security's return. While these are not impressive statistics, when one forms portfolios of say 20–25 securities, the unsystematic portion of a security's return (as represented by ϵ_{it}) averages out and only the systematic part, caused by each security's linear dependence with the market, remains. Thus, at the portfolio level, it is not surprising to find that more than 90% of a portfolio's return can be explained by its linear dependence on the market.

The β of a portfolio is a linear combination of the β_i's of the individual securities in the portfolio and is considered an excellent measure of the risk of the portfolio. The β_i's of individual stocks are to a first approximation stationary over time but, recently, the tendency for the β_i's of individual stocks to be mildly nonstationary has been documented. Portfolio β's however, tend to be much more stable over time because much of the movement in the individual β_i's in the portfolio tends to average out.

In conclusion, we obtain the important relationship that the rate of return of a security is linearly related to its risk where risk is measured by the correlation between the security's rate of return and the market's rate of return. Thus higher-risk stocks tend to have higher rates of return and vice versa. As we shall now see, accounting information may be useful in explaining either unusual returns associated with firm-specific events as measured by the residual term, ϵ_{it}, in equation (1), or the risk of a security, as measured by a security's β_i. Both roles of accounting information are important in attempting to explain or predict the price movement of a security or group of securities.

3. Information Content of Annual Accounting Numbers

In this section I will survey the evidence on the relationship between accounting information derived from annual accounting numbers (those which eventually appear in annual reports) and stock-price movements. At first glance, this may look like another instance of academics attempting to prove the obvious. Any person familiar with the "real world" knows that the market reacts strongly (and perhaps overreacts) to earnings-per-share data. Almost daily, there is a column on the next to the last page of the *Wall Street Journal* analyzing the current year's earnings prospects for one or more companies. Why then is there any interest in confirming the obvious importance of earnings?

First of all, as scientists, we are still interested in seeing whether our methodologies are able to detect this relationship (between earnings and stock prices) and are able to estimate the strength of the relationship. More important, we academic accountants exist in a skeptical world in which we have to prove such relationships to our colleagues, particularly when we attempt to assert the importance of accounting information. Many of our coworkers, especially those in finance and economics, view the accounting process as a tribal rite that must be tolerated for vague institutional reasons not fully understood (except perhaps to create a demand for accountants). A common reaction is to tell us not to bother about aggregating or summarizing all the information on the firm; just to give out the basic data (i.e., cash flows) and leave the evaluation to the informed users of financial information. A prominent economist, attempting to keep accountants in their proper place, once wrote:

A known untruth is much better than a lie, and provided that the accounting rituals are well known and understood, accounting may be untrue but it is not lies; it does not deceive because we know that it does not tell the truth, and we are able to make our own adjustment in each individual case, using the results of the accountant as evidence rather than as definitive information. (Boulding [1962; p. 55])

Further skepticism with respect to the usefulness of accounting income numbers has been provided by a prominent financial analyst:

The accountant defines it [earnings] as what he gets when he matches costs against revenues, making any necessary allocation of costs to prior periods; or as the change in the equity account over the period. These are not economic definitions of earnings but merely descriptions of the motions the accountant goes through to arrive at the earnings number. (Treynor [1972; p. 41])

In one of the earliest empirical studies relating accounting numbers to stock prices, even one of our own found it difficult to find much association between published financial reports and stock prices:

One factor is striking. Only a relatively small, though significant relationship was found between the rates of change of data found in corporate published reports and rates of change of stock prices. . . . Thus, as measured in this study, the information contained in published accounting reports is a relatively small portion of the information used by investors. (Benston [1967; p. 27–28])

It is in light of such skepticism and criticism that academic accountants have attempted to verify the importance of the numbers produced by accountants.

The earliest and most widely quoted study on this issue was performed by Ball and Brown (1968). Basically they were attempting to test the null hypothesis that the annual earnings numbers have no information content because of (1) measurement and aggregation errors of the type suggested by Boulding and Treynor, and (2) alternative and more timely sources of information about firms. The methodology they and others followed depended on an assumption of market efficiency, as described in the preceding section, that security prices incorporate all available information. To detect whether annual earnings numbers are in this set of relevant information, the researchers attempted to determine whether variation in stock prices was associated with the variability of earnings or with the act of issuing such numbers.

Ball and Brown tested whether foreknowledge of the annual earnings number was sufficient to allow an investor to earn superior returns. Certainly, we cannot attach much importance to the earnings number as a factor in determining security prices if knowledge of that number a year in advance of other investors would not allow us to outperform the market. One problem that researchers face when investigating this question is, however, evaluating a given earnings number. When I am told that company ABC's earnings-per-share (EPS) will be $3.00 next year, I don't know whether that is good news, so that I should buy the stock, or bad news. A given realization of actual earnings can only be considered favorable or unfavorable when it is compared with the market's expectation of ABC's EPS. We are all familiar with instances in which a company announced a decline in earnings but the stock rose, or announced an increase in earnings and the stock declined. Rather than view this as yet another example of market perversity, such behavior can be rational if the market, in the first case, expected a sharper decline than actually occurred or, in the second case, a higher increase.

Thus, in order to evaluate whether a given earnings number will be considered favorable or not, we need to have some measure of what the market, in aggregate, expects that number to be. Unfortunately, Ball and Brown did not have access to such expectations data, and consequently, developed some naive models of the expectations process. They used a simple time-series model of earnings expectations (i.e., next year's earnings will equal this year's earnings) as one surrogate for a firm's expected earnings. They also used a cross-sectional regression model in which the change in a firm's earnings was assumed to be consistent with its historical association with an aggregate market index of earnings. Both models produced an estimate of expected earnings. Actual earnings were then compared with these estimates and two portfolios were formed. Firms whose actual earnings exceeded "expected" earnings (called a positive forecast error) were in one portfolio and firms whose actual earnings numbers were less than expected (a negative forecast error) were in another portfolio. These portfolios were formed twelve months prior to the actual release of the earnings number to test whether foreknowledge of actual earnings would enable an investor to earn superior returns. Note that a failure to earn superior returns could be explained by two factors: either earnings are irrelevant to investors, or else earnings do matter but Ball and Brown's simple models for generating market expectation of earnings are woefully inadequate.

Fortunately, the results were positive. Stocks with positive forecast errors tended to outperform the market and stocks with negative forecast errors tended to do worse than the market. (Notice that only the sign and not the magnitude of the forecast error was used to form the two portfolios; an additional factor which would tend to mitigate against strong positive findings.) Thus, when actual income differs in whatever direction from expected income, the price of the associated security tends to move in the same direction. Of even more interest, Ball and Brown found that much of this movement occurs early in the year, well in advance of the actual release of the year's income. This is consistent with an efficient market, in which information is gathered in anticipation of the actual announcement, and stock prices are adjusted accordingly. In fact, Ball and Brown could find little price reaction by the time the actual earnings numbers were released, implying that delays in issuing these numbers cause them to be almost entirely discounted by the time they were issued. More recent evidence provides an alternative explanation: the low reaction may be caused by the increasing unrealism of the mechanical models of earnings forecasts vis-à-vis market expectations as the end of the year approaches.

It is also interesting to note that abnormal returns[1] were not realized

---

1. An abnormal return is the return in excess of what would be expected given the stock's systematic risk, β, and the market return, i.e., for a period, t, in which the market return was R_{Mt}, a stock with risk β and return R_{jt} would have an abnormal return equal to $R_{jt} - \beta R_{Mt}$.

once the annual earnings report was issued, implying that once the information is released publicly there is no opportunity for earning superior returns by careful analysis of the earnings numbers. Ball and Brown reported using a cash-flow figure (they actually used operating income, which still includes noncash income items) which was not as successful in predicting the signs of abnormal returns as the net income or EPS figures.

Gonedes (1974) replicated the Ball and Brown study with a more sophisticated methodology. He used a variety of financial ratios as well as the EPS number to generate surrogates for market expectations of firm performance. (Gonedes, however, did not use a pure cash-flow variable.) He found that the EPS variable captured most of the information content of all that was available from the accounting numbers that he tested. Both Ball and Brown, and Gonedes, point out that their tests do not describe the unique contribution of the net income or EPS figure. These income figures are correlated with many other variables (e.g., sales) and economic events relative to the firm so that even if these figures were not provided, much of the information contained in them might be generated from other sources.

Patell (1976) replicated the Ball and Brown procedure on a sample of firms for which he had management's estimate of earnings for the coming year. Thus he could test whether the procedures are sensitive to the mechanical model used by Ball and Brown to generate the market expectations of earnings. While he found that the management forecast was more accurate, ex post facto, in predicting actual earnings for the year, the margin of superiority was not great. Further, the trading strategy based on management's forecast and assumed prior knowledge of the actual earnings was only slightly better than the strategy based on the mechanical models used by Ball and Brown. Therefore, it would appear that the procedure they used to generate a surrogate for market earnings expectations is a reasonable one.

Recall that Ball and Brown only used the sign and not the magnitude of the forecast error to classify firms. Beaver (1974a) has recently investigated a strategy in which the magnitude as well as the sign of the forecast error is used to form portfolios. Presumably, firms with high positive forecast errors (large amounts of unexpected earnings) will outperform firms with lower positive forecast errors. Beaver found that the most extreme portfolios, the ones containing firms with the largest positive and negative forecast errors, had much larger abnormal returns than portfolios formed from firms whose forecast errors were moderate in magnitude. Patell (1976) formed portfolios where stocks were weighted in proportion to the *magnitude* of unexpected earnings (stocks with negative unexpected earnings [forecast errors] were sold short) and found that the weighted portfolios "outperformed" the unweighted portfolios. Thus the magnitude of unexpected earnings has information content as well as the sign.

Additional evidence on the importance of the magnitude of unexpected earnings was provided by Niederhofer and Regan (1972). They identified the 50 best and 50 worst performers on the New York Stock Exchange in 1970. Where possible, they obtained earnings predictions for these firms from the March 1970 Standard and Poors Earnings Forecaster and compared the actual 1970 earnings to these forecasts. They found that the analysts had consistently underestimated the earnings gains of the top 50 firms and overestimated the earnings for the bottom 50 firms. They concluded that "stock prices are strongly dependent on earnings changes, both absolute and relative to analysts' estimates" and that "the most important factor separating the best from the worst performing stocks was profitability."

Collins (1975) performed a particularly interesting study on the value of disclosing sales and earnings data by segments. In 1970 companies were required by the SEC to start reporting sales and profits before taxes and extraordinary items by product line. In addition, firms had to disclose line-of-business sales and earnings for the previous five years. Collins tested whether a trading strategy developed from segment-based earnings, which were not publicly available prior to 1970, would be profitable. Forecasts from segment-based earnings were compared to forecasts prepared from consolidated statements as a measure of unexpected earnings changes. During 1968 and 1969 such a trading strategy was profitable for firms which had not publicly reported either segment revenue or profit figures, but there was no significant profit from this trading strategy for firms which had voluntarily disclosed this information. This finding could not be replicated in 1970. Nevertheless, the study suggests that segment disclosure is desirable in enabling investors to anticipate changes in earnings which otherwise would be unexpected if only consolidated data were disclosed. In this case, the study is supportive of the SEC disclosure requirement and is similarly relevant to the current FASB discussion on disclosure of operating data by segments.

The above studies provide fairly convincing evidence that the procedures accountants use to arrive at a net income or EPS number do not destroy the information content of these numbers. Investors with advance knowledge of a firm's income number should be able to earn superior returns, and no other financial number has yet been found that one would rather have a year in advance than the net income number.

There is still the question of the timeliness of the annual accounting number by the time it is released; has the information content of this number already been incorporated in market expectations so that the actual announcement has little effect? Beaver (1968) investigated the magnitude of both price changes and volume of trading in the week of the earnings announcement as compared with other weeks in the year. He found that the variance of price changes (which combines the effect of both positive and negative price changes) was 70% higher in the report week than at other times of the year, implying that the announcements led to significant changes in the equilibrium prices of securities. The volume was 30% higher in the week of the announcement, which Beaver interpreted as the extent to which investors are willing to incur the transactions costs of altering their portfolios to reflect the new information contained in the earnings announcement. Both pieces of evidence tend to support the significance of new information in the annual earnings announcement.

These studies should put to rest the idea that accounting earnings are irrelevant. They have information content in that prior knowledge should enable an investor to earn superior returns, and they are timely since significant price and volume reactions do occur at the time they are released. While we are unable to measure the unique contribution of the annual earnings number relative to all other forms of available information, accounting income has been shown to play an important role in investor expectations about the future performance of the firm.

In addition to the role that accounting income numbers play in revising investor expectations about future returns, there is also the question as to whether accounting data could be used to form expectations about the systematic market risk of a security, i.e., the β_i of a stock. Typically, the β_i's of securities are estimated from a historical regression of a security's return with the market return according to equation (1). For predictions in the future it is usually assumed that the historical relation will persist and that the stock will continue to have about the same correlation with the rest of the market as it did in the past. The question that arises is whether accounting information is used by the market in estimating the systematic risk of a firm. Also, can accounting variables be used to predict future levels of systematic risk better than simple extrapolations of past trends? This latter question is important if the firm changes its capital structure or the industries in which it operates so that historical relationships may no longer be indicative of future risk levels.

Beaver, Kettler, and Scholes (BKS) (1970) investigated the association between accounting-determined risk measures and the market risk measure. An accounting beta was defined, analogously to the market-determined beta, as the correlation of the firm's net income with a market index of earnings. A variety of other financial risk measures were also tested (for example, earnings variability, liquidity, leverage and payout). BKS found significant correlations between the accounting risk measures and the market risk measures. Thus accounting risk measures are consistent with the underlying information set used by the market in assessing the riskiness of firms. BKS even found that the accounting risk measures could be used to develop forecasts of future market-determined risk measures superior to the procedure of simply assuming that the future β_i will be the same as the present β_i. More recent evidence on the nonstationarity of β, however, enables us to make better forecasts of future β than the simple extrapolation technique employed by BKS so that the indicated superiority of the accounting-based forecasts may not now exist.

Gonedes (1973) used a slightly different methodology to test the association between accounting-based and market-based risk measures and was unable to detect a strong association between the accounting beta and the market beta as reported by BKS. He attributed the difference in findings to the use by BKS of a market price to scale the accounting numbers which may have introduced a spurious correlation with the market measure of risk.

Beaver and Manegold (1975) attempted to resolve this issue by investigating a variety of specifications to test the association between accounting- and market-based betas. They again found that "across a variety of specifications for accounting and market betas, there is a statistically significant correlation between the two." Especially at the portfolio level, where measurement errors in estimating the accounting beta for individual firms will average out, there is a strong correlation between the two risk measures. Further, this correlation is not caused by scaling the accounting measure by the market price since the effect persists when nonmarket measures are used to scale income numbers. Nevertheless, Beaver and Manegold conclude that the accounting beta appears to be only one of the explanatory factors in determining the market beta.

Gonedes (1975) reran his initial study with a different index of market earnings, and he, too, now found a statistically significant though small association between accounting and market estimates of systematic risk. While Beaver and Gonedes still disagree on some details of the appropriate methodology to use to settle this issue, it seems that both have agreed that accounting-based measures of systematic risk play a significant role (of unknown magnitude) in the market's assessments of the systematic risk of securities. Thus we now have evidence that not only are unexpected changes in earnings associated with unexpected changes in a security's market value, but also that information from the accounting numbers can be used to form expectations about the systematic risk of a security which affects the expected rate of return from holding that security. Accounting data plays a dual role—in giving rise to unexpected security returns as well as affecting the riskiness of a security. This latter effect is especially interesting since it suggests the use of a new aggregation of accounting data not previously used in traditional financial analysis (i.e., the accounting beta).

These results can give us some comfort. It would have been hard to justify our existence if we could not find any evidence of the relation of accounting data to market-based phenomena. Nevertheless, apart from this comfort, we do not have much guidance or insight for the profession. For the auditor who has to decide whether or not to disclose an item as material, or to classify an event as extraordinary, there is little in this research to offer much help. While the studies have demonstrated the importance of an accounting income number, we would not know how to choose a single accounting income number to best summarize the operations of a firm. We really have no idea how the market reacts differentially to extraordinary items, income before or after taxes, primary or fully diluted earnings, operating income or net income available for common shareholders. At this stage, we must fall back on our feelings about efficient market processing of available information to suggest more disclosure rather than less and to recommend against a heavy expenditure of resources in argument about the form of presentation or the production of a single "best" number.

4. Information Content of Interim Earnings Reports and Corporate Forecasts

The previous section documented the importance of the annual-earnings number in the process of setting equilibrium prices by investors. As pointed out in the Ball and Brown study, investors do not wait until the annual-earnings number is released to revise their expectations about the magnitude of this number. A continuing series of adjustments are made throughout the year as investors receive new information about the firm's prospects. Among the potential sources of new information for revising expectations are interim reports issued by management and the announcement, by management, of forecasts of annual earnings. At present, auditors are not responsible for either of these informational items, but there are rumblings that auditors should bear some responsibility for the process that generates the figures in these announcements.

In this section I will review the evidence on the information content of these interim reports to see whether the reports do contain information relevant to investors. A failure to find information content in such reports could be due either to the fact that they are irrelevant or that they are potentially relevant but are not taken seriously by investors because of the lack of an auditor's opinion associated with their release. Alternatively, if the reports are found to have information content, then we may conclude that it is reasonable to have companies continue to issue them, and the case for additional and costly intervention by outside auditors is made more difficult.

One of the earliest empirical studies on the value of quarterly reports was performed by Green and Segall (1967). Their objective was to make an accurate prediction of annual EPS. They wanted to see whether having the actual first quarter EPS figure for a year would enable them to make a better prediction of annual EPS than if they did not have this figure. Presumably, if the first quarter actual EPS could not be used to make a better prediction of annual EPS, it was not a worthwhile piece of information to have.

Green and Segall developed three forecasting models using annual data alone and three models which incorporated quarterly data for forecasting annual EPS. Overall they could not distinguish between the accuracy of the annual models and the quarterly models, which led them to conclude that "first quarter reports are of little help in forecasting annual EPS." This is a surprising result since, on average, knowing one fourth of a figure should enable one to make a better prediction of that figure. Green and Segall suggest that this negative finding may be caused by the arbitrary allocations of annual expenses to four quarters of operations which give an unrealistic picture of operations in any given quarter.

Green and Segall (1966) replicated their study using a larger set of firms, one more quarterly model, and a different year for estimating the annual EPS. (Just how a replication of a 1967 study could appear in 1966 is one of the more intriguing aspects of publishing in academic journals.) They obtained the same general conclusions as in their first study about the difficulty of using the first quarter of actual earnings to make a better prediction of annual earnings.

Brown and Niederhoffer (1968) performed an extended replication of the Green and Segall study with a large number (519) of firms, four annual models, and eight quarterly models. They concluded that the predictors using interim information, as a group, did better than the annual predictors and that the best interim model predicted better than the best annual model. Moreover, as each additional quarterly report is received, the interim predictors' margin of superiority increased.

Green and Segall (1968) disputed the Brown and Niederhoffer conclusions, pointing out, among other things, that the worst interim predictor did more poorly than the worst annual predictor. The dialogue continued for another round (see Niederhoffer [1970] and Green and Segall [1970]) without agreement between the two groups. A dispassionate observation (I hope) on the evidence is that it has proved surprisingly difficult to develop simple forecasting rules, using quarterly data, which can be applied uniformly to all firms to make annual predictions of annual EPS which are markedly better than the predictions made solely on the basis of previous annual data. This is not to say that quarterly numbers are not without information content; just that we have been unable to devise mechanical rules that estimate annual income reasonably well.

Another approach to this problem, using the ideas of market efficiency, was taken by Brown and Kennelly (1972). Rather than take as the ultimate objective of interim reports the prediction of annual EPS, they applied the market test to see whether quarterly earnings were in the information set used by investors. Basically they used the Ball and Brown methodology, which was based on annual data, to see if advance knowledge of quarterly earnings would enable investors to earn higher profits (i.e., than from just knowing the annual EPS in advance). They claimed that "if the disaggregation of annual EPS into quarterly EPS adds information, it should reduce errors in classification for shorter periods."

They found that trading models based on advance knowledge of quarterly earnings outperformed models which used advance knowledge of annual earnings only (transactions costs being ignored). Also, the response of the market to the audited annual earnings reports was lower than the response to the unaudited interim reports. While there may be a variety of explanations for this phenomenon, it is at least consistent with investors responding strongly to interim reports even without the auditors' seal of approval. Brown and Kennelly concluded: (1) the information contained in quarterly EPS reports is useful for predicting aggregate abnormal rates of return of associated securities, and (2) disaggregating the annual EPS into its quarterly components improves the predictive ability (in terms of stock prices) by 30–40%.

Beaver (1974a) replicated the Brown and Kennelly study but formed portfolios on the basis of the magnitude of the quarterly forecast errors as well as just the sign. He too found that using quarterly data, in the weighted portfolios, produced abnormal returns superior to those obtained when annual data alone were used.

Just as Brown and Kennelly (1972) can be viewed as an extension of the Ball and Brown (1968) analysis to quarterly data, May (1971) extended Beaver's (1968) methodology for assessing the information content of the annual earnings report to quarterly reports. May found that the magnitude of price-change responses in weeks of interim and annual earnings announcements was greater than the average price change for non-announcement weeks. Also, the relative price-change response to quarterly earnings, while generally less than the response to annual earnings, was not significantly less. This was consistent with the Brown and Kennelly finding of the relevance of quarterly earnings to investor decisions. May was concerned that the comparable responses to unaudited quarterly earnings announcements and to audited annual reports suggest that "investors may be unaware of or unable to take account of the difference in quality (reliability) of quarterly and annual accounting data." An alternative explanation, which assumes the market is fully aware of the unaudited nature of interim reports, raises the question of the value of auditing annual data, at least as measured by the ability to change investor expectations.

Kiger (1972) also observed generally significant price changes as well as volume changes when interim reports are released. His methodology was somewhat different from that used in the other studies, and he investigated New York Stock Exchange firms, whereas May looked only at firms listed on the American Stock Exchange. Nevertheless his findings were consistent with the previously cited studies.

Additional evidence on the reliability of interim reports was provided by Stickney (1975). He investigated firms which were making their initial public offering more than two or three months past the close of the fiscal year and hence had to present interim data. Clearly, if there is an opportunity to inflate an interim earnings report, such companies would have the motivation to do so to improve the terms of the stock issue. Nevertheless, he found that forecasting models using these interim earnings report outperformed predictors based solely on annual data, and he could find no evidence of manipulation of these interim reports.

Patell (1976) has provided evidence for the information content of forecasts voluntarily made by company officials of annual EPS. He found a statistically significant upward price change during the week of forecast disclosure. This occurred, on average, even for firms for which the forecast was below what would have been expected based on the past earnings history of the firm. This suggests that there is some self-selection among the set of firms that voluntarily issue forecasts; even firms disclosing bad news may be trying to preclude more drastic downward revisions which the market might be making about their prospects. In general, however, forecasts which exceeded estimates of market expectations were preceded by positive price adjustments. Patell also found that the voluntarily issued forecasts were better predictors of year-end earnings than the mechanical rules on annual data used by Ball-Brown and Brown-Kennelly even though the differences were surprisingly small, especially since the forecasts were issued after part of the year had already passed. The fact that these rules performed almost as well as management's own estimates provides additional support for the value of these models in developing surrogates for market expectations of earnings.

Interestingly, the largest errors in management forecasts were associated with firms with the highest risks, as measured by β. This suggests that a significant amount of uncertainty in the accuracy of forecasts is caused by the inability of management to forecast general economic conditions for the coming year. It is therefore most difficult to forecast earnings for those firms whose operations are most strongly correlated with economy wide forces (i.e., high beta firms).

To summarize the results in this section, interim earnings reports and company forecasts provide useful information to investors. Significant price reactions are associated with the release of these reports and advance knowledge of the information contained in these reports provides the basis of profitable trading strategies for investors. While the prediction of the next annual EPS may not be the most important objective of quarterly reports, it is interesting that it has been difficult to develop models using quarterly data which are substantially more accurate than models based on annual data alone. There is no evidence, on the other hand, that investors respond less strongly to quarterly reports than to annual reports, even though quarterly reports are unaudited. The conclusions one draws from this finding differ depending upon the strength of one's prior belief there should or should not be a differential reaction to an unaudited report.

5. Time Series Behavior of Earnings

Studies described in the previous sections have indicated that changes in earnings are associated with changes in stock prices. A variety of theoretical models exist in which the value of the firm is a function of the future earnings of the firm. One question that arises, then, is how can the past earnings history be used to make a prediction about future earnings and hence explain or predict stock price reactions to unexpected earnings changes. We are all familiar with, and presumably chastised by, the growth-stock cult in which a subset of firms was identified which were supposed to be able to maintain a superior rate of earnings growth over long periods of time. Many simple valuation models also use past earnings growth as an important variable for explaining price-earning ratios.

To illustrate the issues here let us consider three hypothetical firms. Firm A's EPS for the past four years has been $1, $2, $3, and $4 respectively. Firm B's EPS has been $4, $4, $4, and $4, while firm C's EPS has been $7, $6, $5, and $4. Suppose now we are asked to predict next year's earnings for these three firms using, as evidence, only these past four years of earnings history. In order to make this prediction, it would be useful to know something about the process which generates successive earnings changes. Two extreme cases have been considered. One is the stationary process, which implies that earnings are a random variable whose expectation is either constant over time or a deterministic function of time. With a stationary process, unusually favorable earnings in a year will tend to be followed by unfavorable earnings as the earnings "revert" to their historic level (or trend line). With a stationary process, successive earnings changes are *negatively* correlated, and the most recent earnings level is not helpful in explaining the future level of earnings. If one believed that earnings followed a stationary process with no trend, one would estimate that, for next year, firm C would have higher earnings than firm B which, in turn, would have higher earnings than firm A.

An alternative process to describe the time-series properties of earnings is the martingale process. A martingale is a generalization of the now famous random walk process in which past earnings and trends are not important in predicting future earnings. With a martingale, successive earnings changes are independent over time (zero correlation instead of negative correlation as with a mean-reverting process) so that the expected value of next period's earnings would be no different from the realized value of last period's earnings. With a pure martingale process generating earnings, one would predict that next year's earnings would be $4 for firm A, B, and C; i.e., only the most recent earnings are relevant, not how the firms happened to reach that level.

If earnings are expected to follow a drift (usually positive) over time, we could be dealing with a submartingale process in which earnings other than the most recent are still irrelevant but the expected value of next year's earnings is now allowed to be greater than the most recent year's (rather than precisely equal to it).

There are a variety of other reasons for attempting to understand the time-series properties of earnings. In the previous two sections a number of researchers needed to construct a surrogate for market expectations of earnings so that realized earnings could be evaluated as being favorable or unfavorable in comparison with those expectations. The particular time-series models one will use to generate market expectations will be strongly influenced by the evidence on the distribution of successive earnings changes as described above. Also, I have described the difficulties that past researchers have had in developing predictors, using interim data, which could substantially improve upon forecasting models using annual data alone. The models that were being tested by these researchers were generated on an ad hoc basis and may be improved as we learn more about the underlying structure of the earnings process.

The evidence will also be useful in understanding the value of smoothing accounting income figures. The accounting literature is filled with articles documenting the attempts of company officials to smooth their income series. The value of trying to smooth this series depends upon the process generating earnings. Smoothing has its basis in the idea that increases and decreases in income are temporary fluctuations about a long-term trend line. Rather than allow these fluctuations to occur, companies would prefer to show a smoother rate of growth, and hence, attempt to lower income in good periods and pick up income (where possible according to GAAP of course) in bad periods. Such behavior is consistent with a feeling that earnings do follow a mean-reverting process. For if one believes that earnings follow a martingale process, one would expect an unusually good earnings report to be followed by earnings distributed randomly about this most recent level and to be unrelated to previous earnings levels. In such a situation, it makes little sense for company management to attempt to smooth their earnings. In fact, Ball and Watts (1972) claim that attempting to smooth a random walk or martingale process could lead to more variability in the earnings series rather than less.

Finally, the underlying process is important for valuing the firm when a new earnings number becomes public. With a martingale process, unexpected increases or decreases in earnings will likely be followed by subsequent earnings about this new level. Consequently, the expectation of all future incomes is changed by each earnings realization and there should be a significant price adjustment to unexpected changes. With a mean-reverting process, however, unexpected changes will likely be followed by changes in the opposite direction in future years so that the effect of one year of unexpected good or bad earnings is much smaller.

Lintner and Glauber (1967) examined whether growth rates in a variety of income measures and in sales persisted over time. They divided the postwar period into four five-year periods and computed the correlation of growth rates for a large number of U.S. companies over these four time periods. They found that the degree of dependence between successive growth rates in the income and sales numbers was extremely small. The evidence suggested, though Lintner and Glauber were reluctant to conclude, that growth rates could almost be assumed to be independent in successive time periods.

Brealey (1969) correlated the change in earnings in successive years for 700 companies over a fourteen-year period. If earnings changes were expected to persist (positive changes followed by more positive changes; e.g., we've found a "growth" stock), then there should be positive correlation between successive changes. If earnings followed a mean-reverting process (which might lead company accountants to smooth out fluctuations), then there should be negative correlations in successive changes. In fact, Brealey found that the correlations were extremely small, suggesting a martingale process in which successive earnings charges are statistically independent. Brealey concluded that simple extrapolation of earnings changes (such as assuming next year's earnings to be $5 for firm A, $4 for firm B, and $3 for firm C) is "likely to prove valueless or almost so . . . and may distract attention from relevant information."

Ball and Watts (1972) performed extensive statistical analysis on 451 firms using four definitions of income (net income after taxes excluding extraordinary items, adjusted EPS, net income/total assets, and net sales) during the 1947–66 time period. They found that changes in both net income and EPS are independently distributed, suggesting a martingale process. Since earnings, on average, increased over this 20-year period, they concluded that the earnings process was best described by a sub-martingale. Ball and Watts emphasize that their results are based on averages (means and medians), which still allows some specific firms to be outliers.

Beaver (1970) also examined the time-series properties of earnings but concentrated more on the accounting rate-of-return series than the undeflated earnings series. He found that the accounting rate of return is a mean-reverting process but the reversion (from unexpected increases or decreases) occurs over some period of time in excess of a year. He attributes this to the smoothing process induced by accounting conventions such as historical cost depreciation. Beaver describes the rate of return through the years as a moving-average mean-reverting (MAMR) process. The undeflated net income series was consistent with a martingale process.

In a subsequent paper, Beaver (1974) argues that the mean-reverting process for accounting earnings is a "straw man" that no one really takes seriously. He maintains that a moving-average mean-reverting process is also consistent with good predictors that place a large weight on the most recent observation. He also claims it is important to distinguish between earnings changes due to profitability (i.e., an increase in the rate of return earned on one's assets) and earnings changes caused by an expansion of the investment base but with underlying profitability remaining the same. For example, it would be reasonable to assume that a firm's investment base follows a martingale process which may induce a martingale process on the income earned from this base. I might add that it would be useful to deduct that component of earnings changes which is due to price-level effects and which exerts an upward bias on any earnings series examined in the post World War II period. The MAMR process proposed by Beaver assumes that each year's unexpected earnings consists of a transitory factor (as in the pure mean-reversion process) and a nontransitory factor (as in a martingale) whose effects will persist for a finite number of periods into the future.

Recent evidence by Griffin (1977) and Watts (1975) suggests that quarterly earnings may be characterized as a moving-average process in first differences. Such a process could be manipulated in a quarterly basis by management's smoothing operations.

While the evidence is still inconclusive between a martingale process and a moving-average mean-reverting one, some tentative conclusions can be drawn. Little evidence can be found to support the practice of extrapolating past growth rates of earnings into the future. It has also been difficult to find evidence of an annual-earnings process which would be amenable to smoothing by management. One possibility, which does not seem to be widely advocated in traditional financial analysis, is to use estimates of the accounting beta for a firm (the correlation of a firm's earnings changes with economy-wide earnings changes) to estimate the change in income for a firm in the current year. In addition to the Ball and Brown (1968) and Brown and Kennelly (1972) papers, which used this as one of the models to generate an estimate of the market's expectation of earnings, Brown and Ball (1967) have documented the strong cross-sectional dependence of a firm's earnings on a market-wide-earnings index and an industry-earnings index. Thus if analysts could generate reasonable estimates of these economy and industry-wide earnings levels, they might be able to get a better prediction of a firm's change in earnings than would be possible by simply attempting to exploit the time-series properties of past earnings numbers for the firm. For the auditor, such a model would be easy to implement at the time of an audit since there should be reasonable estimates of these earnings levels by the end of a year. Such an estimate may prove useful as part of the analytic review to see whether management's presentation of income is consistent with the historical relationship.

Another study of the time-series properties of earnings was performed by Dopuch and Watts (1972). Rather than restricting the earnings process to, say, one of two arbitrary processes (martingale or mean-reverting), they allowed the data to pick out a process from a very large class of linear-autoregressive-integrated-moving-average processes, sometimes known as Box-Jenkins analysis after the principal proponents of this collection of models. Having selected the particular process which seems to best fit the historical time-series data for each firm, Dopuch and Watts attempted to see whether a switch in accounting policy would cause the time-series earnings process to change. If it did, this was construed as a material or significant change in the firm's earnings process. If an accounting change did not change the time-series process, the change could be viewed as immaterial. Testing this methodology on the net income series of eleven steel firms which switched from accelerated to straight-line depreciation, they found a significant difference in eight of these firms (only one, though, had a significant change in the series describing accounting rates of return). Two problems arise with this technique. First, Box-Jenkins analysis requires an enormous amount of time-series data to select the underlying process which presumably is remaining stationary during this time. Second, at the time an accounting change is made there is no evidence of what the future series which could enable one to determine if a different time-series model is operating will look like. It does not seem helpful to recommend that auditors should wait fifteen years to gather enough data to decide whether a change made fifteen years earlier was, in fact, material.

6. Empirical Evaluations of Accounting Alternatives

The existence of alternative accounting methods for reporting the same set of underlying economic effects has occupied the attention of many academic accountants, practitioners, and occasionally even the U.S. Congress. Academic accountants have written an almost uncountable number of papers on the merits and demerits of proposals accounting for cost of goods sold, depreciation, the investment credit, mergers, interperiod tax allocation, intangible drilling expenses, and leases, among others. Practitioners have not only been involved in the above debates in the journals and in policy groups, but also have had to deal with clients who, having found it difficult to generate profits in the factory, have tried to produce profits in the controller's office. Many firms have refused to adopt LIFO because of fears of what impact the drop in reported earnings would have on their stock-price performance. (One of the few good outcomes of the recent U.S. inflation has been a considerable decrease in the number of firms willing to pay heavy indemnities to the government because of such vague and, in my opinion, misguided fears.)

If one believes in an efficient market that correctly processes all available information about a firm, then one is not likely to believe that a fully disclosed change in accounting policy, which does not affect any cash flows, is likely to have much of an impact on a firm's stock price. Even further, if a firm's market price is found to be affected by earnings changes caused by accounting method changes, we might have serious evidence in conflict with the efficiency of the market. A number of studies have investigated whether a change in a firm's accounting policy which tends to increase reported earnings can be associated with abnormal increases in the stock price of the firm.

At a very simple level, tests have been made as to whether the price-earnings ratios of conservatively reporting firms (e.g., using tax allocation before APB 11, or accelerated depreciation) differed from comparable firms that used liberal reporting policies (e.g., flow-through, and straight-line depreciation). If the market is clever about detecting such reporting differences, the P/E ratio of conservative firms should exceed that of liberal firms since the former are using procedures which will, on the same set of economic events, report lower earnings than will the latter group. Since the prices of the two groups of companies should be unaffected by differences in reporting policies, the P/E ratios of the two groups would have to differ. Unfortunately, there are a number of problems associated with building defensible models of P/E ratios (see Gonedes-Dopuch [1974], Section 8) so that one is reluctant to draw definitive conclusions from such studies. Nevertheless, the studies generally found that there were differences in the P/E ratios, of the expected sign, between liberal and conservative firms.

A number of studies have now been performed which examine the stock-price reaction around the announcement of annual earnings for the year in which a company switched a particular accounting policy. The period immediately after date of announcement was selected because the difference in annual earnings from one year to the next would seem to be largest for the first year in which the new accounting policy was in effect. Thus, if the market was to be fooled by a reported earnings increase caused by an accounting change, the maximum impact would likely occur for the first year of the change when the earnings comparison with the prior year would be most dramatic.

Kaplan and Roll (1972) examined two sets of companies; one set switched to the flow-through method (from deferral) for the investment credit, the other set switched from accelerated depreciation to straight line. While a small (and still unexplained) positive effect was noticed around the time of the earnings announcement, this effect was temporary and there were no permanent increases in price caused by adopting either of these more liberal accounting policies. In fact, firms which switched depreciation methods seemed to do worse than the market, implying that such changes were undertaken when the firm was anticipating hard times.

Ball (1972) examined a large number of accounting changes of many different types. He found that shareholders of firms which tend to make such changes have generally received lower than normal returns prior to the year in which the switch was made. The year of the accounting change itself did not exhibit any unusual stock price behavior. He concluded that changes in accounting technique were not associated with market-price adjustments.

Sunder (1973) examined the stock price performance of firms that switched from FIFO to LIFO and from LIFO to FIFO. This is an interesting test since firms switching from FIFO to LIFO will report lower earnings at the same time that their economic earnings have improved because of a lower tax bill. Conversely, firms switching from LIFO to FIFO will report higher earnings, which they hope the market will respond to and thereby overcome the negative impact of their much higher tax bill (e.g., more than $50 million for Chrysler in 1970). The evidence indicated that firms switching to LIFO did not encounter any negative price reactions in the stock market. In fact, the average price of these stocks rose 5% more than would be expected, given general market movements, during the year in which the accounting change was made. The sample of firms that switched from LIFO to FIFO was too small to yield definitive conclusions, but there was a tendency for the stock prices of these companies to decline after this accounting change, which increased nominal earnings. A subsequent paper, which controlled for changes in the riskiness of these firms (Sunder [1975]), indicated no effect for the LIFO to FIFO switchers but the positive effect for the FIFO to LIFO firms persisted. Thus switching from LIFO to FIFO seems a particularly expensive and fruitless way to improve one's stock price, and we now have evidence that the market will not penalize and may even reward the share prices of firms that voluntarily report lower earnings and pay lower taxes.

Patz and Boatsman (1972) investigated the price performance of oil exploration companies around the time that the Accounting Principles Board issued a draft statement requiring companies which previously used full-cost accounting to switch to the successful-efforts method. If adopted, the earnings of such companies would be sharply lowered. If the market could not perceive that such an earnings decrease was merely due to an accounting convention and not to any fundamental economic forces, one might expect the share prices of full-cost companies to be adversely affected. Patz and Boatsman found that there was no adverse effect on the share prices of such companies, which is again consistent with predictions made from a premise of market efficiency.

Merger accounting has been a particularly inflammatory topic in accounting and financial circles. Many observers felt that the growth of conglomerates in the 1960s was attributable to their ability to avoid accounting for the excess of costs over book value of acquired companies through use of the pooling-of-interests method. The more stringent conditions imposed by APB 16 and 17 for merger accounting may even have been considered by some to have led to the decline in merger activity since their promulgation. Most of the controversy centers on the amortization of goodwill associated with a purchase price in excess of book value, an expense which has no effect on the cash flows of the firm. It should not be difficult for an intelligent analyst or investor, familiar with the terms of a merger, to compute such an amortization charge himself if he thought that that was the appropriate adjustment to make. Therefore, the pooling vs. purchase controversy is another instance of an argument over an alternative form of presentation which should not matter in an efficient market. Hong, Mandelker, and Kaplan (1978) investigated 159 mergers during the 1954–64 time period; 122 of these used pooling of interests and had positive goodwill associated with the merger, 37 used purchase accounting to amortize positive goodwill. Despite the use of pooling of interests, which some observers feel leads to inflated earnings, there was no tendency for the 122 pooling firms to earn abnormal returns around the merger date. On the contrary, there was a tendency for firms using purchase accounting to have positive excess returns around the time of the merger. This effect is probably not due to the use of purchase accounting, per se, but could be due to a selection mechanism whereby firms which choose purchase accounting may have been doing well and could therefore "afford" the decrease in reported earnings caused by amortizing goodwill. In any case, we have additional evidence that earnings increases caused solely by accounting conventions do not translate into higher stock prices.

The above studies concentrated on stock-price reactions at the time immediately following an earnings change or important event (APB announcement, a merger) took place. The studies found, in general, that no abnormal price movements were caused by an accounting change at that time. Once a company has switched to a more liberal accounting policy though, it will typically report higher earnings year after year than if it had continued to use the more conservative method. If the market somehow lost track of what set of accounting policies a firm was using, a possibility much more likely before the extensive disclosure rules in recent years, it might not realize that differences in earnings between two companies could be due to their using different accounting policies. Jacobs and

Kaplan (1975) compared the stock-price rates of return between two sets of companies from 1962 to 1968; one set used straight-line depreciation and the other used accelerated depreciation for financial reporting. Both sets used accelerated depreciation for tax purposes. They found that there were no significant differences in the rates of return between the two sets of firms even though the accelerated firms, as a group, were reporting lower earnings than they could while still following generally accepted accounting principles.

The evidence is consistent that the market does not respond to earnings increases which are caused by cosmetic changes in accounting policy. There is even evidence which suggests that companies which change accounting policies in an attempt to increase earnings (or reduce losses) are in the midst of, or anticipating, poor operating results. As a consequence, investors may perceive such manipulations as a negative signal by management about the current and future profitability of the firm. Additional anecdotal evidence on this point occurred earlier this year when both Ford and Chrysler suddenly decided that the flow-through method was more appropriate to account for the investment credit. Coincidentally and within one day of each other, the two auto companies switched accounting methods; this changed a $97.9 million loss in the first quarter for Ford into a $10.6 million loss.

Similar beliefs about the incredible naïveté of the market were expressed in a recent *Business Week* (July 28, 1975) article about establishing deferred tax accounts for oil companies now that the depletion allowance has been repealed. Whatever the merits of deferred tax accounting, one should hardly conclude that this type of earnings restatement should have much effect on the market. Yet two top oil company executives were quoted as saying: "This is going to make oil stocks look a lot less attractive because many investors do not look beyond the net income figure." And "It's going to make equity financing almost impossible at the worst possible time." The writer of the article concluded that reducing the retained-earnings figures of these companies (through a retroactive charge) will cause a major increase in debt-equity ratios which would make borrowing more difficult and affect the financial decisions of the firms. Surely, it doesn't take very much "efficiency" in the market to make such statements appear ludicrous. Only if the market and commercial lenders were wildly inefficient could such statements ever begin to attain plausibility. Enough said!

A different approach has been taken by some to evaluate the impact of accounting alternatives on the market. Recall that in the Ball and Brown (1968) and Brown and Kennelly (1972) studies (among others), mechanical models were used to generate surrogates for market expectations of earnings. These surrogates were then compared to actual earnings to form portfolios and assess the profitability of knowing the earnings numbers one year in advance. Beaver and Dukes (1972) investigated whether the profitability of such a strategy could be affected by changing the accounting method used to measure earnings. In particular, they wished to determine whether earnings prepared under the deferral method for tax allocation would yield lower abnormal returns (because the method involved more allocations and was further from actual cash flows) than earnings generated under the flow-through method. It turned out that the deferral earnings seemed to be most consistent with the information in security prices, with flow through (or nondeferral) and cash flow less consistent, respectively. In a subsequent paper, Beaver and Dukes (1973) viewed tax allocation as an issue of accelerated depreciation rather than of determining a deferred tax-liability account. They found that an earnings measure based on a depreciation charge somewhat greater than straight line was most highly associated with stock-price changes.

In a similar study, Dukes (1976) found that capitalizing R & D expenditures is more consistent with security prices than the actual expensing procedures that were used in his sample of companies. Foster (1975) also found that the earnings numbers of insurance companies had a higher association with security prices when unrealized capital gains and other adjustments were included in income than when these items were excluded, as they are in reporting normal or statutory income.

One implication of these latter studies is that the information that the market uses to assess performance of companies is broader than just reported earnings. Items in footnote disclosure such as R & D expenditures or market value of securities appear to be used by investors even though these items may not have been flowed through the income statement. As such, these findings are consistent with the studies reported earlier in this section which found that the market could properly evaluate the effects of alternative accounting techniques and respond to footnote disclosure.

It is not true, however, that these studies can be used to determine the most preferred accounting alternative, i.e., the one whose use leads to the highest association with stock-price changes. Theoretical reasons why stock-price reactions cannot be used to infer the market preferences for an accounting alternative are developed in Gonedes-Dopuch (1974). Preferences for alternative information systems ultimately require an analysis of social-welfare considerations which cannot be decided merely by stock-price associations. On a practical basis, accountants attempting to generate measures that have maximum association with market prices would eventually be driven to define accounting income as the change in market value over the period.

7. Accounting Ratios as Predictors of Business Failure

Of all the material surveyed in this paper, I believe that the research done in predicting bankruptcies has the most immediate relevance to practicing auditors. While it is important that net income not be in error by more than a material amount and that inventories not be valued at above cost or market, auditors get into much of their troubles when they give an unqualified opinion to a firm which shortly thereafter goes bankrupt. Analytic techniques which help an auditor decide when a firm is approaching default or insolvency would seem to offer significant benefits in reducing legal and insurance expenses. A fair number of studies have been performed which indicate that such techniques exist.

Beaver (1966) examined 30 financial ratios of a paired sample of 79 failed and 79 nonfailed firms from 1954–64. The ratios were in six broad categories: cash flow, net income, debt to total asset, liquid asset to total asset, liquid asset to current debt, and turnover. In his first analysis, he compared the mean values of each of the ratios between the failed and nonfailed firms. This profile analysis revealed substantial differences in the mean ratios between the two sets of firms and the mean difference increased as the year of failure approached (financial statements for up to five years before the actual failure event having been examined).

A second analysis was a dichotomous classification test in which each of the ratios was used to see how well it could discriminate between failed and nonfailed firms. The cash flow to total debt ratio had the strongest ability to predict failure, followed closely by net income to total assets. Each of these two ratios correctly classified 87% of the firms based on the last financial statements issued before failure (of the firms that actually failed, of course). The cash-flow to total-debt ratio correctly classified 78% of firms based on financial statements issued five years before failure. These flow ratios were substantially better in predicting bankruptcies than the liquid-asset ratios advocated in much traditional financial analysis.

Altman (1968) extended Beaver's univariate analysis to allow for multiple predictors of failure (Beaver considered the effects of using only one ratio at a time). Altman used multiple discriminant analysis (MDA), which attempts to develop a linear function of a number of explanatory variables to assign a value to a qualitative dependent variable, e.g., bankrupt or nonbankrupt. Since financial ratios are highly intercorrelated, it is difficult to predict which variables work well together in predicting bankruptcy from examining the effects of variables taken one at a time. Altman had a matched sample of 33 bankrupt and 33 nonbankrupt manufacturing corporations (1946–65) with assets between $1–$25 million. Twenty-two financial ratios, based on data one period before bankruptcy, were examined and Altman eventually selected five of these to be included in his final discriminant function:

1. Working capital/Total assets (liquidity),
2. Retained earnings/Total assets (age of firm and cumulative profitability),
3. Earnings before interest and taxes/Total assets (profitability),
4. Market value of equity/Book value of debt (financial structure),
5. Sales/Total assets (capital turnover rate).

Unfortunately, Altman was not able to use a cash-flow variable, which Beaver found to be the most discriminating in his study; apart from other accruals, Altman did not have depreciation figures.

Running split sample techniques, Altman was able to classify correctly more than 90% of the firms. With a new sample of 25 bankrupt firms, Altman's discriminant function correctly predicted 24 of them would go into bankruptcy. With a sample of firms that had negative earnings but which did not go bankrupt, only 14 of 66 were predicted to go into bankruptcy. One additional company which was classified as bankrupt did subsequently go into bankruptcy. For the original sample, but going back three years before bankruptcy, 48% of the firms were correctly predicted —note, however, that this is below the naïve, ex post facto, sample selection prediction that one half of the firms would go bankrupt.

A number of subsequent studies also confirmed the value of the multiple discriminant technique. Blum (1969) examined 115 failed companies (1954–68) with a paired sample of another 115 nonfailed firms and was able to classify correctly more than 90% of these firms based on financial ratios computed within a year of bankruptcy. Edmister (1972) was able to discriminate correctly 39 out of 42 cases of small business failures using multiple discriminant analysis. Edmister found that dividing company ratios by the average ratio for companies in the same industry improved the classificational ability of the test. Deakin (1972) examined 13 ratios for 32 failed and 32 nonfailed firms (1964–70). He replicated Beaver's methodology and again found that the cash-flow to total-debt ratio had the best discriminating ability of any single ratio though his classification results were not as good as Beaver's. He then constructed a discriminant function using all 14 variables with disappointing results—the function was highly nonstationary in each of five years prior to failure and on a new sample of 11 failed and 23 nonfailed firms, eight of these were incorrectly predicted on the basis of financial ratios computed in the year prior to failure. These results were likely caused by Deakin's inclusion of too many highly intercorrelated variables in the discriminant function. Wilcox (1973) tested a bankruptcy model he developed from an underlying probabilistic model (called the gambler's ruin problem). While this simple model at least has some theoretical underpinning, the statistical analysis is too informal to allow us to draw definitive conclusions as to its value.

Altman (1973) developed a discriminant function to predict railroad bankruptcies. In companies selected from many industries, normal variation in financial ratios across industries weaken the discriminating ability of these ratios. The railroad industry is unique in having had enough bankruptcies in recent history to enable a statistical analysis of factors that could predict bankruptcy for this industry by itself. From an initial list of 14 ratios, Altman developed a discriminant function based on 7 ratios. The model was derived from 21 bankruptcies in the 1939–70 period by comparing the ratios for each of the bankrupt railroads with the in- dustry average for the year of bankruptcy. (There are some problems with this methodology which are not worth getting into here.) When the model was applied to the estimating sample, only one bankrupt firm was mis- classified as healthy while every industry observation was correctly clas- sified, not an unsurprising result given the large number of independent variables used and the strong serial correlation of industry averages from year to year.

The model was applied to a randomly selected group of 50 railroads between 1946 and 1969. Six railroads were classified as bankrupt prone, two did go bankrupt, one discontinued all railroad operations, two were merged into larger systems, and one was operated by the Canadian government. None of those classified as nonbankrupt had gone bankrupt by 1970. The model was also tested on 55 large railroads in 1970. Of these, 14 were classified as bankruptcy candidates. Of the 14, six were already in bankruptcy, five had been classified by railroad analysts as being on the brink of failure, and the other three were controlled by larger, more solvent railroads (with a deep pocket, presumably).

In a good summary article for this section, Altman and McGough (1974) describe the relation between the multiple-discriminant analysis prediction of failure and an auditor's qualification or disclaimer as to the going-concern nature of the firm. They used the five-variable discriminant function developed in Altman's 1968 paper. Of 34 companies entering bankruptcy since 1970, 28 of them would have been predicted to be bankruptcy candidates based on multiple-discriminant analysis of their last financial statement. In only 16 of these 34 companies did the auditors indicate going-concern problems in their opinion.

Of a sample of 21 companies which had a going-concern problem expressed in the auditor's opinion, six did subsequently go bankrupt and all six would have been predicted by the MDA model. Seven of these firms have recovered and are no longer receiving a qualified opinion; of these seven, five had MDA scores which would not have predicted bankruptcy. Thus, this study certainly suggests that a multivariate model could be of significant help for auditors attempting to assess the going-concern probability of a firm.

Despite the reasonable success of multiple-discriminant analysis for predicting bankruptcy, I think that much better and more powerful statistical techniques can be used to work on this important problem. MDA is a rather heuristic technique with only limited tests of significance and internal checks on its validity available. Samples have been mostly drawn on a matched-pair basis when there is no logical reason why there have to be as many failed as nonfailed firms in a sample. As a consequence, most tests are made on samples of failed firms. The auditor's task, however, is to assess the validity of the methodology on *all* firms and then see which get misclassified. If only a .5% of all firms fail each year, but the model predicts that each year 10% are bankruptcy candidates, we cannot expect auditors to qualify their opinion on 10% of their clients. More work has to be done to relate levels of ratios to the norms for an industry, as Edmister did. Also the impact of inflation on net income figures and on the desirability of including more debt in the capital structure needs to be included.

As I said in the introduction to this section, I believe this area offers the most potential for research impact on practice. It is therefore disappointing that statistical analyses done to date have been so cursory. Even granting the limitations of MDA, it might still be interesting for auditors to apply Altman's discriminant function to their clients' numbers this year to seen how many of their clients they should start to worry about. At the very least, such a test could be the first step in an analytic review. Failure to pass this test might lead to more stringent testing of the marketability of inventory and the collectibility of receivables.

8. Summary

How do we evaluate the impressive number of empirical studies of the information content of accounting messages? I am very positive and enthusiastic about the contribution of empirical research over the last ten years. Nevertheless, I view the future possibilities for empirical accounting research with much less optimism. While I reserve the right to change my mind in the light of new research, I now think that we are unlikely to maintain the momentum of empirical research into the next ten years. But first, let us start with the good news.

The studies in Section 3 demonstrate that accounting numbers do have information content. The stock market responds to the release of these numbers and stock-price revisions are associated with unexpected changes in earnings. Moreover, the income number produced by accounting procedures appears to be more closely associated with the underlying economic operations of the firm than are cash-flow variables. Interim reports including quarterly announcements and corporate forecasts of earnings are also viewed as timely information sources and are used by the market in forming expectations about the future prospects of the firm. This occurs despite the unaudited nature of these reports.

We have gained much knowledge about the time-series behavior of earnings. In particular, the idea of growth stocks which can maintain a steady percentage growth of earnings, over a period of several years, has been shown to be the exception rather than the rule. Simple models in which next year's earnings equal this year's appear to forecast better than extrapolation of past growth trends into the future.

A number of studies have shown that the market is able to evaluate properly the increase in earnings caused by fully disclosed changes in accounting policy. Such changes and accompanying earnings increases are fully discounted by the market so that there is no apparent benefit from this earnings manipulation. If anything, earnings increases manufactured in the controller's office may be viewed by the market as a negative signal about the firm's future prospects for sustaining earnings from continuing operations.

The concept of an efficient market which processes all available information in an unbiased and timely manner has important implications for accounting policy-makers. For one thing, it implies that many debates about selection among various forms of accounting procedure may not be worth the resources currently devoted to them. Typically, disclosure of the particular procedure used by the firm, along with enough supplementary data to enable the computation of income and balance sheet effects under alternative procedures, is a relatively costless course of action. In many cases, enough information already exists in footnote disclosure to permit alternative income and valuation computations.

An efficient market also implies that we should not be greatly concerned about whether readers can understand more complex and complete disclosure. Worries about the naïve investor seem misplaced since, to an excellent approximation, such investors face a fair game in which stocks are correctly priced according to risk-return relationships. As long as such investors hold diversified portfolios and avoid incurring heavy transactions costs by excessive trading, they can expect about the same return, for their level of risk, as more sophisticated investors. Accountants need not feel either paternalistic or responsible for investors who hold improperly diversified portfolios or who trade constantly on every piece of information that emerges in the marketplace.

An efficient market also gives some guidance on a limited set of accounting policies such as marketable securities. Once one accepts the idea that the market is rational and that prices respond to all available information, then there can be little justification for valuing securities at other than market value. Current policy, in which securities are written down to market value (below cost) only when the decline is expected to be permanent, implies that the accountant has greater knowledge and insight than all the participants in the market. If the accountant could know which price declines were only temporary, he would be silly to be spending his time verifying receivables and signing opinions. Much more profitable opportunities would await him. Again, as long as the market value of securities is disclosed somewhere in the financial statements this is not a crucial issue, but it provides an example of how research can occasionally give a clear preference for an accounting procedure. More extensive policy implications that follow from the idea of market efficiency, and the empirical evidence in support of this idea, are presented in Beaver (1973), and the reader is referred to this highly readable source.

What then are my reservations about the future value of empirical research in accounting? I think that we have now gotten all the easy results and that major new findings are going to be much harder to obtain. In effect, we have taken an extremely important advance in finance, tested it successfully on a variety of accounting data, and drawn some straightforward conclusions from this research. Current research is involved with cleaning up some of the past studies by controlling for or testing a number of factors that were not included in the original research. Future work may extend our testing procedures from NYSE firms to OTC firms which may be more representative of most of the clients of CPA firms. At best, though, these studies will confirm the findings of the earlier studies by showing that the results follow even under more careful testing or using a more sophisticated methodology, and the conclusions from such studies will therefore be consistent with our current beliefs.

I am more pessimistic about the ability of empirical research to give us many insights into many varied and important questions now confronting the accounting profession. While it is typical, when confronted with a difficult policy issue, to call for more research on the question, it is not clear to me how empirical research in particular can provide much guidance in current debates over issues which involve costly disclosure. An example of such an issue is how or whether to adjust financial statements for the effects of inflation or changes in the price level of specific assets. As another example, should quarterly statements or earnings forecasts be audited? Both issues potentially involve having more information disclosed but with some cost associated with such disclosure. (While general price level accounting may be the least costly of the above possibilities, many critics, myself excluded, argue that the benefits are commensurate with or even below these low costs.) At present, empirical research cannot offer much help for policy-makers trying to decide whether to implement any of the above proposals. The situation is even worse than this, though. Let us assume that a new form of costly disclosure is selected. Present methodology does not allow us to look at the subsequent price and return series to make a judgment as to whether there has been an improvement in resource allocation or any form of social welfare to warrant the costs of increased disclosure. I find this a particularly frustrating state of affairs.

I should mention one particularly ambitious and clever attempt at such a policy evaluation. Benston (1973) tried to determine whether there were any measurable benefits from the Securities Exchange Act of 1934 which established more costly disclosure requirements. Benston could not find any empirical measure of market performance that improved in the post-SEC area. Unfortunately, many other factors could have led to this finding besides the ineffectiveness of the SEC (see Gonedes-Dopuch [1974], Section 8), so that we are unable to conclude from this study alone that the SEC has had no positive impact on the functioning of securities markets.

Therefore, I am unable to conclude this survey of ten years of empirical research in accounting with an optimistic forecast of what the next ten years of such research will yield. On particular issues, the evidence from empirical research may be used to provide support for a particular alternative. I have already mentioned the marketable securities question. Another possibility for future research is to incorporate the recent advances in the pricing of options and convertible securities so as to improve drastically the current arbitrary and irrational features of computing earnings-per-share in APB 15. The research cannot be used to justify the computation and disclosure of a figure such as fully diluted earnings per share, but since policy-makers have decided that such a figure should be computed, research can be used to derive a figure that has some basis in economic theory and evidence. A third area where empirical research may prove useful is on materiality in financial reports. By observing market responses to unexpected changes in financial statements, we might be able to determine the sensitivity of the market to small differences in reported income. Thus, on particular issues, empirical research may provide a significant amount of guidance. We should not expect, however, that such research will resolve many of the fundamental disclosure and reporting issues addressed by the FASB and the SEC.

References

Altman, Edward. "Financial Ratios, Discriminant Analysis, and the Prediction of Corporate Bankruptcy." *Journal of Finance* (September 1968): 589–609.

———. "Predicting Railroad Bankruptcies in America." *Bell Journal of Economics and Management Science* (Spring 1973): 184–211.

———, and Thomas McGough. "Evaluation of a Company as a Going Concern." *Journal of Accountancy* (December 1974): 50–57.

Ball, Ray. "Changes in Accounting Techniques and Stock Prices." *Empirical Research in Accounting: 1972,* Supplement to *Journal of Accounting Research,* vol. 10, pp. 1–38.

———, and Philip Brown. "An Empirical Evaluation of Accounting Income Numbers." *Journal of Accounting Research* (Autumn 1968): 159–78.

———, and Ross Watts. "Some Time Series Properties of Accounting Income." *Journal of Finance* (June 1972): 663–81.

Beaver, William. "Financial Ratios as Predictors of Failure." *Empirical Research in Accounting: 1966,* Supplement to *Journal of Accounting Research,* vol. 4, pp. 71–111.

———. "The Information Content of Annual Earnings Announcements." *Empirical Research in Accounting: 1968,* Supplement to *Journal of Accounting Research,* vol. 6, pp. 87–92.

———. "The Time Series Behavior of Earnings." *Empirical Research in Accounting: 1970,* Supplement to *Journal of Accounting Research,* vol. 8, pp. 62–99.

———. "The Behavior of Security Prices and Its Implications for Accounting Research (Methods)." *Committee Reports,* Supplement to *Accounting Review,* vol. 47 (1972), pp. 407–37.

———. "What Should Be the FASB's Objectives?" *Journal of Accountancy* (August 1973): 49–56.

———. "The Information Content of the Magnitude of Unexpected Earnings." Stanford University Working Paper, presented to 1974 Stanford Research Seminar (1974a).

———. "The Evolution of Security Price Research in Accounting." Stanford University Working Paper, presented to 1974 American Accounting Association Doctoral Consortium (1974b).

———. "Financial Statements: Issues of Preparation and Interpretation." Stanford University Working Paper presented to 1975 Stanford Research Seminar (1975).

———, and R. E. Dukes. "Interperiod Tax Allocation, Earnings Expectations, and the Behavior of Security Prices." *Accounting Review* (April 1972): 320–32.

———, and R. E. Dukes. "Delta-Depreciation Methods: Some Empirical Results." *Accounting Review* (July 1973): 549–59.

———, Paul Kettler, and Myron Scholes. "The Association Between Market

Determined and Accounting Determined Risk Measures." *Accounting Review* (October 1970): 654–82.

————, and James Manegold, "The Association Between Market-Determined and Accounting-Determined Measures of Systematic Risk." *Journal of Financial and Quantitative Analysis* (June 1975): 231–84.

Benston, George. "Published Corporate Accounting Data and Stock Prices." *Empirical Research in Accounting: 1967,* Supplement to *Journal of Accounting Research* vol. 5, pp. 1–14, 22–54.

————. "Required Disclosure and the Stock Market: An Evaluation of the Securities Exchange Act of 1934." *American Economic Review* (March 1973): 132–55.

Black, Fischer. "Yes, Virginia, There is Hope: Tests of the Value Line Ranking System." *Financial Analysts Journal* (September–October 1973): 10–14.

Blum, Mark P. "The Failing Company Doctrine." Unpublished Ph.D. dissertation, Columbia University, 1969.

Blume, Marshall. "Betas and Their Regression Tendencies." *Journal of Finance* (June 1975): 785–95.

Boulding, Kenneth. "Economics and Accounting: The Uncongenial Twins." In W. Baxter, and S. Davidson, eds., *Studies in Modern Accounting Theory.* Homewood, Ill.: Irwin, 1962, pp. 44–55.

Brealey, Richard A. *An Introduction to Risk and Return from Common Stocks.* Cambridge: M.I.T. Press, 1969.

————. *Security Prices in a Competitive Market.* Cambridge: M.I.T. Press, 1971.

Brown, Philip, and Ray Ball. "Some Preliminary Findings on the Association between the Earnings of a Firm, Its Industry, and the Economy." *Empirical Research in Accounting: 1967,* Supplement to *Journal of Accounting Research,* vol. 5, pp. 55–77.

————, and John Kennelly. "The Information Content of Quarterly Earnings: An Extension and Some Further Evidence." *Journal of Business* (July 1972): 403–15.

————, and Victor Niederhoffer. "The Predictive Content of Quarterly Earnings." *Journal of Business* (October 1968): 488–97.

Collins, Daniel W. "SEC Product-Line Reporting and Market Efficiency." *Journal of Financial Economics* (June 1975): 125–64.

Deakin, Edward. "A Discriminant Analysis of Business Failure." *Journal of Accounting Research* (Spring 1972): 167–79.

Dopuch, Nicholas, and Ross Watts. "Using Time-Series Models to Assess the Significance of Accounting Changes." *Journal of Accounting Research* (Spring 1972): 180–94.

Downes, David, and Thomas Dyckman. "A Critical Look at the Efficient Market Empirical Research Literature as It Relates to Accounting Information." *Accounting Review* (April 1973): 300–17.

Dukes, R. E. "An Investigation of the Effects of Expensing Research and Development Costs on Security Prices," proceedings of the conference on Topical Research in Accounting, 1975. New York University, 1976: 147–93.

Dyckman, Thomas, David Downes, and Robert Magee. *Efficient Capital Markets and Accounting: A Critical Analysis.* Englewood Cliffs, N.J.: Prentice-Hall, 1975.

Edmister, R. O. "An Empirical Test of Financial Ratio Analysis for Small Business Failure Prediction." *Journal of Financial and Quantitative Analysis* (March 1972): 1477–93.

Fama, Eugene F. "Efficient Capital Markets: A Review of Theory and Empirical Work." *Journal of Finance* (May 1970): 383–417.

Foster, George. "Accounting Earnings and Stock Prices of Insurance Companies." *Accounting Review* (October 1975): 686–89.

Gonedes, Nicholas. "Evidence on the Information Content of Accounting Messages: Accounting-Based and Market-Based Estimates of Systematic Risk." *Journal of Financial and Quantitative Analysis* (July 1973): 407–44.

————. "A Note on Accounting-Based and Market-Based Estimates of Systematic Risk." *Journal of Financial and Quantitative Analysis* (June 1975): 355–65.

————. "Capital Market Equilibrium and Annual Accounting Numbers: Empirical Evidence." *Journal of Accounting Research* (Spring 1974): 26–62.

————, and Nicholas Dopuch. "Capital Market Equilibrium, Information Production, and Selecting Accounting Techniques: Theoretical Framework and Review of Empirical Work." *Studies on Financial Accounting Objectives: 1974,* Supplement to *Journal of Accounting Research,* vol. 12, pp. 48–129.

Green, David, and Joel Segall. "The Predictive Content of Quarterly Earnings: A Replication," *Empirical Research in Accounting: 1966,* Supplement to *Journal of Accounting Research,* vol. 4, pp. 21–36.

————. "The Predictive Content of Quarterly Earnings." *Journal of Business* (January 1967): 44–55.

————. "Brickbats and Straw Men: A Reply to Brown and Niederhoffer," *Journal of Business* (October 1968): 498–502; "Return of Strawman," *Journal of Business* (January 1970): 63–65.

Griffin, Paul. "The Time Series Behavior of Quarterly Earnings: Preliminary Evidence." *Journal of Accounting Research* (Spring 1977): 71–83.

Hakansson, Nils. "Empirical Research in Accounting, 1960–70: An Appraisal." In N. Dopuch, and L. Revsine, eds., *Accounting Research, 1960–1970: A Critical Evaluation.* Urbana: Center for International Education and Research in Accounting, Univ. of Illinois, 1973, pp. 137–73.

Hong, Hai, Gershon Mandelker, and Robert Kaplan. "Pooling vs. Purchase: The Effects of Accounting for Mergers on Stock Prices." *Accounting Review* (January 1978): 31–47.

Jacobs, Bruce, and Robert Kaplan. "Accounting Alternatives and the Steady State Rates of Return of Stock Prices." GSIA Working Paper #54–74–75, Carnegie-Mellon University, presented to 1975 Stanford Research Seminar (1975).

Jaffe, Jeffrey, F. "Special Information and Insider Trading." *Journal of Business* (July 1974): 410–28.

Jensen, Michael. "Capital Markets: Theory and Evidence." *Bell Journal of Economics and Management Science* (Autumn 1972): 357–98.

Kaplan, Robert, and Richard Roll. "Investor Evaluation of Accounting Information: Some Empirical Evidence." *Journal of Business* (April 1972): 225–57.

Kiger, Jack E. "An Empirical Investigation of NYSE Volume and Price Reactions to the Announcement of Quarterly Earnings." *Journal of Accounting Research* (Spring 1972): 113–28.

Lev, Baruch. *Financial Statement Analysis: A New Approach.* Englewood-Cliffs, N.J.: Prentice-Hall, 1974.

Lintner, John, and Robert Glauber. "Higgledy Piggledy Growth in America." Presented to the Seminar for the Analysis of Security Prices (May 1967) Univ. of Chicago; printed in Lorie, James and Richard Brealey, eds., *Modern Developments in Investment Management.* New York: Praeger, 1972.

Lorie, James, and Mary Hamilton. *The Stock Market: Theories and Evidence.* Homewood, Ill.: Irwin, 1973.

May, Robert. "The Influence of Quarterly Earnings Announcements on Investor Decisions as Reflected in Common Stock Price Changes." *Empirical Research in Accounting: 1971,* Supplement to *Journal of Accounting Research,* vol. 9, pp. 119–163.

Niederhoffer, Victor. "The Predictive Content of First-Quarter Earnings Reports." *Journal of Business* (January 1970): 60–62.

———, and Patrick Regan, "Earnings Changes, Analysts' Forecasts, and Stock Prices." *Financial Analysts' Journal* (May-June 1972): 65–71.

Patell, James. "Corporate Earnings Forecasts: Empirical Tests and Consumption-Investment Model." Ph.D. Dissertation, Carnegie-Mellon University, 1976.

Patz, Dennis, and James Boatsman. "Accounting Principle Formulation in an Efficient Markets Environment." *Journal of Accounting Research* (Autumn 1972): 392–403.

Stickney, Clyde. "Window Dressing the Interim-Earnings Report: An Empirical Assessment for Firms Initially Going Public." *Journal of Business* (January 1975): 87–97.

Sunder, Shyam. "Relationships Between Accounting Changes and Stock Prices: Problems of Measurement and Some Empirical Evidence." *Empirical Research in Accounting: 1973,* Supplement to *Journal of Accounting Research,* vol. 11, pp. 1–45.

Sunder, Shyam. "Stock Price and Risk Related to Accounting Changes in Inventory Valuation." *Accounting Review* (April 1975): 305–15.

Treynor, Jack. "The Trouble with Earnings." *Financial Analysts Journal* (September–October 1972): 41–46.

Watts, Ross L. "The Time Series Behavior of Quarterly Earnings." University of Rochester Working Paper, presented to 1975 Stanford Research Seminar (1975).

Wilcox, Jarrod. "A Prediction of Business Failure Using Accounting Data." *Empirical Research in Accounting: 1973,* Supplement to *Journal of Accounting Research,* vol. 11, pp. 163–79.

Discussion

Robert K. Mautz

Professor Kaplan has performed a task well beyond either my competence or my patience; he has—as nearly as I can tell—not only read all the papers included in the bibliography of his critique, but has also understood them, an impressive achievement. As part of a good faith effort on my part, I referred to a limited number of those papers to obtain some feel for their appeal to practicing accountants. Let me give you a few selections from what I found.

The result is a time-state preference theory which is extremely general and yet simple in specifying the nature of the multi-period consumption-investment decision process faced by investors. The effect of security price behavior upon the multi-period consumption-investment decisions is immediately obvious when viewed within the context of the time-state preference formulation. In the Hirshleifer analysis, the investment decision is viewed as a decision to exchange current consumption for future consumption in such a manner that utility is maximized. The sole arguments of the utility function are time-dated, state-contingent consumption claims. However, the optimization problem is subject to the constraint that the present certainty equivalent value of all consumption (present and future) must be equal to the present certainty equivalent value of current wealth (which includes current and future endowments as well as securities).[1]

Moreover, generally accepted accounting principles currently permit only a very limited class of depreciation to be used. In the context of our model, they only permit δ of τ or one. There is no reason why such a constraint need exist. If a broader class were allowed (i.e., if δ were permitted to vary over a wider range), the resulting depreciation methods would still possess all the traditionally required properties such as objectivity, allocation of cost over the life of the asset, and historical-cost base, and yet they would permit the selection of depreciation methods more consistent with the underlying cash flows of the assets. This is an important option to allow for at least two reasons. (1) Empirically, it appears as if the average δ across our sample firms is greater than δ but less than one. (2) Moreover, the δ assessed in our empirical analysis is only an average across firms, and it would be expected that the δ would vary across firms.

Finally, if moving to a broader class of depreciation is considered to be infeasible, there is a sense in which tax allocation might be viewed as a correct

1. William H. Beaver, "The Behavior of Security Prices and Its Implications for Accounting Research (Methods)" in *Research Methodology*, (Lawrence, Kansas: Scholars Book Co., 1972), p. 10.

policy. The APB could consider requiring all firms (including A/A firms) to report as A/S firms, disclosing the amount of the tax deferral due to depreciation, so that the market can assess its own δ at a potentially lower processing cost.[2]

The drift downward in the Abnormal Performance Index computed over all firms and years in the sample reflects a computational bias. The bias arises because

$$E[\underset{m}{\Pi}\,(1 + v_m)] \neq \underset{m}{\Pi}\,[1 + E(v_m)],$$

where E denotes the expected value. It can readily be seen that the bias over K months is at least of order $(K - 1)$ times the covariance between v_m and v_{m-1}. Since this covariance is typically negative, the bias is also negative. While the bias does not affect the tenor of our results in any way, it should be kept in mind when interpreting the values of the various API's. It helps explain, for example, why the absolute changes in the indexes in the bottom panel of Figure 1 tend to be greater than those in the top panel; why the indexes in the top panel tend to turn down shortly after month 0; and finally, why the drifts in the indexes in the bottom panel tend to persist beyond the month of the report announcement.[3]

Table 1 reports summary statistics relating to the performance of the various models. Based upon these results, several tentative conclusions are offered.

(1) There is a wide variety of models that exhibit significant association between the sign of the forecast error and the API. An analysis was conducted of the percentage of times that the forecast error and the API had the same sign. The percentage of occurrences when both had the same sign is reported in the final column. The significance of these departures from the null hypothesis that the "true" percentage is .50, can be computed from the binomial test. Based upon this test, 48 out of the 60 models are significant beyond the .01 level (the critical p = .549). Of the remaining 12 models, another five are significant at the .05 level (critical p = .534). The remaining seven models have percentages less than .50 and all seven involve the same earnings variable, undeflated earnings (from B). An analysis of the magnitudes of the API's also indicates that knowing the sign of the forecast error in advance of the market can lead to substantial abnormal returns. In fact, for the better models, the magnitude of the abnormal return averages approximately 10 percent per year. Compare the magnitudes of these API's with the API that could be attained if a clairvoyant revealed perfect information about u itself 12 months in advance (i.e., more precisely the sign of u for the next twelve-month period). If a buy and hold policy was initiated based upon such information, the average API

2. William H. Beaver and Roland E. Dukes, "Interperiod Tax Allocation and δ-Depreciation Methods: Some Empirical Results," _Accounting Review_ (July 1973): 558–59.

3. Ray Ball and Philip Brown, "Empirical Evaluation of Accounting Income Numbers," _Journal of Accounting Research_ (Autumn 1968): 172.

of the positive and negative groups would be 21 percent. Thus, merely knowledge of the sign of the earnings forecast error accounts for approximately half of the total.[4]

Some of these selections are taken from the "Summary" portion of the paper, the part to which a practicing accountant might turn first to get an idea of the writer's conclusions. What do they tell him? He would be unlikely to read further. You can now appreciate why I feel so indebted to Professor Kaplan for reading and summarizing these papers in his lengthy critique.

Yet I do have at least one small quarrel with him. Frankly, I was a little confused at the contrast between his strong assertion: "I am very positive and enthusiastic about the contribution of empirical research over the last ten years" and his summary of that research which followed almost immediately. The results of ten year's efforts, when summarized in his terms, are something less than overwhelming. And please remember that because I am unable to understand the papers themselves, I must rely on Professor Kaplan's summary.

Among the "good news" he finds proceeding from the research he has reviewed are such gems as the following:

1. "The studies in Section 3 demonstrate that accounting numbers do have information content." Practicing accountants may find this something less than startling.

2. "The stock market responds to the release of these numbers and stock price revisions are associated with unexpected changes in earnings." Again, the experience of any practitioner will tell him that this should have been expected.

3. "Moreover, the income number produced by accounting procedures appears to be more closely associated with the underlying economic operations of the firm than are cash-flow variables." Might not a practitioner be excused if he were to conclude from this that researchers had rediscovered the accrual system together with its advantages over the cash basis?

4. "Interim reports including quarterly announcements and corporate forecasts of earnings are also viewed as timely information sources and are used by the market in forming expectations about the future prospects of the firm." Even the most polite practitioner may be a little incredulous

4. William H. Beaver and Roland E. Dukes, "Interperiod Tax Allocation, Earnings Expectations, and the Behavior of Security Prices," *Accounting Review* (April 1972): 327.

at this point. Just how much effort has it taken for scholarly researchers to discover what his own activities have long since convinced him are incontrovertible facts? But we go on to additional exciting findings.

5. ". . . growth stocks which can maintain a steady percentage growth of earnings, over a period of several years, has been shown to be the exception rather than the rule." And, ". . . the market is able to evaluate properly the increase in earnings caused by fully disclosed changes in accounting policy." Practitioners will undoubtedly welcome this last conclusion. For some years they have been trying to convince their critics that disclosure is the best solution for a number of difficult accounting issues.

6. ". . . earnings increases manufactured in the controller's office may be viewed by the market as a negative signal about the firm's future prospects for sustaining earnings from continuing operations."

Not one of these conclusions, nor all of them together, are likely to impress many practitioners as any great contribution to his knowledge. The typical researcher's response to this may be expressed in terms such as: "But now we have hard evidence. Formerly, you just thought you knew but your belief was not based on evidence as firm as we now have." Such an argument will impress my practitioner friends no more than will the conclusions themselves. Some knowledge, they will respond, is so self-evident that time spent in "proving" it is time wasted.

Professor Kaplan proceeds with some additional conclusions which are more likely to be given serious consideration, at least by some practitioners. He finds "that many debates about selection among various forms of accounting procedure may not be worth the resources currently devoted to them." Those practitioners who contend that disclosure is a satisfactory solution to many accounting problems are likely to agree outright and to let the matter drop. Other practitioners, especially those who find themselves involved in arguments with analysts, regulatory bodies, and other accountants about the number of alternative procedures now available are not likely to be so readily convinced.

Again: "Worries about the naïve investor seem misplaced since, to an excellent approximation, such investors face a fair game where stocks are correctly priced according to risk-return relationships." The hardbitten practitioner, a little bitter from bearing the burden of much litigation, is likely to suggest that you tell this one to the judge. To my knowledge, this proposition has never been offered seriously as a defense in a lawsuit, where the accountant feels his work receives its final test, but I doubt that it would wear well if it were. Perhaps that is because those investors who sue accountants and others are not willing to offset the gains in other parts of their portfolios against the losses on which they sue. Professor Kaplan notes that "as long as such investors hold diversified portfolios and avoid incurring heavy transaction costs by excessive trading, they can expect about the same return, for their level of risk, as more sophisticated investors."

But we seldom are sued on the basis of an investor's luck with his entire portfolio. One unsatisfactory investment is all he needs to make life most unpleasant for us. Professor Kaplan's gratuitous advice that "accountants need feel neither paternalistic nor responsible for investors who hold improperly diversified portfolios or who trade constantly on every piece of information that emerges in the marketplace" would strike us as the greatest good news we could receive if we could get it written into a Supreme Court decision. Until then, it provides cold comfort indeed.

Professor Kaplan also finds in the workings of the efficient market guidance on certain accounting policies, one of them being the proper accounting valuation of marketable securities. ". . . there can be little justification for valuing securities at other than market value." The fact that the FASB now has outstanding an exposure draft on the accounting for certain marketable securities that does not agree precisely with Professor Kaplan's conclusions appears to constitute ample evidence that the research on which he bases his views has not had a similar impact on the world of practice.

If I am to make any useful contribution to the deliberations of this symposium, it might be in offering some thoughts about the practitioner's attitude toward accounting research. Generally speaking, he is friendly but cautious. Research is "a good thing" and he is not about to take a position in opposition. Yet his experience with research somehow has been disappointing. He can cite very few instances in which research has come to his rescue in time of need or helped him with a difficult problem. He recalls that the Wheat Committee found research to have been of little aid to the APB and he has yet to see any great contribution by research to the work of the FASB.

Those researchers who actually desire to have some impact on practicing accountants might do well to think of practitioners as "primitive empiricists"—and I mean nothing derogatory in my selection of that term. My dictionary tells me that *empiric, empirical,* and *empiricism* all have to do with experience. An empiric is "one who believes that practical experience alone is the source of all knowledge. None of my practitioner associates would wish to go that far, but they do place a great deal of emphasis on experience, their own and that of their colleagues.

They are not empirical researchers in the sense that the papers reviewed by Professor Kaplan constitute empirical research. But they have had, as practicing accountants, a great deal of varied experience and they tend to formulate their views and guide their actions on the basis of the knowledge thus gained. Practical experience has been a hard teacher and they have learned their lessons well. The total empirical evidence that a practitioner of thirty years' experience has garnered may not be marshaled and presented as neatly as can be done in a research paper, but it carries at least equal weight. His evidence is as convincing to him as any evidence you may gather is convincing to you.

Because the nature of their work is always to question assertions and to call for satisfactory supporting evidence, accounting practitioners must refuse to accept that which they do not understand. My reading of extracts from some of these papers was not intended to be facetious. Do you really expect an intelligent professional to accept conclusions related to his profession solely on faith, completely in ignorance of their meaning? If you cannot or will not explain your research results to him in terms meaningful to him, you can expect no impact whatever. He should not and will not accept what he cannot understand. Neither will he seriously consider that which is contrary to his own experience unless you can present convincing evidence in opposition, evidence that he can understand and evaluate.

If you will take the time to become acquainted with them, you will find that practicing accountants, whether in industry or CPA practice, take a thoroughly rational approach to the resolution of issues, given their objectives and the perceived constraints within which they practice. If you wish to have impact on them, you must learn what those objectives and those perceived constraints are. The easiest generalization in the world is one that begins, "I can see no reason . . ." when the person making the assertion has made no effort to discover any reason. Practicing accountants are neither stupid, completely emotional, nor venal in their thinking. They operate at least as rationally and as morally as other reasonable men. My own research experience convinces me that practitioners' minds are always open to understandable, persuasive evidence. That is the basis on which they must operate in their own enlightened self-interest. In business as elsewhere, to press blithely on, ignoring evidence of danger, is to court disaster. So if you would have an impact on their thinking, the presentation of persuasive evidence is your best opportunity.

A factor of increasing importance in determining the impact you will have is that of time; practitioners have minimal time for trivia, for speculation, for "rapping" for the joy of it. The article that begins with an admission that the data are not convincing but "you may be interested in the details of my procedure" is unlikely to get a reading. The practitioner has so many items pressing for his attention that he must select from among them with care. His total reading burden is impressive. Professional magazines, authoritative releases, interpretations prepared by his own firm, industry developments, the general economic situation as portrayed in business periodicals, books, research studies, all these pile up on his desk in increasing numbers. Our national technical partner recently commenced his remarks at our annual partners meeting with the admonition: "Read, read, read." Those of you who keep up with current developments have some idea of how technical and time-consuming some of this material is.

In addition, the practicing CPA faces a continuing demand for help with position papers on a variety of subjects from a variety of authorities. He never knows when an important client will call with a request for a discussion of a recent release or with a question of how it relates to the client's current situation. Given the flood of proposals before us today, anyone in practice has the constant feeling that he is not quite prepared for his next telephone call.

Now putting this all together, what does it mean? I suggest it means that if you want to have an impact on practice—and of course you may do research solely for your own entertainment—then you must make your work relevant to those you wish to impress; you must make it accessible in that it is published in magazines that he regularly sees, understandable enough that he does not require an interpreter, and incorporating evidence sufficiently convincing that he will consider it the equal of his own experience.

Another thought or two appear relevant to the subject. Two weeks ago, Bob Sterling and I shared a session at the Alabama Convocation on Accounting Research. My portion was a strong plea for more applied research in the development of accounting standards. With his usual blend of whimsy, folklore, appeal to scientific method, personal charm, and oratorical skill, Bob enthusiastically destroyed my case. At least, judging from the relative applause, he did so.

Well, "If you can't lick 'em, join 'em," so I will try to emulate some of Bob's work. He has contended in a number of his papers that accounting should be scientific, that it should be predictive, and that predictive ability is demonstrated through "If-then" statements. "If such-and-such is true, then so-and-so will follow." In an earnest effort to apply his recommendation, I have constructed a number of such predictive propositions which seem reasonably relevant to the topic before us. Before offering them to you, a word or two about the convocation will be in order.

It brought together a number of young faculty members who had recently completed their doctoral work and were either commencing or early into their personal research programs. Extensive opportunities for small group discussions were provided. I came away with one overwhelming impression: this group of academics was up absolutely tight over the necessity, and especially the difficulty, of immediate and continuing publication in periodicals which they feared were biased against them. My "If-then" propositions link that impression with some of the thoughts expressed earlier in this paper. Here is the first one.

"If publication is essential to academic acceptance, then upward ambitious academics will place premium priority on publication." You may feel that this, like some other conclusions before us in this session, is so obvious as not to be useful. But remember this is a first attempt and there is at least a commendable effort to incorporate unnecessary jargon.

Permit me to attempt another.

"If the *Accounting Review* and the *Journal of Accounting Research* are the most prestigious publication possibilities, then research activities, the results of which are acceptable for publication therein, will command primary attention." Conversations at the Alabama convocation were convincing on this score.

"If the formal or informal editorial policies of the *Accounting Review* and the *Journal of Accounting Research* favor research topics and methods culminating in conclusions not comprehensible or not interesting to practitioners, then one should not be surprised if the impact of such research on practice is minimal."

The discussion and parts of the papers presented here appear to confirm this assertion. The proposal, offered as a remedy, that practitioners rely on summary articles would be more acceptable if the conclusions themselves were not contested by other articles. This suggests that we practitioners had best be cautious in accepting such summaries as reliable.

Sidney Davidson has been another of my mentors over the years and I borrow a bit from the introduction to his paper in the following:

"If one's teaching interests are influenced by one's educational and research experience, then the editorial policies and practices of the *Accounting Review* and the *Journal of Accounting Research* may exert significant influence on the nature of educational programs in accounting." You may note that these last propositions appear to stray a little from the topic of this conference. But be patient, we may tie back to our topic again before my scientific excursion terminates.

"If control over the editorial policies of the *Accounting Review* and the *Journal of Accounting Research* could be obtained and maintained, the nature and direction of academic activities, both teaching and research, could be influenced." Obviously, this proposition depends on the previous propositions. Some who find such an implication a little disturbing may raise the old question of which came first, the chicken or the egg. Does editorial policy influence the nature of research or do research interests determine what is available for publication? To borrow an expression, the man suffering from a surfeit of chickens will regard this as something less than a nontrivial question. But just a couple of more proposals.

"If conclusions similar to Professor Kaplan's are justified, then the editorial policies of the *Accounting Review* and the *Journal of Accounting* in recent years leave something to be desired." Apparently, a great deal of effort and much valuable publication space have been devoted to the work he summarizes very briefly. This same proposition could be stated a little differently.

"If one views accounting practice as essentially utilitarian in nature, then undue emphasis in the *Accounting Review* and the *Journal of Accounting Research* on the kind of research evaluated by Professor Kaplan may be wasteful, at best."

And one final statement that reveals my fears: "If the editorial policies of the *Accounting Review* and the *Journal of Accounting Research* are and remain 'out of sync' with the interests of practitioners, then educational policy may become increasingly irrelevant to accounting practice."

And this last proposition brings us back to the impact of research on practice. It would be little short of tragic if the major impact of empirical research on accounting practice were to diminish the usefulness of accounting education to future practitioners.

Discussion

Charles A. Werner

Professor Kaplan has indeed presented a most interesting and challenging paper. In my view, he has done an excellent job of surveying recent empirical research about financial accounting numbers.

Is There Cause for Pessimism? Toward the end of his article (pages 168 and 169), Professor Kaplan concludes: "I think that we have now gotten all the easy results and that major new findings are going to be much harder to obtain." A little later on he says: "I am much more pessimistic about the ability of empirical research to give us many insights on a whole variety of important questions now confronting the accounting profession." I would suggest that there are indeed grounds for pessimism about the future of empirical research, but not for the reasons which appear to trouble Professor Kaplan. If I may extrapolate a bit, I think we are being told that all of the frontiers which can be dealt with in empirical accounting research have been addressed and that no significant new advances can be made in the research process itself or in its findings. Even if this conclusion is so (and I have my doubts), it is not the reason why I am pessimistic about the future of empirical accounting research. There is another more important reason for pessimism.

We should all be most pessimistic about the future of research which presumably had as one of its principal motivations the desire to affect changes in practice, and yet has had virtually no such discernible effect. In short, I see as a reason for pessimism—but also as a challenge for the future—the fact that we have been unable to "sell" the results of the empirical accounting research studies already completed to the business community and to the rule-making bodies.

Professor Kaplan presents several interesting examples of our inability to sell valid empirical research findings to the rule-making bodies of the profession. For example, as to marketable securities he states (and I agree): "Once one accepts the idea that the market is rational and that prices respond to all available information, then there can be little justification for valuing securities at other than market value."

Accounting Alternatives—or Does Monkey Business Pay Off? From the empirical research literature surveyed at pages 156 through 162 of his paper, Professor Kaplan demonstrates amply that the answer to the above question is a ringing "no." In particular, I found the commentary about FIFO to LIFO switches for inventory valuation to be most interesting, although I received this information with somewhat mixed feelings, believing as I do, that LIFO is a pretty poor accounting principle, although to be sure it is one which is generally accepted. It appears from the article that companies that switched from FIFO to LIFO did better from the standpoint of stock price than those companies which switched from LIFO to FIFO. It is possible, of course, that this finding can be explained away by the same type of "selection mechanism" which Professor Kaplan uses to explain the results of empirical research in the business combinations area. One might suspect that the companies which are able to accept making a FIFO to LIFO switch are companies with good earnings and a sound economic position in the first place. Nevertheless, I view these findings as significant.

The findings of the depreciation studies such as Kaplan and Roll (1972) are also interesting. If the empirical research studies are correct, why shouldn't we have only one acceptable method of depreciation for financial reporting purposes? Again assuming the empirical research is right in this area, the only thing that continuing alternative depreciation methods (and the attendant switching between methods which seems to occur depending on a company's financial situation) is to worsen the public's view about the integrity of financial accounting.

Another recent troubling excursion in this area is the developments on deferred-tax accounting for the oil and gas producing companies. Even if one were to accept the somewhat specious arguments about oil and gas deferred-tax accounting in the past, failure to provide deferred taxes now on the full amount of "timing differences" is troubling in the face of present accounting literature on deferred taxes for other entities. More disturbing, however, are the two quotations which Professor Kaplan includes in his article at page 160 from certain oil company executives. Assuming that they are men of good will—and I have every reason to believe that they are—it is distressing that they could honestly believe something which is so patently untrue in the face of the related empirical accounting research. The lesson of the Patz and Boatsman 1972 study (cited at pages 158 and 159 of Professor Kaplan's article) is that even a potential required switch from full-cost accounting to successful-efforts accounting for oil and gas producing companies did not affect stock prices. If anything, such a change could have been construed as more pervasive than a change requiring oil and gas producing companies to adopt deferred tax accounting in the face of an obviously changed fact situation due to the new tax legislation. In any event, presumably the efficient marketplace will take care of any differences among the methods that companies select pursuant to FASB Statement No. 9, and maybe that is some consolation.

Forecasting. Professor Kaplan discusses forecasting in a number of places in his paper. One thing that pleased me very much was the conclusion at page 141 that "stocks with positive forecast errors tend to outperform the market and stocks with negative forecast errors tend to do worse than the market." In short, if you are not conservative about your forecasting, the marketplace may burn you. This little lesson has some interesting implications which do not appear to have been learned either. For example, the proposed SEC release on filed forecasts (Release No. 33–5581) would apparently permit companies to "sail into the safe harbor" only if the earnings forecast turned out to be within a range of $\pm 10\%$ of the actual results of operations. While there are other problems with the way the SEC has stated this permissible range, the interesting implication of the empirical research cited by Professor Kaplan is that perhaps a larger amount of latitude should be given for forecasts which tend to be conservative because of the effect that this would have on stock prices.

While I cannot resolve the Green and Segall v. Brown and Niederhoffer controversy about the effect of first-quarter-earnings information on accuracy of annual forecasting, I would suggest that there is a missing piece of information which would be helpful in analyzing what the results of these studies mean. If we knew what the company's forecast was for the first quarter and how much the actual first-quarter results varied from such forecast, we would be in a better position to make a prediction of annual results of operations.

Ignorance in the Marketplace. As Professor Kaplan suggests (page 136) we have all run into "presumably financially knowledgeable individuals who show a disconcerting amount of ignorance about the assumptions under which financial reports are prepared." In this regard, it is interesting to hear what the "ignorant masses" are saying about the annual reports they receive.

In a recent study published by the Bureau of Business and Economics

Research at California State University of Los Angeles, Marc Jay Epstein has gathered some statistics about what round-lot shareholders on the American and New York Stock Exchanges want in annual reports, what they do not particularly like, and how they make their investment decisions. A high percentage of these shareholders (76.9%) said that they would like to see financial information in less technical terms included in the annual report. At the same time, when asked whether there was any additional information they would like to see included in the annual report, 61.3% of the respondents said "No." When asked to describe the basis on which they normally made investment decisions, ranking such factors in order of importance, nearly 50% of the respondents said that they made decisions on the basis of advice from their stockbrokers. Analysis of the annual report, listed only by 15% of the respondents, was a poor fourth in the ranking. Taken at their face value, these are disturbing figures because they could be construed to mean that information in present annual reports is enough, although it is somewhat hard to understand, and that it is seldom used by shareholders for making investment decisions. However, this conclusion would not appear to be supported by the studies discussed in Section 3 of Professor Kaplan's paper on the basis of which he concludes that they "demonstrate that accounting numbers do have information content."

Predicting Bankruptcy. The results of the empirical accounting research studies relating to predictions of bankruptcy are distressing (particularly such studies as Altman and McGough), implying as they do that a mathematical model can do a better job of predicting bankruptcy than can an auditor in giving a qualified or disclaimer report relating to going concern. I would, however, like to see a little more research done in this area before deciding. For example, I think we should know whether there is a closer correlation between actual bankruptcy and auditors' report letters or between actual bankruptcy and statistical model prediction. What I'd really like to find out is how many times the statistical model predicts bankruptcies that do not occur compared with how many times the auditor's report letter "predicts bankruptcies that do not occur. Another thing that such a study might put to rest is the theory widely held in the business community that an auditor's report qualified as to going concern is the equivalent of a "self-fulfilling prophecy" or a "death sentence."

In Conclusion—a Suggestion to Academe. As I noted at the beginning of this discussion paper, I am deeply troubled and pessimistic about our chances of getting the business community and the rule-making bodies to understand the results and importance of empirical accounting research. I do believe that part of the difficulty rests with the preparers of such papers. For example, I seldom read the *NAA Journal* anymore because the papers are generally so full of formulas and explanations of mathematical methodology that I am bored to death by the time I get to the third or fourth page of an anticle. Gentlemen, you must make yourselves interesting, readable, and understandable. If you do not, the results of your fine research will surely fall by the wayside. Of course, I can't promise that empirical accounting research will be used anyway, but the least we can do is give it a fair chance.

PART IV
Where to Go from Here

Directions for Future Research

Frank T. Weston

Other papers at this symposium have discussed the impact of various types of research on accounting practice. As might be expected, the evidence of a heavy impact is neither clear nor convincing. One of the objectives of the symposium is to provide guidance on the directions which research might take in the future to have the greatest potential impact on the development of accounting practice. In pursuing this aim, it seems desirable first to outline some broad goals for future research, then to discuss the objectives of financial accounting, which should give some indication of the optimum direction for research in the future, and finally to make a few observations on the techniques which appear to have the greatest potential. These comments are based on the experience of a practitioner in the public accounting profession who has had an unusual opportunity during his career to observe—and to participate in—the processes by which accounting practice is moulded and accounting principles become "generally accepted."

Broad Goals for Future Accounting Research

The goal of accounting research in the future might be simply stated: "to have a maximum beneficial effect on the financial accounting and reporting process, within reasonable limits of time, effort, and monetary costs." In addition to the usual difficulty with the familiar "cost-benefit" notion, the trouble with such a broad goal is that it is difficult to make the words "maximum beneficial effect" operational. This difficulty in turn is caused to some extent by the shortcomings of research in the past. Thus, to determine whether a particular change in accounting practice is beneficial requires that we have a clear notion of what the objectives of financial accounting and reporting are. As we all know, a widely accepted agreement as to the objectives of accounting is still being sought. Given this condition, the researcher has difficulty deciding on the subject areas to be researched and the criteria to use in establishing his research plan.

A similar problem arises in attempting to furnish guidance for future research. The only approach which appears reasonable to the writer is to agree upon certain assumptions about objectives for the financial accounting and reporting process and then to attempt to determine which types or areas of research would be most productive in moving the process towards those objectives. This approach, of course, is based on the conclusion that research as to the objectives of accounting is not part of the scope of the research contemplated by this symposium.

Objectives of Financial Accounting and Reporting. For purposes of this paper the writer accepts the following statements of the objectives of the financial accounting and reporting process: The objective is to furnish information, primarily in monetary terms, about the resources and obligations of an entity—and changes therein during a period—useful to investors and creditors in making decisions as to the commitment of their capital. The information should assist these investors in evaluating, comparing, and predicting the timing and amounts of returns on their investments and the related risks and uncertainties. (It will be noted that these objectives are basically the same as those submitted in the Report of The Study Group on the Objectives of Financial Statements, of which the writer was a member.[1]

The writer also assumes that the basic structures of business and of the various professional groups will continue as at present, and that investors will be primarily interested in equity and debt securities of corporations, generally available in the public markets or by private placements. The writer also assumes that the basic format of financial statements will not change in the foreseeable future, although that in itself might be an interesting area for research.

Areas for Future Research

Adopting the above broad approach, there then follow four significantly different but related areas on which future research could concentrate: (1) How do investors use the financial accounting information which is now available to them? (2) What (additional) information of a financial accounting nature would be useful to investors? (3) Can the financial

---

1. Report of the Study Group on the Objectives of Financial Statements (New York: American Institute of Public Accountants, 1973).

accounting and reporting process furnish any or all of such information? (4) If so, how can this best be achieved?

One of the frustrating aspects of adopting a broad approach such as that outlined above is that one has the feeling of having to "begin at the very beginning"—a tremendously large and difficult task. Unfortunately, this is true. In the last two decades the emphasis on the accounting process has shifted from a management-oriented scorekeeping system to a user-oriented investment-process system. This trend has parallels in other social areas, as the move towards "consumerism" has swept the country. In addition, the importance of accounting in achieving the optimum allocation of capital resources has become apparent.

Thus, for example, it is not a simple exercise for an academic researcher, an accounting practitioner, a member of management, or even a representative of a regulatory commission to decide whether a particular measurement method or accounting treatment is "preferable," since at present we do not know how this information is used by the investor-user. And, by and large, the investor-user, as well as the professional analyst who is presumably his representative, cannot effectively communicate his needs or define the manner in which he uses accounting data. This is due in part to the fact that preparers and, particularly, users have not given much thought to the improvements which might be made in the accounting process and how such improvements might affect the decision processes of users.

Where does all this lead us? It seems to the writer that first we must have general agreement among all the interested parties as to the broad objectives of accounting. This would presumably be based on (1) macro-economic notions as to the optimum allocation of capital resources among competing organizations in our business community, and (2) the perceived needs of investors who are making capital-investment decisions. Then we can proceed with research seeking improvements in the financial accounting and reporting process.

Decision Processes of Investors. It seems obvious from the above analysis that the first major research task is to delineate the various decision processes of investors. This problem will be made difficult because of the fact that investors are influenced by a great deal of information in addition to that generated by the financial accounting process. As indicated in earlier discussions at this symposium, this problem of multiple variables is a recurring one for researchers. Whether we can ever isolate or identify the impact on an investment decision of a particular bit of accounting information is a challenging question. In the writer's opinion, this will not be possible. However, this does not mean that we should not attempt to identify the information which is—or should be—relevant to the investor. Future research should attempt to find some answers here.

In this general area of research it seems clear that new methods and approaches will be needed. It is the writer's view that a single candidate for an advanced degree will not have the financial or operative resources to do an effective job in this type of research. It may be that the large professional organizations will have to finance such projects. Of equal importance will be the need to arrange for introductions of researchers to analysts, investors, preparers, etc. In many ways this type of research will be open-ended—that is, the decision processes of investors may be found to be affected by the mere process of inquiring into their nature. Thus the time required may be considerable.

An example of such a study would be a project whereby a group of researchers would spend a period of time with the investment managers of a large institutional investor—say, an insurance company or a pension fund or a bank. The researchers would study the investment decisions made during a certain period and would attempt to determine the bases on which individual decisions were made. Such a study would, of course, entail considerable time, effort, and expense, together with a very cooperative attitude on the part of the investors, but in the writer's view, it is only in this way that useful research as to the decision processes of investors can be conducted. It may even be feasible to test the decision processes of a few "average investors," if any can be found. A sampling of professionals—doctors, lawyers, engineers, accountants—might prove interesting.

A second facet of the research on the decision processes of investors would be an attempt to determine what information, presumably in addition to the information presently available, would be useful to investors, once their decision processes are identified. This type of research would involve the creation of financial statements reflecting different measurement methods, different disclosures, different means of reporting risks and uncertainties, and also new approaches to financial reporting, including such items as financial forecasts, share of market data, management-succession plans, new-product developments. This second type of research would also be extensive and would require the cooperation of an even larger group of interested parties. For such research to be successful, there would have to be significant assistance from management—the preparers of the statements and those in the best position to furnish information necessary to create some of the novel presentations mentioned above. In order to obtain the help of management, it would be necessary first to develop a sincere interest in improving the process. The next requirement would be an understanding of the needs of users and an agreement that their needs should be the predominating criteria in seeking to improve the system. Management would also have to be willing to spend the necessary time, effort, and money to make the activity worthwhile, and would have to be willing to publish the results and to discuss the relative advantages and disadvantages—both from the users' point of view and from management's point of view. There are some indications, although relatively few, that managements in this country are finally beginning to be willing to participate in a meaningful way in improving the financial accounting and reporting process. In the writer's view, however, management's reluctance will be the greatest hurdle to be overcome in future research of all types. And, without the cooperation of management, no significant advances can be made in the areas under discussion.

The Financial Accounting and Reporting Process. When research in the future gives us some indication of the decision processes of investors, it should also be possible to determine through research whether changes can and should be made in the financial accounting and reporting process to be responsive to their needs. This process would also entail the cooperation of all the interested parties—preparers, reporting public accountants, analysts, governmental regulatory agencies, and academics. For this type of research to be of maximum usefulness, it may be necessary to establish some sort of priority—particularly in terms of widespread testing of the practicality of various proposals. For example, as present conditions confirm, it would not be wise to attempt to test on a large scale a major change such as the introduction of current-value data into financial statements at the same time that preparers and users are being asked to prepare and evaluate financial statements adjusted for changes in the general price level. Priorities will have to be established. One of the most important decisions will be whether or not to proceed with research on modifications within the historical cost framework, postponing for the present any major widespread research in the use of current-value measurements. In the writer's opinion, a decision to proceed in that manner would be a sound one. Others doubtless feel to the contrary. While the writer believes that some form of current-value measurements should eventually be incorporated into the financial accounting and reporting system, he believes that there are limitations on the nature and extent of changes which can be made in the process within a reasonable time. Furthermore, testing changes first within the historical cost framework will enable all interested parties to evaluate the proposed changes more effectively than would be the case if major changes were all made at one time, including a shift from historical cost measurements to current-value measurements. The establishing of priorities will be a major challenge for those responsible for mounting the major research efforts envisaged by this paper.

Specific Subjects for Future Research

Let us turn now to a discussion of those areas as to which research in the future will have the greatest—or most beneficial—impact on the development of accounting practice. Some of these will be significant regardless of whether or not a decision is made to remain with historical cost in the near future.

Uncertainty. In the writer's view, financial statement presentations at present fail to communicate adequately to users the uncertainty inherent in the financial accounting process. There is no indication that almost every item in the balance sheet and income statement has been measured initially or evaluated or allocated subsequently under conventions which either do not attempt to measure economic changes or attempt to do so under circumstances which defy exactitude. It is probable that this failure to communicate to current users is the inadvertent result of the shift in the emphasis of the objectives of financial statement presentations. When the primary use was for internal or management scorekeeping or for the presentation of the operations of an entity as viewed by management, preparers were aware of the weaknesses in the process. Now that a wider and less knowledgeable group of users is the target, no significant efforts have been made to communicate the uncertainties underlying the apparently precise data in the statements.

Thus, research could well be conducted to determine the best ways in which the inherent uncertainties could be communicated to users. This would entail questions such as: How much understanding should the investor be expected to have of the accounting process? How can the customary circumstances of uncertainty be described? How can unusual conditions be described? This should be a fertile field for research. As indicated above, these areas would be important regardless of the primary measurement system in use—in fact, introduction of current values would make communication of uncertainties much more important and relevant to investor needs. An added facet would be determining whether the general risks of the business or of the economic environment should somehow be communicated by or in conjunction with the financial statements.

Disaggregation of Data. The disaggregation of data included in financial statements of complex business entities may be useful to investors in evaluating, comparing, and predicting investment returns. This subject has recently received added attention with the issuance by the Financial Accounting Standards Board of a proposed standard for *Financial Reporting for Segments of a Business Enterprise.*[2] To be helpful to this project, any pertinent research would have to be commenced in the near future. It is interesting to note that the Board requested that, during the exposure period, business enterprises test the preparation of information for compliance with the lines proposed in the draft and that written comments indicate the results of those tests. The Board also solicited views as to whether the information would be useful in analyzing and understanding an enterprise's financial statements. It is unfortunate that the Board did not specifically request investors and other users to comment on the usefulness of this type of information. Many filings with the Securities and Exchange Commission presently contain segmented operating data. These could be the basis for research among users as to usefulness. The proposed addition of information as to assets identifiable with each segment would add another dimension in this area.

As in the area of uncertainty, research on disaggregation would be pertinent to financial statement data prepared on either the historical cost basis or the current-value basis.

Forecasts of Financial Data. Another fruitful area for research is that of forecasts of financial data. While one might engage in a semantic argument as to whether a forecast is a financial statement, or whether a forecast should be part of the financial-statement "package," it seems clear

2. *Financial Reporting for Segments of a Business Enterprise, Exposure Draft,* Financial Accounting Standards Board, Stamford, Conn.: September 30, 1975.

that a financial forecast fulfills very well many of the objectives of financial accounting and financial statements. It is one more bit of information of a financial nature which would assist investors to evaluate, compare, and predict the results of activities of a business enterprise and thus the returns to them from investments.

Research in this area would also involve cooperation among all the groups mentioned in previous sections. This subject would be pertinent regardless of whether the decision is made to remain with the historical cost system for the present, or to move into current values on a rapid schedule. The major challenge to research in this area would be similar to that involving objectives—the need to contact and work with significant and responsible investor groups who would be willing to participate in a lengthy and complex project.

Some observers believe that the introduction of forecasts into the financial statement "package" would make academic the need to disclose certain costs on a replacement cost or current cost basis. Many of the arguments in favor of these disclosures emphasize the need to advise users as to the relationships among current costs, past costs, current and past selling prices, and future costs and selling prices. A financial forecast would appear to handle this particular problem nicely. Research might attempt to determine whether the introduction of financial forecasts would justify postponement for a limited time period of the introduction of current cost data. While this determination of priorities would be a very difficult research exercise, it might prove very valuable to the long-term improvement in financial accounting and reporting.

Elimination of Discretionary Alternative Methods. In addition to the above discussed areas, which involve introduction of new or different data into the system, there remain for potential research the areas in which current accounting principles permit the choice of alternative methods at the discretion of the preparer. Could future research be effective in improving the accounting process by attempting to limit discretionary choice in a particular set of circumstances? While these areas— e.g., inventory-costing methods and depreciation-allocation methods— appear to be fruitful fields for research, it seems clear that any attempt at research should await completion of a rather detailed specification of the objectives of accounting. When such a specification is available, it seems there will still probably be a need for a decision by an authoritative body— e.g., the Financial Accounting Standards Board—to specify the particular criteria which would justify the use of a particular method. Stated another way, a selection of an inventory or depreciation method may have to be made to achieve consistency and thus comparability under similar circumstances, rather than on a clearly observed revelation of the "right" method based on supporting principles and concepts. Much of the accounting process will continue to be based on conventions, and research should enable those responsible for that process to make informed decisions based on evidence of usefulness.

Other Areas for Research. One might discuss in turn each of the subjects which have plagued the Accounting Principles Board over recent years—lease capitalization, business combinations, pension costs, income-tax allocation, income-statement format, translation of overseas financial data, the investment tax credit, accounting for return on investments (leveraged leases; interest and other carrying costs), reflecting changes in the general price level, and complex earnings-per-share situations. Whether research should concentrate on each one of these is, of course, an interesting question. As indicated previously, a general consensus must first be reached as to the objectives of financial accounting and reporting. When such agreement is reached, certain of these topics will be logical subjects for research. Assuming agreement on the user orientation of financial statements, research on each topic would necessarily be involved with users' reactions to possible changes in each area. Useful research would be possible, on an even smaller scale than indicated above.

The question of lease capitalization, for example, seems to involve the simple question of whether financial statements would be more useful if they displayed the resource (the right to use the property for a fixed period) and the related obligation (the present value of the contracted lease payments) in the balance sheet, with appropriate related treatment in the income statement. The major objections to this process are (1) that the obligation is not a "liability" and (2) that inclusion in the balance sheet would impair the credit rating or borrowing capacity of the entity. As for the first point, it seemed clear to the Accounting Principles Board that assets and liabilities are what accountants say they are. The Objective Study Group suggested definitions in terms of sacrifices for which potential benefits have not yet been received (assets) and benefits for which sacrifices have not yet been made (liabilities). A sympathetic reading of a lease agreement would indicate that the first objection is largely a semantic problem of no great moment. Research could well make a contribution as to the second objection—whether in fact the inclusion of these items in the face of the balance sheet and in the totals would, of itself, change the credit standing of the entity. While sophisticated credit specialists have termed this notion nonsense, a good many business executives still maintain that such changes would result. An in-depth research effort involving discussions with investors and credit-rating agencies could help in this area. Once these matters had been investigated, the central question of whether the communicative ability of financial statements would be enhanced by capitalization could be considered on its own merits. This question in turn might involve considerable research into user needs and cost-benefit considerations.

As is evident from the above brief discussion of a single issue, in order for research to have a significant impact on the financial accounting and reporting process it oftentimes must consider more than one facet of a problem and must involve consecutive decisions. Such research will be costly and time-consuming.

Several of the topics mentioned above involve an analysis of transactions to determine their substance (e.g., business combinations), or the allocation of costs to time periods under conditions of extreme uncertainty (e.g., pension costs), or the allocation of benefits or sacrifices to various periods (e.g., return on investments, investment tax credit). Research could be helpful in these areas by exploring the various alternative possibilities and attempting to determine which method or approach most closely correlates with the substance of the transaction and the objectives of financial statements. Such determinations will not be easy. In fact, many of the final determinations may have to be made by the body responsible for the establishment of accounting principles on a judgment basis—which may appear arbitrary to many. However, adequate research, presumably of the type common today in various journals, could lay the groundwork for such decisions. Certain problems are amenable to research on a limited basis, as opposed to the broad research discussed in previous sections.

Conclusion

If future research is to be effective in improving accounting practice, the results must be more convincing than in the past. Achieving more convincing results will continue to be difficult even when the research involves limited coverage of subjects of the type addressed in the past, and will be doubly difficult for the broad user-oriented projects of the type discussed above. As users' needs begin to dominate the scene, accounting research will experience a frustrating period because of the complex nature of the subject matter and the increased costs. As indicated above, it is to be hoped that major projects may be undertaken through the cooperation of all the interested groups. Test data covering a large number of entities or situations should be made available. Given these conditions, it is not going to be easy for any single researcher to undertake an important project with any assurance of satisfactory completion in a relatively short period of time. It will be difficult to conclude that any suggested change or new accounting approach will be an improvement, since the conclusions will usually involve a subjective determination of users' reactions.

The difficulty facing the researcher in the complex world of business is well demonstrated by a suggestion made by Ray Chambers:

> Researchers and practitioners both entertain the expectation that research will lead to advances in practice. But there would be more disciplined research if practitioners refused to take notice of research work unless or until the products of inquiry had been thoroughly debated by researchers themselves, were substantially supported by evidence and were in the form of tightly constructed and well-defined proposals. At that point, but not before, it would be profitable to have a small committee of practitioners as appraisers or referees of research conclusions.[3]

It seems extremely unlikely to the writer that we will ever achieve the research utopia envisioned by Chambers. Quite the contrary—researchers will not, by themselves, be able to deliver the well-wrapped, complete research package Chambers proposes. Researchers will instead be involved in a complex process of cooperation with many interested groups in very broad projects, involving considerable time, effort and expense.

The above is not to say that research in the future will not have an impact on accounting practice. Its impact may well be greater than at any time in the past. However, it will be part of a bigger scheme of formalized improvement in the financial accounting and reporting process in which various groups will participate actively. It should be a challenge to all those with research capabilities.

3. R. J. Chambers, "The Anguish of Accountants," *The Journal of Accountancy* (March 1972): 73.

Some Comments on Directions for Future Research in Accounting

Sidney Davidson

As I consider the topic of directions for future research in accounting, I am reminded again how much each of us is a creature of his own background, training, and recent interests. At this moment of confession let me concede that my thoughts about future accounting research are heavily influenced by the economics orientation of my early training and of the institutions with which I have been connected and by my own recent research and writing activities. What follows then will be a highly personal view of accounting research.

To put the effect of the first influence another way, it seems to me that the underlying goal of financial accounting must be to present financial statements that depict economic reality as best we can. Within broad limits of objectivity, we should accept as the major goal of accounting the presentation of those data that will portray the world in a realistic manner and thus facilitate the making of sound economic and social decisions. Accounting research should seek to make financial accounting more decision-oriented.

This leads to the second, and even more personal, major influence on my feelings about the future direction of accounting research—my own recent activities. I served recently, along with Frank Weston and others, on the Study Group on the Objectives of Financial Statements. I think the report that emerged from our nearly three years of deliberations—the Trueblood Report—is a sound and judicious document. However, it begins on the first page of the first chapter with a troublesome admission, "Users' needs for information [in making economic and social decisions] are not known with any degree of certainty. No study has been able to identify precisely the specific role financial statements play in the economic decision-making process. This study is therefore dependent upon certain assumptions about users' information needs and their decision processes."[1] Certainly providing a better understanding of users' decision models must rank high on our list of basic goals of accounting research.

1. *Report of the Study Group on the Objectives of Financial Statements,* AICPA, October, 1973, p. 13.

One of the few things we know about users' decision models is that they are future oriented. To me this means that information about management's future plans and expectations would clearly be in line with users' needs. High on the list of projects for future research should be those that seek to make the reporting of forecasts more effective. Ideally this would include techniques for making forecasts more accurate, but I am not optimistic about what can be done by accountants on this score. Attention by accountants should instead be focused on improved forms for reporting of forecasts, for stating of the underlying assumptions, and for consideration of appropriate methods of freeing those who prepare and attest to forecasts from excessive legal liability if the forecasts are prepared with care and in good faith.

This need for further work on users' models has been brought home to me even more forcefully in my recent work with Roman Weil on general price-level adjusted financial statements. I am not an enthusiastic supporter of the publication of such statements, but I am troubled when opponents of that approach ask its supporters to demonstrate *specifically* how purchasing-power adjusted accounting statements would help users make sounder economic decisions. It seems to me that an appropriate response is to ask supporters of the status quo to show specifically how *present* conventional financial statements assist economic decision-making. In each of the ways in which conventional accounting is now useful, would general price-level accounting (or current-value accounting) be more useful? That to me is the central question, but one we are unable to answer effectively because we know so little about how accounting data are now used. Proper evaluation of purchasing-power accounting awaits our obtaining a clearer view of users' decision models and the place of financial statement data in them.

It may be that research by academic scholars in accounting and finance may make the greatest contribution to accounting practice by continued emphasis on securing a better understanding of users' decision processes. Accounting Principles Board Opinion No. 20 prescribes that a change in accounting principle is permitted "only if the enterprise justifies the use of an alternative [new] accounting principle on the basis that it is preferable." The Opinion adds that "The burden of justifying . . . changes rests with the entity proposing the change," but nowhere does it spell out the criterion of what makes one accounting principle "preferable" to another (except to say that any principle that has received the blessing of the Board in an Opinion is ipso facto preferable).

Can a criterion for preferability be established? This may be another way of asking is it important to try to decide on a "best" income number or is disclosure of the alternative acceptable accounting principle sufficient, if the results of the other alternative are also shown?

Does geography matter? Is it important in user decisions whether an item is labeled extraordinary or operating, discontinued or continuing? Is it important whether it appears in the body of the statement or in the footnotes?

Here the vast literature on efficient capital markets that has come into being in the last decade or so may give some clues, but, again, reverting to personal confession, there are some parts of this literature that leave me troubled.

An efficient capital market is one where the security prices of the issues traded there fully and promptly reflect all of the publicly available data about those issues. The other papers at this symposium have marshaled much of the evidence indicating that most securities markets are indeed efficient, that they see through changes and differences in accounting principles, and they detect significant information wherever it is found in the financial statements or elsewhere. The evidence for the efficient markets view seems overwhelming whether we apply the "weak form," or the "semi-strong form" tests.[2] Accounting research providing some additional tests of this view might provide some incremental assurance of the efficiency of most markets, and so would be marginally useful.

More helpful than additional tests of this sort would be research that (1) sought to determine the cost of having efficient markets translate accounting data and (2) considered those individual cases where the market, although efficient in a macro sense, did not seem to deal adequately with individual company shifts in accounting principles or statement geography. Let us consider each of these two in somewhat greater detail.

Almost all descriptions of efficient markets treat the market as a large, mysterious "black box." All publicly available information enters at one end, and a set of rational, carefully determined prices emerges at the other. What mysterious bits of alchemy are performed within the box, aside from vigorous bargaining of buyers and sellers, remains largely unexplained. The processing of information, even publicly available information, is a costly, time-consuming process. Individual processing of all information by

2. See E. J. Fama, "Efficient Capital Markets: A Review of Theory and Empirical Work," *The Journal of Finance* (May 1970).

the multitude of participants in the market would add substantially to that cost. Management and accountants could release the information about a firm in the form of a "computer dump"—a vast outpouring of non-summarized, unclassified data. To operate efficiently, the market would have to, and undoubtedly would, digest this mass of data—but at an enormous cost.

The long history of financial statement preparation demonstrates that some summarization, some classification is valuable. At what point does it become worthwhile to give up efforts at further classification (which in our world probably means better definitions of income) and settle for mere disclosure? The classification must be done by someone if the market is to work efficiently. (In the hundreds of models hinting at the way securities prices are determined, earnings or some surrogate for them have appeared in every one that I have ever seen.) How much cheaper is it to have that classification done once by a well-trained analyst of economic affairs familiar with the data (I hope that is a description of the chief financial officer of the traded corporation) and attested to by a similarly well-trained independent analyst (the CPA, of course), both operating within an economically realistic set of concepts (what GAAP should be), than to leave such income determination to the efforts of each participant in the market? A better definition of income would save substantial amounts of "transactions costs," even if reports embracing it included disclosure of data that could be used to meet "inferior" definitions of income.

The research that is needed here is an effort to measure the costs of individual processing of data that is required because of a lack of consensus on the best definition of earnings. This is not an easy effort, and cooperation from groups that must participate if it is to be successful will be hard to obtain because it may threaten their economic position.

Turning to the second question about efficient markets that affects accounting research, one must ask, Do efficient markets always work? There are a reasonably large number of individual cases in which a change in accounting policy or a questioning of existing policy in the press, with no discernible change in underlying economic conditions, and little, if any, increase in publicly available information, brought about sharp initial market reaction. The market collapse when Career Academy announced its change in policy in accounting for franchise income is but one example. Some of the cases cited in Abe Briloff's *Unaccountable Accounting*[3] and

3. Abraham J. Briloff, *Unaccountable Accounting* (New York: Harper & Row, 1972).

in Ray Chambers's *Securities and Obscurities*[4] would make a good initial list of cases for study.

To date most of the analysis of these seeming exceptions to the efficient market concept has been of an anecdotal (and polemic, I fear) nature. An analysis in depth of these situations, comparing in each case the individual stocks performance relative to the market and industry for periods both before and after the change or the publicity would be helpful. This would include a study of whether the announcement of the change or the publicity was a "signal" that underlying economic conditions for the firm had changed in a manner not previously expected. It would help us to decide whether these cases were mere aberrations—real outliers—or whether they give us a clue to some important modifications that should be made in some aspects of the efficient-markets hypothesis.

As with study of users' decision models, this research on efficient-market qualifications is likely to be time consuming and costly. Yet it is the sort of thing that academic researchers do best. It is the sort of research that would be helpful to the FASB as it continues on its most important task—the effort to prepare a statement on the conceptual framework for accounting and reporting. Nowhere has the need for prompt efforts for preparing such a statement been better illustrated than by the Board's recent exposure drafts on leases and on certain marketable securities.

In both of these areas there have been substantial research and writing. Bob Sterling's prize-winning article in the *Journal of Accountancy*[5] sketched the long history of academic research on valuation of marketable securities—a history that was completely ignored by the FASB in its proposed action. Similarly, substantial work has been done on the subject of leases by practitioners as well as academics. How the FASB could issue an exposure draft on leases with its questionable criteria for capitalization, choice of interest rates, and provisions for nonretroactivity in the face of such research is puzzling to say the least.[6]

These two instances do not make me optimistic about the effect of re-

---

4. Raymond J. Chambers, *Securities and Obscurities: A Case for Reform of the Law of Company Accounts* (Melbourne, Australia: Gower Press, 1973) Inclusion of the Chambers material would give the study an international flavor.

5. Robert R. Sterling, "Accounting Research, Education and Practice," *Journal of Accountancy* (September 1973): 44–52.

6. Since this paper was delivered, the FASB has issued its final ruling on leases, Statement no. 13. The Statement calls for retroactive recognition of lease capitalization and presents sounder criteria for capitalization. This provides additional support for my optimistic conclusion that sound academic research (and perhaps a little prodding from the SEC) has an effect.

search on changes in practice. My minority position on so many questions
at the APB (assuming, of course, that my positions were based on sound
research—a point I never doubted) was also discouraging. Yet time does
have the virtue of giving us some perspective on these matters. When
I think back on the state of the accounting art when I took my first
course from Bill Paton some 35 years ago, I am amazed at how much
progress we have made. Most of the progress has been slow, much of it
grudging on the part of preparers of financial statements. I have sometimes felt that a major obstacle to progress in accounting principles has
been that those "generally accepted" principles have been enunciated
by auditors who were more concerned with auditability than economic
reality. Dealing with such attitudes has led me to fall back time and time
again on Lord Keynes' comment, "I would rather be vaguely right than
precisely wrong."

With all its slowness, with all its pain, progress in accounting has been
steady. Accounting has indeed been a dynamic art in the last quarter
century. I feel that much of that progress has come as the fruit of academic
research efforts. Many of those efforts seem to go unnoticed and unread,
unappreciated by the practicing profession. But cumulatively and through
time they have had their effect. The practicing accounting profession is
much the better for our efforts and I am proud of them. Still, there is
much yet to be done and my prescription for academic research is to keep
on doing that which we have done well in the past.

PART V

Conference Synthesis

The Impact of Research on Practice— A Synthesis

Nicholas Dopuch

After reading the main papers of this conference it occurred to me that it would be useful to begin this synthesis by considering a question that has largely been ignored here: Why study or evaluate the impact of accounting research on accounting practice? As one who earns part of his salary because of research efforts—my own and, as editor of the *Journal of Accounting Research,* those of others—I see no threat from the academic employers that research efforts will cease to be rewarded. In fact, it appears that the importance of research to the academic's career is even increasing as more schools base promotion decisions on the quantity and quality of the research outputs of their faculties. Hence, an evaluation of the impact of research on practice does not seem to be linked to some movement under way in which academic research is now coming under suspicion.

We should also realize that the academic's research is largely at the discretion of the researcher who chooses his topics and his methodologies on the basis of his perceived reward function. This may be at the heart of the problem regarding the lack of any major impact of research on practice, as noted by each of the main authors. That is, an academic's research decisions will be guided by the criteria imposed at his school concerning promotions and salary increases. If those criteria are controlled wholly or in part by colleagues in other disciplines, then the practical implications of accounting research may be of secondary importance. This may be an argument in favor of professional schools of accounting, but it is certainly not offered with that objective in mind.

Returning to the question posed above, I think we can answer it by relating this conference to two predecessors and to the events which might have prompted all three. This is the third conference held within the last five years at which a review of accounting research studies was a major part of the program. Coincidentally, I have been involved with all three. I helped organize the first of the three, held in 1971 at the University of

Illinois,[1] I coauthored a paper presented at the second conference, held at the University of Chicago in 1974,[2] and now I find myself on the program of the third one as well. These three conferences can be related if we reflect on what might give significance to the issue of what impact research has had on practice. I believe that the significance of the issue stems from the need to make policy decisions, just as it does in other professional areas. For example, the medical profession exhibits a concern over this issue because of the potential impact current research results may have on the optimal treatments of patients. Similarly, we observe physical scientists striving to communicate the results of their research because those results may be critical to the technological developments in the applied or engineering areas. Even economists become involved with the issue when they attempt to relate their research results to the policy-making decisions underlying monetary and fiscal policies. In contrast, a concern over the impact of economic research is totally absent in the areas of economics in which theories are developed to explain rather than to influence behavior.

I conclude then that the motivation for this type of conference can be linked to the problems we face regarding the policy-making activities of the FASB (APB) and the SEC and the extent to which research results can be relied upon to guide policy decisions. As such, I view this conference as fitting the same mold as the previous two referred to above.

This is not to say that the relationship between research and practice has been totally ignored prior to say the creation of the APB, our first private regulatory body. Rather, were it not for regulatory bodies our interest in the ways in which reseach could have impact on practice would proceed in a much different manner, as proposals would then be made by researchers and firms would accept or reject them on the basis of their perceived merits. In effect, practice would be affected through time as part of a competitive process. But when policies are issued which affect all firm's managements and their auditors then it becomes cost-effective, on intuitive grounds, to investigate the extent to which research may provide the means of resolving policy questions.

In line with that, let me suggest an area of research that would have been

1. N. Dopuch and L. Revsine, *Accounting Research 1960–1970: A Critical Evaluation* (Urbana, Ill.: Center for International Education and Research in Accounting, 1973).

2. *Studies on Financial Accounting Objectives: 1974,* Supplement to *Journal of Accounting Research,* vol. 12.

appropriate to review at this conference but that has not received explicit consideration. The area I have in mind deals with the whole question of competitive vs. regulated markets. Recall that accounting decisions were governed by private decisions until the early 1930s when we first moved into a regulated structure for accounting information. The movement was given additional impetus during the 1960s and 1970s through the creation of the APB and the FASB. When we note that a decision by the SEC or the FASB to change the present system of measurement and disclosure can alter the costs and benefits faced by four sometimes competing interests, then it is clear that the degree to which regulatory bodies can derive optimal decisions on accounting issues becomes an important area to consider.

Let me be more specific. Our present system relies on the interactions between corporations issuing information, auditors who pass judgment on the integrity of the issued information, users of information from corporations and from other sources, and the suppliers of other information. Each set of interests attempts to balance the costs and benefits of producing and using information. Suppose that either the SEC or the FASB wishes to evaluate a potential change in the present system. Such an evaluation would require first an assessment of the changes in costs and benefits affecting each interest, should a change be made, followed by the imposition of a set of priorities which would allow the agency to resolve any conflicts between the various parties. Needless to say the normative models describing how (whether) optimal decisions can be made by regulatory agencies have not yet been developed, and some have argued they may never be.[3] Therefore, it may be more socially beneficial to move back toward more competitive markets regarding information-production decisions rather than toward more regulation.[4] Whatever the optimal strategy, research on the issue of competitive vs. regulatory market systems would have been an appropriate one for such a conference.

Once we have established a motivation for evaluating the impact of different types of research on practice, the next step would be to compare what the impact should be—a normative question—against what is the actual impact—a positive question. If a discrepancy exists, we would then

3. See the discussion by W. Beaver and J. Demski, "The Nature of Financial Accounting Objectives: A Summary and Synthesis," in *Studies on Financial Objectives,* ibid.
4. N. Gonedes, N. Dopuch, S. Penman, "Disclosure Rules, Information-Production and Capital Market Equilibrium: The Case of Forecast Disclosure Rules," *Journal of Accounting Research* (Spring 1976).

have to devise ways to adjust the actual impact to the optimal level. Incidentally, the adjustment might involve reducing the actual impact, to the extent we find practice relying on research results which are invalid or which are at least premature. As an aside here, the December, 1974, issue of the *Journal of Accountancy* includes an article[5] in which the authors survey the implications of the results of various empirical studies for the materiality decision. Some of the studies they reference are so deficient from a methodological standpoint that the auditor would be wise to ignore the results. Unfortunately, the authors do not provide an evaluation of the quality of the various studies, but merely provide their results.

Returning to the papers of this conference, how did the main authors treat the normative and positive questions posed above? Basically, they confined themselves to a consideration of only the first question. Of course, this was to be expected from Davidson and Weston, who could merely speculate on what types of practical issues should be researched in the future. However, neither Bedford, Kaplan, nor Dyckman et al. provided an explicit discussion of the actual impact of the set of studies they were asked to review. In the case of Kaplan and of Dyckman et al. I believe they did so on the implicit assumption that the empirical studies using past financial data and the behavioral studies have not had any impact on practice. Given that these two classes of studies are of recent vintage, this is probably a reasonable assumption.

When we consider the a priori models, however, I think a more explicit discussion of what (if any) impact these models have had would have been useful. Bedford did give us some of his findings in his oral remarks, but not enough details were supplied for us to determine whether we agreed or disagreed with his findings. As for what he included in his paper, his main conclusion is that practice has been affected primarily by the matching principle formally enunciated by Paton and Littleton. This principle may be giving way, though, to the communication model recommended formally in ASOBAT[6] and embraced to some extent by the Trueblood Committee.[7] What surprises me is why he did not trace this communications orientation further back to his own writings in the 1950s and to earlier ones of Vatter, both of whom argued against the traditional

5. M. O'Connor and D. Collins, "Toward Establishing User-Oriented Materiality Standards," *Journal of Accountancy* (December 1974).

6. *A Statement of Basic Accounting Theory,* American Accounting Association (Sarasota, Fla., 1966).

7. Report of the Study Group on *Objectives of Financial Statements* (New York: American Institute of Certified Public Accountants, 1973).

practice of developing accounting theory around an income concept. I was also surprised that he did not comment on what relationships exist between present theoretical discussions of current cost and price-level adjusted statements and discussions presented in prior periods of high rates of inflation. It would seem that earlier writings on alternative bases have influenced our current thinking here.

Granted then that the three main authors did not consider explicitly the actual impact of their set of studies on practice, how did they approach an evaluation of the normative question of what impact should the studies have had on practice? Bedford approached the problem by attempting to define a meta-model which could be used to evaluate a priori models. According to him, an a priori model *should* have an impact on practice if it possesses his set of criteria. While we may disagree about the specific criteria he proposes, the idea itself is appealing.

Both Kaplan and Dyckman et al. followed a somewhat different approach. They attempted to ascertain what impact their studies should have on practice mainly by assessing the relevance of the issues studied to practical problems.[8] Dyckman et al. went one step further and included an assessment of the competence with which behavioral studies were conducted, which would also influence the degree to which such studies should have an impact on practice. Recall though that Kaplan accepted the quality of the studies he reviewed, confining his attention to the relevance of the issues studied. This was a reasonable strategy for him to follow since the studies he reviewed are generally considered to represent the most competent examples of empirical work in accounting.

The same strategy would not have been inappropriate for Dyckman et al. for, as they indicate in their paper, the typical behavioral study in accounting exhibits severe if not condemning methodological deficiencies. Personally, I welcome this type of honest assessment of the behavioral area by two behavioral accountants since for years we have been admonished by others in their group for not paying attention to the results of behavioral studies. We can now feel comfortable in the knowledge that we were correct in not doing so.

Even though the studies reviewed by Kaplan are more impressive methodologically, he nevertheless ends with essentially the same conclusion—that his studies also should not have had much of an impact on practice. The primary reason for this outcome is simply that the studies

8. Note though that the approach taken by Kaplan and Dyckman, et al. fits well with the first requirement of Bedford's meta-model.

do not address themselves to the mainstream of practical problems, especially if the problems have policy-making implications. Kaplan's conclusion was echoed by Mautz, who even suggested that the potential impact of empirical studies using past financial data may be closer to zero.

Mautz suggested this conclusion mainly on the basis that the results of the empirical studies reviewed by Kaplan border on being trivially obvious. While it may be difficult to get excited about results which demonstrate that accounting income numbers have information content, and about some of the other results pointed out by Kaplan, I doubt that practitioners are so committed to the evidence on the efficient-capital-markets hypothesis that they would predict the market is capable of seeing through accounting changes and other managerial manipulations. If they *were* so committed, it would be hard for them to justify the extensive concern recently exhibited over such "trivial" questions as (1) how to handle the deferred-tax problem in the oil company, (2) whether it matters that the leasing opinion is not made retroactive, given that the capitalized values of past contracts will be parenthetically shown on the balance sheet, and (3) what is the correct concept of earnings per share. The discussions at this conference have clearly indicated that it is quite difficult for practitioners to reconcile the evidence presented here on efficient capital markets and the anecdotal evidence gained from their experiences with users and managers.

A similar difficulty is revealed in Davidson's paper on the future issues to be researched. For example, Davidson argues for income calculations, yet it is not clear that such summary calculations provide much utility in efficient capital markets. Similarly, he expresses some doubt about the consistency of the evidence on efficient capital markets and his observations of market reactions in cases of the kind typically described by Briloff and Chambers. Unfortunately, his call for research which can explain away such "inconsistencies" will have to go unheeded for awhile since the market model used in such research requires that the researcher work with large samples at an aggregate level.

Turning to some of Davidson's other research proposals, I believe I can comment on them in conjunction with some of Weston's suggestions. Both Davidson and Weston seem committed to the view that progress will not be made until we agree on the objectives of financial statements. It may be more than a coincidence that they assign a high priority to this task after serving on the Committee to Define Financial Accounting Objectives. I also believe we could settle a number of issues if we could in fact agree on the objectives of financial statements. Yet disagreements on the objectives of financial statements are merely manifestations of the fact that we cannot agree on a normative theory of accounting. The profession has been trying to develop a theory of accounting since the 1930s. For example, here is a representative quotation on the nature of the problem:

> If the practitioners, after sufficient time has elapsed, have not come to some substantial agreement as to what are or should be considered accepted accounting principles and practices, we may well expect the Commission's (i.e., the SEC) staff accountants to prepare and the Commission to publish what it shall demand in the way of such practices. . . .

This quotation was taken from an article by C. Aubrey Smith published in *The Accounting Review* back in 1935. As we know, the profession has not yet achieved this goal, and it is not because of a lack of attempts to do so. The fact that we have not been able to obtain agreement on a normative theory suggests that additional pleas to do so, which have also come from discussions here, will not much change matters. I would recommend that the FASB recognize the futility of trying to develop *the* theory of accounting and merely enunciate the objectives it intends to follow in its deliberations. Its opinions will then be evaluated in terms of its objectives. As new members arrive on the scene and major events occur, the objectives could be revised. Incidentally, I would not expect many changes over time, since accountants are more in agreement on objectives than we are led to believe. For example, I find a great deal of overlap between the APB's set of objectives in its Statement No. 4 and those adopted by the Trueblood Committee. Where disagreements arise is in the interpretations of these objectives as they may apply to specific accounting issues. But such interpretation is the main task of a body such as the FASB.

The other main proposal of Davidson and of Weston deals with the problem of not knowing enough about the decision processes of investors. I, personally, am not alarmed about this since (1) investors do not know much themselves about their decision processes, and (2) in a highly competitive market, with heterogeneous expectations and utility functions, it is not clear that we can ever generalize across decision processes or that we even need to do so. There are methodologies which enable us to study the decision processes of decision-makers, and next year's annual Chicago conference will be devoted to this area of research. For the most part, however, such studies are designed to understand decision-making at the individual level. It is not clear how knowledge of individual decision processes can improve the workings of an aggregate competitive market.

I will elaborate by way of an analogy. I take it for granted that everyone present here has at least one automobile and that just about everyone of us is ignorant about the relative mechanical features of his automobile(s). Yet, when we go to a dealer to purchase an automobile we expect and receive a fair game. The game is fair because of guarantees from the dealers and the makers of the cars and because there are a sufficient number of knowledgeable people studying and communicating the relative features of the different makes of automobiles to lead to an efficient market. It is not obvious that forcing all of us to become automobile experts will improve the efficiency of that market, although specific individuals may be able to improve their individual decisions. The basic question, though, is whether the aggregate level of costs incurred in having individuals increase their expertise will be compensated by the aggregate benefits from doing so.

It seems to me that these types of reservations apply to the objective of relating financial reports to the specific needs of individual or even group decision makers. We have a market mechanism for evaluating how aggregate decisions are affected by accounting choices. This mechanism has been used to evaluate accounting choices made in the past and it can be used in the same way to evaluate future decisions to supply accounting information not yet contained in accounting reports. An analysis of individual decision-making processes may allow us to improve the decision-making ability of individuals. However, we are not justified in inferring then that the overall efficiency of the market will similarly be improved.

That is the extent to which I will comment about the main papers presented here. As I indicated above, all of the attention of these authors centered on the normative question of what should be the impact of research on practice. Only Moonitz, in his discussion of Bedford's paper, considered the second or positive question—i.e., what has been the actual impact of research on practice?

Suppose we wished to consider the latter question. How might we assess the actual impact of research on practice? One possibility would be to interview practitioners regarding changes induced in their thinking by specific research studies. But this would be expensive and we would run into the various methodological problems associated with questionnaire studies (as pointed out by Dyckman, et al.). A second possibility would be to follow the approach illustrated by Moonitz who attempted to trace developments in a particular area of controversy. But this approach requires the skills of a historian, and there is evidence to suggest that few accountants qualify as such.

As a third possibility we could examine the footnote references in practitioner journals to determine what schools of thought seem to be influencing the thinking of practitioners. This type of footnote analysis is not as straightforward as it might seem since it runs into tracing problems because of secondary referencing and the like. Nevertheless, an example of what can be done along these lines is a paper recently published in the *Journal of Accounting Research* which relies on citation analysis to examine features of the accounting literature.[9]

As in the above approach, we might go back one step and examine the influence of research on practice as conveyed through textbooks. Since this is not a difficult type of research, I had an assistant summarize the footnote references of several of the more popular financial and managerial (cost) texts. Except for the typical APB (FASB) Opinions, only one research paper was referenced in a sample of four introductory or principles texts; one was found in the Welsch, et al. intermediate text, and several each were found in the Meigs, et al. intermediate text, and in the Hawkins text. The financial text he found which clearly dominated the others in research references was the Kieso/Weygandt intermediate text. But even the latter was fairly silent on the efficient-capital-markets literature. In the very near future a new principles book (by Davidson et al.) will appear which does include a chapter on the implications of the efficient-capital-markets hypothesis on accounting.

The situation is quite different with managerial texts. Managerial texts are not heavily influenced by regulatory bodies and this may explain their reliance on research studies. References in a few (well-known) managerial texts are generally current and even include several from the behavioral literature.

As a final approach to the question I scanned the little survey book compiled by Tom Burns of Ohio State,[10] which contains outlines and course objectives from a wide range of schools. Although a number of academicians do not bother to describe what they are doing in their courses, it does appear that research findings of current studies find their way into the graduate and seminar-type courses. However, very few readings courses are available at the undergraduate level. At that level, the students exposure to research is usually confined to discussions of past and current opinions of regulatory agencies. I have talked to other colleagues

9. T. W. McRae, "A Citational Analysis of the Accounting Information Network," *Journal of Accounting Research*, vol. 12, no. 1 (Spring 1974).

10. See his annual series, *Accounting Trends* (New York: McGraw-Hill).

and they agree that one negative result of the activities of the APB and the FASB is simply that so much classroom time is spent debating (searching for?) the rationale of these committees' pronouncements.

As a final comment let me suggest that this conference and others like it may lead to a greater impact of research on practice. Several of the discussants here have complained about the technical styles of research papers which tend to discourage a practitioner from attempting to read them. Yet the technical details of research papers are necessary in order to permit academicians to evaluate the competence of the research studies. What we need is some type of filtering service which can provide reviews of research studies and communications of their practical implications to practitioners. The review papers presented here and the related discussants' comments provide one mechanism for achieving this objective.

Index